NEW DEVELOPMENTS IN EATING DISORDERS RESEARCH

New Developments in Eating Disorders Research

Pamela I. Swain
Editor

Nova Science Publishers, Inc.
New York

For permission to use material from this book please contact us:
Telephone 631-231-7269; Fax 631-231-8175
Web Site: http://www.novapublishers.com

LIBRARY OF CONGRESS CATALOGING-IN-PUBLICATION DATA

New developments in eating disorders research / Pamela I. Swain, editor.
p. cm.
Includes bibliographical references and index.
ISBN 1-59454-542-1
1. Eating disorders. I. Swain, Pamela I.
[DNLM: 1. Eating Disorders. WM 175 N532 2006]
RC552.E18N42 2006
616.85'26--dc22 2005015093

Published by Nova Science Publishers, Inc. ✢New York

CONTENTS

PREFACE

The abundance of food in the developed countries of the world has seemingly spawned an epidemic of disorders connected to the food. Extremes such as intensive concern about one's body image and total disregard for it have resulted in countries which contain enormous segments of the population who are either obese and proud of it or bordering on anorexia nervosa. This new book gathers state-of-the-art research from leading scientists throughout the world which offers important information on understanding the underlying causes and discovering the most effective treatments for eating disorders.

Body dissatisfaction and eating disorders have emerged as important issues among young men. Research has revealed that the clinical diagnosis of eating disorders, sub-clinical body image issues, disordered eating and exercise disorders are prevalent among adolescent boys and young men. In addition, the reluctance of males to recognize their problem behaviors and present for treatment as well as the methodological limitations with the measurement of male body image and eating disorders suggest that the current prevalence figures may be underestimates.

Disordered eating, poor body image and dangerous weight loss and weight gain techniques may have damaging physical, mental and social effects on young males. The importance of safe and effective preventive programs for body image improvement and eating disorder prevention is needed, yet very few school or college based prevention programs have included males, and even fewer have achieved beneficial attitudinal or behavioral change. It is recommended that programs to prevent body image issues and eating disorders that are relevant to the concerns of adolescent and young males are designed and implemented in order to curb this emerging public health problem. Chapter 1 outlines the occurance of body image issues and eating disorders in boys and young males; research findings from our studies of Australian boys, male adolescents and young men and a summary of international prevention programs that have included males.

Various biological, psychological, and sociocultural factors have been considered in the attempt to understand the etiology of eating pathologies such as anorexia nervosa and bulimia nervosa. Psychosexual issues are neither sufficient nor necessary for the development of an eating disorder in a young person, and it should be considered as only one factor in the multidimensional, multifactorial framework needed to clarify this complex and still poorly understood set of disorders. In particular, gender roles and sociocultural expectations appear strongly implicated in the development of eating disorders, since anorexia nervosa and bulimia nervosa occur predominantly among women as described in chapter 2. This is frequently attributed to the continued emphasis on physical attractiveness and a thin physique for women. In consequence, women reportedly express greater dissatisfaction about their bodies, more concern with appearance and body weight, and more frequently engage in weight-control efforts. Since at least 90 per cent of eating disordered patients are females, then it would therefore seem plausible to suggest that the female role might play a part in the genesis of these pathologies. This fact strongly supports that the meaning of femininity in Western society has some relationship with the development of eating problems. Eating disorders are common, serious illnesses that present major challenges to physicians and other health care professionals. Sociocultural body norms for ideal size and shape may be reinforced by participation in activities, sports, or membership in groups that promotes weight loss and shape change. Eating disorders are furthermore reinforced when high status individuals (e.g. parents, teachers, coaches, doctors) encourage a susceptible individual to diet. Studies indicate that a complex combination of genetic and sociocultural-developmental factors is responsible for the onset of these illnesses.

Previous studies into the role that culture plays in shaping attitude and behavior to food and weight have provided limited insight as most of the research is cross-national. The present study compared Omani, Indian and western adolescent schoolchildren attending three schools in Muscat, Oman. Assessment with cross-cultural valid measures such as *Eating Attitude Test-26*, subscale of *Eating Disorder Inventory* to gauge the presence of fat-phobia and Bradford *Somatic Inventory* to elicit presence of somatization were used. Significant differences in attitudes to eating, body image and somatization between the western and non western children were found. Chapter 3 suggests trajectories of eating disorder such body image disturbance as expressed in fat-phobia and somatization tend to vary from culture to culture and underscores the view that some of the health related behavior among adolescent needs to be examined within socio-cultural context.

Adolescence is certainly the age of experimenting with a wide variety of rituals aimed at reaching full control on body changes, as well as on the social context teen-agers live within and start gaining their autonomy. As explained in chpter 4, dieting is one of these rituals frequently tried by adolescents as a fascinating way to deal with the body changes typical of puberty.

Eating disorders are today an increasing problem among teenagers and young adults specially females. In the case of bulimia the estimated prevalence is between 3 and 5% and the average age it starts is around 20 years. It is known that its etiology is complex and depends on biological, psychological, and social factors as well as more specific characteristics as, for example, the practice of sports that in some cases leads to these disorders. The close relation between corporal image and performance makes the female athletes a group particularly vulnerable to problems of bulimic behavior due to the emphasis in weight control that they are frequently submitted. However the studies available are still insufficient to characterize the amplitude and distribution of the problem. The aim of chapter 5 is to evaluate bulimic components of behavior among adolescent female endurance runners. From a total of 40 athletes affiliated with the Track and Field Federation of Rio de Janeiro, 17 female endurance runners (16 ± 1.8 years old) and 32 post-menarche, non-athletic adolescents (15.0 ± 1.4 years) were examined. The athletes were training for at least 2 years (15 ± 7 hours/week). The body composition was esteemed by the anthropometric method and percent body fat (%F) and Body Mass Index (BMI) were calculated. Bulimic behavioral components (frequency and severity) were evaluated using the Portuguese version of BITE (Bulimic

Investigatory Test, Edinburgh), a self-rating scale. A control group of 32 non-athlete volunteers in the same age group were also evaluated. Calculation of parameters, descriptive data statistics and comparison (Anova one way) of the variables were performed with the softwere Statistica for windows (5.1, 1998), with a significant level of $p \leq 0{,}05$. Scores above the normal limit of 10 were recorded for 35.3% of the athletes (6 individuals), including 29.4% (4 individuals) that reported unusual behavioral components, suggestive of a tendency toward bulimia. One individual scored above 20, indicating a possible clinical case of bulimia. On the scale of severity of the symptoms, a score of 5 (considered moderately severe) was recorded in one case. The athletes in this group are in risk to develop eating disorder, considering their preoccupation with weight control and the use of inadequate means of keeping within the desired range – including restrictive practices such as fasting along with intense physical activity.

Independence and self–esteem are strongly related to physical and mental function which in turn are largely determined by nutritional status and physical activity. Food is an integral part of our well-being and quality of life. It extends beyond simply satisfying hunger and providing nourishment. Specific foods have a symbolic meaning and particular food habits are influenced by religious, cultural, social and emotional experience. Elderly people showing interest towards food, nourishment and keeping a good appetite, in most cases still are vital human beings full of interests and quite independent. Behavioural characteristics before mentioned describe the picture of the elderly aging with "a good health", known in medical literature as *Healthy Aging*. Aging is normally associated with body weight gain in individuals who fail to decrease food intake in proportion to the age-related decline in energy expenditure. However, decreases in body weight are common in elderly individuals (over 70 years of age) who do not eat enough to meet energy demands. Age related reduction in energy intake is largely a physiologic effect of healthy aging and reveals itself with a loss of eating need and pleasure. As described in chapter 6, this reduction intake may predispose to the harmful anorexic effect of psychological, social and physical problems that become increasingly frequent with aging. The physiological anorexia of aging increases the propensity for developing pathological anorexia and weight loss when an older person falls ill with either a medical or a psychological illness. A 10% loss of body weight over 10 years is consistently associated with increased mortality and functional disability. Weight loss is one of the pathognomonic signs of malnutrition (whether energetic or protein-energy) which may negatively influence the clinical outcome of rehabilitation programmes, confirming that a convenient nutritional status helps the achievement of such a condition and it is absolutely essential when recovering from acute illnesses. A further demonstration of the importance of nutritional status has been pointed out by several studies showing that, after sixties of age, weight loss is associated to a decline in muscle mass and consequently in muscle strength. The picture just mentioned is well-known as *sarcopenia*, which plays a main role in the beginning of: frailty, functional and metabolic impairments, physical disabilities that expose the elderly to an increased risk of falls and protein-energy malnutrition. The obese elderly also affected by protein malnutrition configure the so called *fat frail* who obtains worse outcomes in rehabilitation programmes.

The exploration, the comprehension and the definition of the underlying psychopathological dimensions and/or concomitant to Eating Disorders are everything but exhaustive. On the one hand, the ED present themselves as dysfunctional, transnosographic and multiform behaviour, on the other hand, they tend to mask various underlying pathologies, including structural, pathological descriptions. While the coexistence of the depressive, anxious and personality spectrum pathology is recognised, it is not yet clear if the eating pathology, in its various forms, should be understood as an expression of illness, therefore also structured in an organic dimension, or if, on the other hand, it is a defensive attempt to 'self-cure' another affection of psychic nature and origin. Both theories are probably valid, and in the clinical practise we can outline syndromes of the first kind, the second kind, or even mixed. The main purpose of a psychiatric interview is that of expanding the observation viewpoint of the problem, to look for new connections with other hidden dimensions and to "reframe" the symptom in a more complex and integrated dimension with the other parts of the personality. But what are the themes that are frequently more noticeable in people affected by ED? For this purpose, using some cases as starting points for reflection, chapter 7 will present psychopathological focus areas that seem to be particularly significant in the observation clinic of the ED: feelings and emotions, the depressive spectrum, the rapport with the body, and that with the family.

Eating disorders are complex conditions characterized by disturbances to eating behavior. Anorexia nervosa is a syndrome consisting of a combination of weight loss, amenorrhea and behavioral changes, whereas bulimia nervosa is characterized by recurrent episodes of binge eating. AN affects about 1% of all women between the ages of 15 and 25, and long-term follow-up studies have shown that AN has a mortality rate of about 1-6%, with ventricular arrhythmias being one of the probable major causes of sudden death. The risk of sudden death is thought to be higher in eating disorder patients, compared to coeval women, and therefore it is important to evaluate arrhythmogenicity in eating disorders. The evaluation of arrhythmogenicity requires assessment of cardiac electrical instability, in which three factors need to be considered: 1) modulating factors, 2) triggers, and 3) substrates. Many previous studies have focused on the risk of fatal arrhythmia by evaluating substrates, and there have also been previous studies on substrates and modulating factors in anorexia nervosa. Chapter 8 reviews previous studies on cardiac arrhythmias and function in eating disorders, including our own studies on substrates in eating disorders. Hence, in one of our previous studies, substrates were evaluated for assessment of arrhythmogenicity in patients with bulimia nervosa, as well as in patients with anorexia nervosa. It was found that QT intervals were prolonged and QT dispersion increased in both anorexia nervosa and bulimia nervosa patients.

In: New Developments in Eating Disorders Research
Editor: Pamela I. Swain, pp. 1-36
ISBN 1-59454-542-1

Chapter 1

BODY IMAGE AND EATING DISORDERS IN MALE ADOLESCENTS AND YOUNG MEN

Jennifer A. O'Dea **and** ***Zali Yager***
Faculty of Education; University of Sydney; NSW 2006; Australia

ABSTRACT

Body dissatisfaction and eating disorders have emerged as important issues among young men. Research has revealed that the clinical diagnosis of eating disorders, sub-clinical body image issues, disordered eating and exercise disorders are prevalent among adolescent boys and young men. In addition, the reluctance of males to recognize their problem behaviors and present for treatment as well as the methodological limitations with the measurement of male body image and eating disorders suggest that the current prevalence figures may be underestimates.

Disordered eating, poor body image and dangerous weight loss and weight gain techniques may have damaging physical, mental and social effects on young males. The importance of safe and effective preventive programs for body image improvement and eating disorder prevention is needed, yet very few school or college based prevention programs have included males, and even fewer have achieved beneficial attitudinal or behavioral change.

It is recommended that programs to prevent body image issues and eating disorders that are relevant to the concerns of adolescent and young males are designed and implemented in order to curb this emerging public health problem.

This chapter outlines the occurance of body image issues and eating disorders in boys and young males; research findings from our studies of Australian boys, male adolescents and young men and a summary of international prevention programs that have included males.

* j.o'dea@edfac.usyd.edu.au

INTRODUCTION

Body image problems and eating disorders have long been regarded as female illnesses by the general public and research communities. Recent investigations into body image, weight control and exercise behaviors have revealed dangerous behaviors similar to those identified in studies of young women being used by men to achieve the mesomorphic body ideal. It is not clear whether this reflects an actual increase in prevalence of these behaviors, or an increase in awareness and research into the area of male body image.

This chapter aims to describe these recent discoveries in the prevalence of body dissatisfaction, weight control and disordered eating and exercise behaviors in young, adolescent, and adult males. Possible reasons for these trends as well as interventions to prevent proliferation of this dissatisfaction and behaviors will also be discussed.

Eating disorders in men were well described in early records by Morton (Morton, 1694) and Gull (Gull, 1874), but the majority of research acknowledging the presence of disordered eating in males has only developed in the late 1990's. The majority of studies of male body image to date have been case reports conducted in eating disorder treatment facilities rather than large scale randomized population based studies. These clinical case studies focus on describing similarities and trends among small groups of male sufferers, or comparing eating disordered males with female sufferers rather than a control group of non-eating disordered males. The low clinical diagnosis of disordered eating behaviors in men has therefore resulted in limited sample sizes that have precluded meaningful statistical analyses.

It is also known that individuals with eating disorders are extremely reluctant to present for treatment and this may be even more profound in males (Anderson, 1984; Anderson & Mickalide, 1983). In the largest study of 135 males with eating disorders in the USA, over one third of participants had never actually attended the eating disorders unit of the Massachusetts hospital (Carlat, Carmargo, & Herzog, 1997). Therefore, studies of males who have presented for treatment must be interpreted with extreme caution due to their limited generalizability to the general population.

These small case studies of males with eating disorders have tentatively but consistently agreed that men and women who present for treatment with clinically diagnosed eating disorders generally display similar symptoms and phenomenology; and that with increased severity of the disorder, similarities between genders increases (Anderson & Holman, 1997; Carlat et al., 1997). In fact, in most reports it was agreed that male and female patients diagnosed with anorexia nervosa and bulimia nervosa differed more between disorders than gender (Carlat et al., 1997; Pope, Hudson, & Jonas, 1986).

PREVALENCE OF EATING DISORDERS IN MALES

The currently accepted incidence of clinically diagnosed eating disorders suggests that 5 to 10 percent of sufferers are men (Carlat et al., 1997). However, it is widely acknowledged that men may be underrepresented due to inherent methodological and socio-cultural issues of detection and diagnosis. Prevalence statistics regarding males are generally limited to those who present for treatment due to the lack of large randomized controlled community or population-based studies. It is known that men typically avoid health services (Anderson &

Holman, 1997) and the added feminized stigma of body image issues and eating related problems may increase the reluctance of men to seek treatment (Drummond, 1999). In addition, many men who engage in disordered eating behaviors do not attract attention, as they do not appear to lose large amounts of weight. Men appear to use exercise rather than dieting as a form of weight loss with the overall objective of achieving a more muscular body (Drummond, 2002). Exercise has become a socially accepted and somewhat virtuous behavior which may restrict the detection of excessive, compulsive or obligatory exercise (Yates, 1991). These factors may increase the reluctance of men to seek assistance for body image-related eating disorders and may also result in the current unknown prevalence of disordered eating behaviors and eating disorders among men.

Methodological Difficulties in the Measurement of Body Image Dissatisfaction and Disordered Eating in Males

There are many inherent methodological issues that have inhibited accurate prevalence statistics in males. These include methods of detection, case definition and diagnosis, response rates and generalizability of samples (Carlat & Carmargo, 1991). The body dissatisfaction and disordered eating instruments used in research have generally been derived from those used for women and have largely failed to detect cases of eating disorders in men (Turnbull, Freeman, & Barry, 1987).

Body image scales, such as the Body Dissatisfaction subscale of the Eating Disorder Inventory [EDI] (Garner, Olmstead, & Polivy, 1983) generally measure body dissatisfaction in terms of drive for thinness and usually focus on the hips, thighs and buttocks as the predominant areas of body dissatisfaction. The discrepancy between men who desire a thinner body, and those who want a more muscular body shape has limited the efficiency of many of these widely used body dissatisfaction scales as they exclude a measure of the drive for muscularity. Traditional scales based on silhouette drawings (Fallon & Rozin, 1985; Stunkard, Sorenson, & Schulsinger, 1980) measure satisfaction based on degree of adiposity, not muscularity and may therefore be considered irrelevant by many men, especially adolescent males. Males may then select an ideal figure that is a compromise between composition of fat and muscle rather than a true indication of their current and ideal body, which would impact on their body satisfaction score.

A recent development in body dissatisfaction scales, the Somatomorphic Matrix (Cafri, Roehrig, & Thompson, 2004) is a computerized scale developed to assess both body image satisfaction and perceptual accuracy in regard to body fat and muscularity (Cafri & Thompson, 2004). This scale uses figure drawings along two separate axes of fat and muscularity and has shown males to choose an ideal body far more muscular, but not fatter than their own (Cafri et al., 2004). The Drive for Muscularity Scale [DMS] (McCreary & Sasse, 2000) is another recent development in the more gender-appropriate measurement of the extent to which individuals desire a more muscular body on a 6 point likert-type scale.

Prevalence of Eating Disorders

Prevalence estimates of eating disorders in men vary greatly due to differences in diagnostic criteria and study design, including case detection, response rates and generalizability of data (Braun, Sunday, Huang, & Halmi, 1999; Carlat & Carmargo, 1991). The most accurate estimate of the prevalence of eating disorder in males is that males represent 5-10 percent of all individuals with eating disorders (Braun et al., 1999; Carlat & Carmargo, 1991; Lucas, Beard, O'Fallon, & Kurland, 1991). An increase in the prevalence of eating disorders in men has also been reported, with Braun and colleagues (1999) describing the number of males presenting for treatment in a New York facility to have increased from 0.1 percent in 1984 to 9.8 percent in 1995. It is not clear whether this apparent rise is a result of increased incidence of new cases or an increase in the number of men being identified, diagnosed and presenting for treatment. Olivardia and his colleagues in the USA (Olivardia, Pope, Mangweth, & Hudson, 1995b) have reported that while 53 percent of women with Bulimia nervosa seek treatment, only 16 percent of males do.

Population Based Studies

After a comprehensive literature review of 24 studies of the prevalence of bulimia in community samples, Carlat and colleagues (1997) estimated that men comprise 10-15 percent of all people with Bulimia Nervosa in the community. The population-based studies have been conducted among college students, which may also limit the generalizability of data. Studies have found that between 30 to 41 percent of college males self report binge eating (Halmi, Falk, & Schwartz, 1981; Katzman, Wolchik, & Braver, 1984; Pyle, Halvorson, Neuman, & Mitchell, 1986), and that 13 percent experienced all of the major symptoms of Bulimia Nervosa (Halmi et al., 1981). However these predictions must be interpreted with caution due to low response rates, the possibility of selection bias, and the known reluctance of people with body image and eating problems to participate in such studies (Fairburn & Beglin, 1990).

Exercise disorders, compulsive exercise and obligatory exercise are beginning to gain recognition as clinically diagnosable disorders. Although no DSM-IV criteria for exercise disorders has been established, time spent exercising as well as factors such as concern if unable to exercise, importance placed on exercise and presence of withdrawal symptoms from exercise are known to predict the possibility of a problem (O'Dea & Abraham, 2002; Pasman & Thompson, 1988). Prevalence figures for exercise disorders in college males range from eight percent using the Eating and Exercise Examination- Computerised [EEE-C] (O'Dea & Abraham, 2002) to 21.8 percent (Garman, Hayduk, Crider, & DHodel, 2004) using an un-validated scale to 47.5 percent (Zmijewski & Howard, 2003) using a DSM-IV based Exercise Dependence Questionaire [EDQ] (Ogden, Veale, & Summers, 1997).

Clinical Studies

Clinical studies describe an incidence of disordered eating in males that ranges from one to 11 percent of all disordered eating patients who present for clinical assessment and treatment (Braun et al., 1999; Carlat & Carmargo, 1991; Sharp, Clark, Dunan, Blackwood, & Shapiro, 1994; Touyz, Kopec-Schrader, & Beumont, 1993). The majority of these statistics are derived from admissions to specialist eating disorder units. The Australian study of Touyz et al. (1993) reported that 1.5 percent (three out of 199 patients) presenting for treatment of

Anorexia Nervosa over a three year period were male (Touyz et al., 1993). Anderson, (1984) reported that 10 percent of those presenting for treatment for an eating disorder in a three and a half year period were male.

In a Norwegian study of 364 patients in a psychiatric unit, lifetime prevalence of a serious eating disorder for males was 21.8 percent (Taraldson, Eriksen, & Gunner Gotestam, 1996). In Rochester, Minnesota, Anorexia Nervosa was reported as 8.1 times more likely to appear in females than males with a crude prevalence rate of 22.2 per 100, 000 in males residing in that town (Lucas et al., 1991). However it is believed that these rates represent minimum estimates of the true rate of Anorexia Nervosa in the population as only those people who presented to a doctor or clinician were included in the study (Lucas et al., 1991).

Body Image and Eating Disorders in Studies of Australian Males

A table of research results showing the prevalence of body image concerns, disordered eating and eating disorders among 1, 231 Australian males aged 6-25 years is given below.

In studies of adolescents, from three separate studies (O'Dea et al., 1996; O'Dea & Rawstorne, 2001; O'Dea & Caputi, 2001), an average of 12-15 percent of males reported being "too thin" and around 30 percent wanted to gain weight. The apparent increase from 1996 to 2001 in the number of male adolescents who were actually trying to gain weight (3 percent to 28 percent) may be a reflection of an actual increase over time or may simply reflect the increased desire to gain weight in the older age group of boys in the 2001 study.

Similarly, around one third of the adolescent males in our studies from 1996 to 2001 reported wanting to lose weight, with a greater number reporting actual weight loss behaviors in 2001 (13 percent in 1996 vs. 23 percent in 2001). These results may reflect a change in the trends over time or they may reflect age effects. Future research should further investigate these interesting trends and in particular, longitudinal studies should be designed to examine whether body image concerns and weight change behaviors increase with age and pubertal development among boys.

The results in Table I among young college males suggest that 20 percent exhibit disordered eating behaviors consistent with eating disorders, and that exercise disorders exist among 7 percent of college men. In addition, a surprisingly high level of shape and weight concerns was found (O'Dea & Abraham, 2002). Using a the Eating and Exercise Examination- Computerized [EEE-C], it was found that 25 percent of college males had significant concerns about their weight and regularly employed restrictive eating behaviors such as following specific rules about eating. Findings also demonstrated the possibility of significant and well entrenched exercise disorders, with 34 percent of males reporting that they would be significantly distressed if they were unable to exercise as much as they wanted and one third exercising specifically for weight and shape (O'Dea & Abraham, 2002). A concerning finding of the study was that nine percent reported that they currently suffered from disordered eating, 18 percent reported weight control problems and 22 percent reported a binge eating problem. In addition, 8 percent scored high enough on the clinical eating disorder examination to be diagnosed as having an exercise disorder.

Table I. Studies of body image and eating disorders among 1231 young Australian males aged 11-25 years

	Adolescents (n = 1091)			College males (n=140)	
	n = 173 11-15 yrs (a) %	n = 521 6-19 yrs (b) %	n = 397 13-18 yrs (c) %	n = 47 21-23 yrs(d) %	n = 93 20-28 yrs (e) %
Body Image					
"Too Thin"	12	12	15	16	-
"About right"	69	61	67	72	-
"Too fat"	19	27	18	12	-
Desired Body Weight					
A lot heavier	2	-	4	8	-
A little heavier	23	-	34	46	-
Present weight	37	-	32	26	-
A little lighter	33	-	26	15	-
A lot lighter	5	-	4	5	-
Current weight loss/gain					
Currently trying to lose weight	13	15	23	18	20
Currently trying to gain weight	3	18	28	29	-
Dangerous/ unhealthy weight loss methods					
Starvation	4	-	-	9	-
Vomiting/ attempted vomiting	4	-	-	0	3
Laxative abuse	4	-	-	0	
Slimming pills	0	-	-	0	
Smoking for weight loss	3	-	-	6	
Excessive exercise	13	-	-	22	23
Current eating disorder diagnoses	**%(n)**	**%(n)**	**%(n)**	**%(n)**	**%(n)**
Anorexia Nervosa	0.1(1)	-	-	2.1(1)	0(0)
Bulimia Nervosa	0(0)	-	-	0(0)	1.1(1)
Eating disorder not otherwise specified (EDNOS)	4(7)	-	-	-	20(19)
Exercise disorder	-	-	-	-	7(7)
Believe currently have an eating disorder	-	-	-	2.1(1)	8.6(8)

- Data unavailable
(a) (O'Dea, Abraham, & Heard, 1996)
(b) (O'Dea & Caputi, 2001)
(c) (O'Dea & Rawstorne, 2001)
(d) (O'Dea & Abraham, 2001)
(e) (O'Dea & Abraham, 2002)

Current Research among Physical Education Teachers in Australia

The following is an overview of our current study into the susceptibility to body image problems and eating disorders among college students in physical education majors. Our current research is based on the observation that physical and health education teachers are in a unique position to teach about and prevent eating disorders and child obesity, and yet there is generally no prior investigation of their personal and professional capability to do so. These teachers are exposed to similar socio-cultural pressures as other adults, yet their career path is highly involved with food, exercise and weight control, and their job may demand that they achieve an ideal aesthetic appearance to convey expertise in their field. A preoccupation with food and exercise is known to be characteristic of individuals with eating disorders (Larson, 1989; Worobey & Schoenfeld, 1999), and this may cause them to gravitate towards careers that are food and exercise related (Crockett & Littrell, 1985; Reinstein, Koszewski, Chamberlain, & Smith-Johnson, 1992; Sours, 1980).

Individuals in food and exercise related career paths such as personal trainers, aerobics instructors and dietitians as well as home economics and physical education teachers have been found to be at an increased risk for and engage in disturbed dieting and exercise behaviors to the same or higher extent as the general population (Kinzl, Traweger, Trefalt, Mangweth, & Biebl, 1999; McArthur & Howard, 2001; O'Dea & Abraham, 2001; Palmquist-Fredenberg, Berglund, & Dieken, 1996; Worobey & Schoenfeld, 1999). Furthermore, Kinzl and colleagues (1999) reported that 14 percent of the dietitians studied had chosen their career path partly due to their own preoccupation with food and exercise. The existence of these inappropriate knowledge, attitudes and behaviors in physical education teachers has implications for their own and their student's health. Both anecdotal and empirical evidence exist to demonstrate the occurrence of modeling and transfer of body dissatisfaction, inadequate knowledge and inappropriate beliefs and attitudes about food, exercise and weight control from teachers to students (O'Dea, 2002; O'Dea & Abraham, 2001; Rutz, 1993; Stewart, 1998).

Methods

In order to investigate the hypothesis that physical education majors are at a greater risk than other college students for body image concerns, disordered eating and eating disorders, we designed a cross-sectional study of 232 college students from two major universities in New South Wales, Australia.

Participants were randomly selected from first year Physical Education [PE] courses and first year Non-Physical Education [NonPE] courses including faculties of education, geography, and business studies. In these preliminary findings we will report the initial eating disorder prevalence results among the 77 male participants, which consisted of 33 physical education majors, and 44 non physical education majors.

Male participants completed an anonymous questionnaire in which they self reported whether they had experienced a history of eating disorders. Participants answered detailed yes/no questions about previous diagnosis, treatment or hospitalization for Anorexia Nervosa, Bulimia Nervosa, an "eating disorder", a "low weight problem" or an exercise disorder.

In addition, current treatment of the same disorders was assessed as well as the participants' current belief that they may have one of the eating disorders listed. Participants also answered questions about weight loss techniques that they had employed in the last 12 months.

Results

None of the NonPE education males reported any previous or current eating disorders or any of the weight control techniques that indicate disordered eating (vomiting, laxative abuse, starvation or fasting, diet pills, or smoking for deliberative appetite suppression and weight control). Two of the NonPE males indicated that they currently believed they had a "low weight problem" which specifically related to their desire for weight gain and more muscle mass.

Males in the PE group were more likely to indicate the presence of eating disorders. Two of the PE males (2/33, 6.1 percent) reported that they believed that they currently had an eating disorder. Both of these young men reported smoking for weight control as well as the use of disordered eating methods such as vomiting, laxative abuse, starvation and dieting pills. One of the PE males (3.1 percent) indicated that he believed that he currently had an exercise disorder. The number of PE males who reported employing "excessive exercise" (defined in the questionnaire as more than two hours per day not related to your professional career or training in order to lose weight) was three (9.1 percent) indicating the probable existence of an exercise disorder.

Discussion

There is a substantial lack of research into the body image, dieting and eating behaviors of males to be used as a comparison to the present study. However, in a study of American college students, 121 of which were male, a similar percentage (5.9 percent) of the males reported exercising for weight control for two or more hours per day (Zmijewski & Howard, 2003). This was used as just one part of a DSM-IV based Exercise dependence questionnaire finding that 47.5 percent of college males had current symptoms of exercise dependence, and 35.6 percent had symptoms within the previous 12 months (Zmijewski & Howard, 2003).

The current prevalence of eating disorders in males is relatively unknown, however the personal lifetime prevalence of eating disorders among male eating disorder treatment professionals was self reported as 2.3 percent (Barbarich, 2002; Bloomgarden, Gerstein, & Moss, 2003). Our current finding of 6.1 percent of college males reporting that they believed they currently had an eating may be higher than the studies of Barbarich (2002) or Bloomgarden et al. (2003) due to a college sample being closer to the age of onset and development of eating disorders. The preliminary results of the current study are also similar to our study of 93 college males (O'Dea & Abraham, 2002) in which 8.6 percent reported that they currently believed that they had an eating disorder.

One explanation for our apparent finding that males participating in PE majors may be at a high risk for eating problems is that they are educated about eating disorders during their undergraduate studies and that they may therefore be better able than non-PE males to identify and detect eating disordered behavior in themselves. This explanation seems unlikely in the current case because the males participating in our study were in their first year of undergraduate study and they had not yet undertaken any coursework about eating disorders.

Implications

The results of this preliminary study into the eating disorder risk among males majoring in physical education appears to tentatively confirm our hypothesis that these young men involved in physical education careers may be more susceptible than other NonPE males to develop disordered eating and eating disorders. College and university training programs should take note of this proposed trend and provide referrals to appropriate treatment and counseling facilities.

Future Research

We are currently collecting more data among PE and NonPE college students and we are undertaking further analysis of our data to examine the comparative risk of eating disorders among both male and female undergraduates in PE and NonPE courses to further elaborate on our preliminary hypothesis and initial results. We also intend to follow our students in a three-year longitudinal study to examine the hypothesis that focusing on eating disorders in undergraduate studies in PE may actually exacerbate the body image concerns of students in PE majors.

We are also designing an intervention study aimed at improving the body image and weight related knowledge, beliefs and attitudes of undergraduate PE students

PREVALENCE OF BODY DISSATISFACTION AND DIETING

Young Males

Body Dissatisfaction

Studies of body dissatisfaction among adolescent males and young boys are relatively new. The majority of questionnaires used to measure body image were originally developed for girls, and the one-dimensional scale of figures presented to males fails to evaluate a desire for increased fat, bulk, or muscle size or tone (Cohane & Pope, 2001; McCabe & Ricciardelli, 2004).

It is known that some young males are dissatisfied with their bodies. This can present itself as either a desire to lose weight (fat) or to increase weight (muscle) (Cohane & Pope, 2001). Even from the ages of six to eight years, boys are detecting and responding to socio cultural messages reinforcing the lean, muscular male body ideal (McCabe & Ricciardelli, 2003; Spitzer, Henderson, & Zivian, 1999). Studies of body dissatisfaction and dieting behaviors conducted among young boys have found varying results that are highly dependent upon the methodological approach taken. A recent study found preadolescent boys to be predominantly satisfied, with a small minority wanting to be either smaller or bigger (McCabe & Ricciardelli, 2004). Another study reported that 60 percent of male and female 4th grade children (aged 9, 10 and 11 years) indicated that they often or sometimes wished to be thinner (Gustafson-Larson & Terry, 1992).

Dieting

The reasons that boys begin dieting to lose weight are reported as primarily, in order, to reduce overweight, but also to avoid medical complications of obesity that have affected their parents; avoid teasing; avoid weight gain when sidelined by injuries or to improve sports performance (Anderson & Holman, 1997). A study of 969 third grade children in public schools in the USA found 25.5 percent of the boys wanted to lose weight, and that 17.2 percent had attempted to do so by dieting (Robinson, Chang, Haydel, & Killen, 2000). In a large study of 16, 114 nine to fourteen year olds, 17 percent of the nine year old boys self reported trying to lose weight (Field et al., 1999).

Young boys have also been found to desire weight gain, and to engage in behaviors to achieve this goal. Reasons for desired weight gain included increased physical strength (67 percent); better self protection, greater fitness, improved body image (51 percent), improved attractiveness, increased toughness, enhanced self esteem and as a hobby (35 percent) (O'Dea & Rawstorne, 2001). Behaviors used to try to increase weight included eating more food in general in combination with exercising less or increasing exercise, especially lifting weights. Male adolescents also reported dietary changes for weight gain such as eating more fatty, fried and junk foods; eating more healthy foods; or using supplements and protein foods and formulas (O'Dea & Rawstorne, 2001).

Adolescent Males

The main body image concerns of adolescent boys is to gain weight, size and strength (Dwyer, Feldman, Seltzer, & Mayer, 1969; O'Dea & Rawstorne, 2001) in order to attain the male body ideal and to avoid teasing or criticism about their appearance (Anderson, 1984). In contrast to girls, who grow further away from the thin ideal with weight gain during puberty, male pubertal weight gain in the chest, shoulders and arms tends to bring them closer to the cultural ideal. Nevertheless, body dissatisfaction does occur, with approximately equal numbers of adolescent males desiring weight loss and weight gain. A study of 16-18 year old high school students in England found 69 percent of 12th grade males reported that their current weight was different from their ideal with 31 percent desiring weight loss and 38 percent desiring weight gain (Furnham & Calnan, 1998). Particular groups of males, such as those participating in school sport, were more likely to desire weight gain, with an American study of athletic high schools finding that 47 percent of adolescent men in athletic teams wanted to gain weight (Wang & Yesalis, 1994). This desired weight gain may have implications for both the physical and mental health of these young people, with a correlation found between high school males with a high drive for muscularity having a lower self esteem and higher incidence of depression (McCreary & Sasse, 2000).

Dieting

Studies have recently begun to investigate the incidence of dieting to gain weight among adolescent boys. 21.2 percent of adolescent boys in a state wide school survey conducted in Connecticut in the USA were deliberately eating more food or using food supplements in order to gain weight, with boys in the 7th grade reporting dieting, exercising and engaging in more disordered eating practices than boys in 9th or 11th grade (Neumark-Sztainer, Story, Faulkner, Beuhring, & Resnick, 1999). Another American study found 28.4% of adolescent boys were currently attempting to gain weight by exercising and increasing calories (Rosen & Gross, 1987). An Australian study found that 25.9 percent of male high school students in grades 7-12 reported deliberately trying to gain weight in the past 12 months (O'Dea & Rawstorne, 2001).

Dieting to lose weight is a difficult construct to measure as differences in the wording of a question, and individual perceptions of what it means to be on a diet all affect the results found. A large cross sectional school based study of 6728 young people in grades 5-12 found

20.2 percent of the males had dieted to lose weight at some point (Neumark-Sztainer & Hannan, 2000). Seven percent of males reported engaging in "disordered eating" binge-purge cycle at some point, with 4.1 percent binging and purging daily (Neumark-Sztainer & Hannan, 2000). In a smaller Australian study, (Paxton et al., 1991) found 11.4 percent of male high school students to report ever having dieted; and 26 percent using one extreme weight loss behavior at least occasionally. In terms of current dieting, 12.4 percent of 7th, 9th and 11th grade public school students in Connecticut had dieted to lose weight in the last seven days, and 3.1 percent had used disordered eating behaviors (Neumark-Sztainer et al., 1999). Exercise appears to be the predominant method of weight loss followed by decreasing calories and cutting out snacks, junk food and sweets (Rosen & Gross, 1987).

Several studies have concluded that males at higher BMI have more weight concerns and engage in increased dieting and disordered eating behaviors (Carlat et al., 1997; Field et al., 2001; Neumark-Sztainer & Hannan, 2000; O'Dea & Abraham, 1999). This increases the difficulty of diagnosis of body image and eating problems in young men as they may not appear to be experiencing weight problems and are known for their lack of discussion and disclosure about their body, their weight and their health.

Age of Onset of Eating Disorders and Body Image Problems

Epidemiological trends tend to suggest that eating disorders may develop later in males than in females. In most studies of eating disorders that compare males and females directly, mean age of onset of illness was found to be later for males than for females (Pope, Harrison et al., 1986; Schneider & Agras, 1987; Sharp et al., 1994) and was described as statistically significant in some of the reports (Bramon-Bosch, Troop, & Treasure, 2000; Pope, Harrison et al., 1986). In a study of admissions to the eating disorders unit of a New York hospital, the mean age of onset of illness was found to be 21 for males and 17 for females (Braun et al., 1999). In a larger study of 135 men in a Massachusetts hospital the mean age of onset of illness was reported to be 19 years (Carlat et al., 1997). Males also appeared to have a longer treatment delay in that they presented for treatment at an average of 26 (Carlat et al., 1997) and 30 (Bramon-Bosch et al., 2000) years of age.

These trends are supported by theoretical reasoning for the later age of onset of eating disorders in males. Puberty is known to be a high-risk period for the onset of dieting, disordered eating and eating disorders(Pederson Mussel, Binford, & Fulkerson, 2000; Stice, 2002). On average, puberty occurs one and a half to two years later in males than in females (Offer, Schonert-Reichl, & Boxer, 1996), which may explain the apparent later onset of eating disorders in male patients.

Men

Body Dissatisfaction

It is believed that there is generally no difference in absolute body dissatisfaction between men and women (Tiggemann, 1994), but that men are typically divided between a desire for weight loss and weight gain. Men without eating disorders are reported to want a more muscular build (Collins & Plahn, 1988) with a particular preference for a "V-shape" (Kearney-Cooke & Steichen-Asch, 1990) and larger upper body (Thompson & Tantleff,

1992). This body shape is said to be intimately tied to cultural perceptions of masculinity and is associated with power and strength (Olivardia, Pope Jr, Borowiecki, & Cohane, 2004). Men are also described as being less concerned with exact weight or clothing size and to concentrate more on achieving the masculine, muscular male ideal of a large upper body and narrow hips and waist (Anderson, 1984). Men with eating disorders express a preference for a thin, lean, and toned shape (Kearney-Cooke & Steichen-Asch, 1990). The ineffectiveness of traditional, female focused body image scales to identify, diagnose and detect problems among men is therefore apparent, and this may be part of the reason for the lack of, and difficulty in describing male body image.

It is commonly accepted that women are dissatisfied with their bodies. Body dissatisfaction is now recognized as well entrenched among males, with a large survey of college men revealing that 95 percent expressed dissatisfaction with some aspect of their body, in particular the chest, waist and weight (Mishkind, Rodin, Silberstein, & Striegel-Moore, 1986). Research has consistently agreed and confirmed that approximately half of the males who are dissatisfied with their body desire weight gain, and half desire weight loss and that muscularity is more important to men's body satisfaction than fat (Leit, Gray, & Pope Jr, 2002; Pope,. et al., 2000). Early studies of body dissatisfaction in men revealed that 40-45 percent of men wanted to lose weight and 40-46.8 percent desired weight gain (Drenowski & Yee, 1987; Silberstein, Striegel-Moore, Timko, & Rodin, 1988). A more recent study found that 46 percent of men wanted to gain weight and 32 percent wanted to lose weight; and only 22 percent did not desire a weight change (Drenowski, Kurth, & Krahn, 1995). Further, a recent exploration of body dissatisfaction in males has shown that those men who show the greatest drive for increased build also show the highest levels of body dissatisfaction (McCabe & Ricciardelli, 2004).

Recent studies have employed measurement techniques that allow males to specify a desire for increased muscularity rather than "weight". Using the newly developed somatomorphic matrix (Cafri et al., 2004) to measure body dissatisfaction, college males chose an ideal body with an average of 25 pounds more muscle and eight pounds less fat than their own actual body (Olivardia et al., 2004). This study was then replicated in France, Austria and America, with men desiring an average of a 28 pound increase in muscularity(Pope, Jr. et al., 2000). The men in both studies also chose a figure that they perceived females found attractive that was significantly more muscular and lean than the females themselves had indicated (Olivardia et al., 2004). This finding is consistent with earlier studies (Connor-Greene, 1988; Fallon & Rozin, 1985; O'Dea, 1999; Thompson & Tantleff, 1992)

Reasons for the apparent increased drive for muscularity and investment in appearance among males may be explained as a cultural shift towards the objectification of men's bodies. Some researchers postulate that men's attitudes towards their bodies have become highly related to their aesthetic appearance rather than being based on what they are capable of doing (Morrison, Morrison, & Hopkins, 2003; Rohlinger, 2002).

Further, the muscular male body has been "overwhelmingly assigned" personality traits such as attractive, strong, and powerful, while skinny and obese body types have attained negative associations such as lazy, sneaky and weak (Cafri & Thompson, 2004). This is reflected in qualitative studies, showing that the predominant reason for men wanting to increase muscularity was for social benefit; so that they would be attractive, especially to women; and as a sign of status(Morrison et al., 2003). Men report that they would feel stronger and more confident if they were more muscular; and it has been found that an involvement in weight training increases body satisfaction in males regardless of overall muscle mass (McCreary & Sasse, 2000).

Diagnosis of Eating Disorders among Men

The large amount of research and media attention focusing on body image issues and eating disorders in women may perpetuate the acknowledgement of eating disorders as female problems, and therefore teachers, counselors and doctors often fail to suspect males of eating problems; and males are discouraged from admitting to them. Males may also be excluded from diagnosis on a definitional basis when amenorrhea is required as criteria (Anderson & Mickalide, 1983). Furthermore, the low known prevalence of mild or sub-clinical cases in males (Anderson & Holman, 1997) may represent the fact that body image issues and eating problems are not detected in men until they are well-entrenched and are usually only diagnosed when significant psychiatric co-morbidity is present, for example depression and anxiety disorders.

Disordered Eating Behaviors

Men see physical activity as a masculine and effective method of weight loss (Drummond, 2002; Yates, 1991) and it appears to be the primary method of weight loss and weight control in males rather than a restrictive diet or disordered eating behaviors (Drenowski & Yee, 1987; Yates, 1991). This complicates the diagnosis of eating and exercise disorders in males as they are unlikely to attract attention to their behavior, as they do not tend to lose a large amount of weight. An overzealous dedication to exercise has become a socially acceptable and culturally praised activity which is admired, valued and equated with health and fitness; and a commitment to exercise is highly valued rather than questioned in Western culture.

Males are less likely to engage in typically well known disordered eating behaviors, such as diet pills and laxatives (Braun et al., 1999). An early study of college students found that 14 percent of American college men self-reported bingeing an average of at least once a week and nine percent reported engaging in one or more behaviors including: fasting, diuretics, laxatives, or self induced vomiting for weight control (Zuckerman, Colby, Ware, & Lazerson, 1986). In another early study, four percent of males admitted that they had self-induced vomiting to lose weight (Connor-Greene, 1988).

Men with eating disorders have been found to perceive less pressure to be thin than women. A recent trial using the somatomorphic matrix found that when compared to a control group, men with eating disorders had a realistic body fat ideal, but perceived themselves to be at least twice as fat as they actually were (Mangweth et al., 2004). This has important implications for interventions involving men as it redirects the focus of education towards eating disordered men's perceptions of their body fat rather than what level of body fat is normal and acceptable (Mangweth et al., 2004).

Muscle Dysmorphia

Pope and colleagues describe muscle dysmorphia, which replaces their earlier term of "reverse anorexia" (Pope, Katz, & Hudson, 1993). Muscle dysmorphia is a form of body dysmorphic disorder involving a pathological fear of being too small, and a persistent desire for, and engagement in activity to achieve a more muscular body that interferes with an individual's social and occupational functioning due to the long periods of time spent thinking about, planning, and actually exercising (Pope, Gruber, Choi, Olivardia, & Phillips, 1997). Men with muscle dysmorphia differ from other men who train with weights in that they aspire to unrealistic levels of muscularity and body size, have increased rates body dissatisfaction, may abuse anabolic steroids, consume excessive amounts of protein and creatine supplements, engage in dieting and disordered eating practices and have increased levels of anxiety and mood disorders.

Muscle dysmorphia has not been formally recognized as a mental illness or psychological problem despite the potentially harmful dietary, exercise and drug related practices that are employed (Anderson, Barlett, Morgan, & Brownell, 1995; Davis & Scott-Robertson, 2000). In fact, the practices and attainment of this figure is often perceived to be the epitome of health, fitness, strength and sex appeal. While thinness and underweight are associated with sickness, achievement of the muscular male ideal is closely linked to health, vitality, strength and power (Olivardia et al., 2004).

Causes and Risk Factors of Body Image Issues and Eating Disorders Specific to Males

Mass Media

Both men and women in Western societies receive pressure from a variety of sources to adhere to an ideal body shape and to change their appearance. Sources of body image pressure include the family, peers, and the media.

It has been argued that males are predominantly visual beings and therefore may be particularly affected by visual advertising material, finding it more evocative than females do (Barthel, 1992). Recent investigations of the effect of the mass media on males have been in the form of controlled clinical studies where participants are shown magazine and television advertisements or media images depicting ideal or hyper-mesomorphic males. In many of these studies, it has been found that experimental groups had heightened body dissatisfaction compared to the control group in terms of perceived-ideal muscularity levels (Agliata & Tantleff-Dunn, 2004; Humphreys & Paxton, 2004; Leit et al., 2002; Morrison et al., 2003). The most recent of these studies (Agliata & Tantleff-Dunn, 2004) concluded that viewing ideal male images in advertisements significantly increased muscle dissatisfaction and depression. Another smaller American study of college students found that although females were significantly more likely to be affected by the images, both male and female high body dissatisfaction groups were sensitive to the images shown (Hausenblas, Janelle, Gardner, & Hagan, 2002).

The mass media have been held liable for the perpetuation of the thin ideal for women. In addition, the mass media are known to run articles that serve to provide information about dieting and eating disorders which is known to both normalize and glamorize these behaviors (O'Dea, 2000). This media attention to body image problems and eating disorders in women may create a perception these are issues that are only experienced by girls and women. This may further discourage men to present for treatment for these problems (Anderson & Mickalide, 1983).

It is traditionally believed that there is less media pressure on males to conform to an ideal body shape, however it has now become apparent that the hyper-mesomorphic ideal for men is as equally pervasive and dangerous as the thin ideal for women. The size of males in both the population and the media has been reported to have increased from the 1950's (Spitzer et al., 1999), however this study made no distinction between fat free mass and adipose tissue. The average *Playgirl* centerfold man has been observed as becoming increasingly lean and muscular between 1973 and 1997, shedding 12 pounds of fat and gaining 27 pounds of muscle (Leit, Pope Jr, & Gray, 2001). In addition, it has been found that action figures such as GI Joe and Star Wars figurines have increased in muscularity over time, with major increases in the chest and shoulder measurements (Pope, Olivardia, Gruber, & Borowiecki, 1999). Current models of these toys far exceed levels of muscularity that are achievable by adult human beings, let alone pre-pubertal boys.

The degree to which the mass media affects male body image and eating and exercise behaviors is still largely unknown. Murray and colleagues (1996) proclaim that although the media affects men's awareness and knowledge of health-related issues, they are less likely than females to try to become like the ideals portrayed by the media (Murray, Touyz, & Beumont, 1996). In 1992, it was found that popular male magazines contained less diet and shape related articles and advertisements than popular women's magazines (Anderson & DiDomenico, 1992). However, by 1994, the use of qualitative research techniques, and in particular, content analysis, revealed an increased focus on weight loss in men's magazines, and a decrease in diet and weight related articles in women's magazines (Nemeroff, Stein, Diehl, & Smilack, 1994). This change may be even more marked if conducted today, as male's magazines seem to have increased the weight and shape related content; while women's magazines have had to change their focus from diet and weight, and some have even developed policies revolving around the use of underweight models in response to the consistent blaming of the media for women's body image issues and the development of eating disorders.

Overweight

Studies have found a higher prevalence of eating disorders and disordered eating behaviors in males who were previously overweight (Beumont, Bearwood, & Russell, 1972; Braun et al., 1999; Carlat et al., 1997; Neumark-Sztainer & Hannan, 2000; Neumark-Sztainer et al., 1999; Touyz et al., 1993). In a study of 135 men at a Massachusetts hospital, it was found that bulimic men were significantly more likely to report a parental and personal history of obesity and were heavier than those being treated for Anorexia Nervosa and other eating disorders at the beginning of their treatment (Carlat et al., 1997). In a much smaller report of 12 men being treated for anorexia nervosa in an Australian hospital, six patients reported a history of being overweight (Touyz et al., 1993).

History of Psychiatric Illness

Research consistently shows males with eating disorders to have high co-morbid rates of depression, suicidal intent or suicide attempts, substance abuse, anxiety disorders and personality disorders (Anderson & Mickalide, 1983; Bramon-Bosch et al., 2000; Carlat et al., 1997; Olivardia, Pope, Mangweth, & Hudson, 1995a; Striegel-Moore, Garvin, Dohm, & Rosenheck, 1999; Woodside et al., 2001); with males suffering from bulimia nervosa experiencing higher levels of substance abuse (Carlat et al., 1997; Striegel-Moore et al.,

1999). In addition, a study of 24 males with Anorexia Nervosa noted that these men were more likely to exhibit obsessive character traits during childhood such as being "meticulous", "thorough" or "ruled by the clock" (Sharp et al., 1994).

By surveying the patient records of two English hospitals, two separate studies found a family history of psychiatric illness was a prominent feature of their development of Anorexia Nervosa in males. A family history of psychiatric illnesses including severe alcoholism, chronic agoraphobia, anxiety, depression and suicide were found among one in four of the 24 patients studies, together with a recurring theme of social phobic avoidance patterns (Crisp & Toms, 1972). Chronic psychiatric illnesses were found in one third of male patients that had undergone treatment for Anorexia Nervosa in another English hospital (Sharp et al., 1994). These illnesses were predominantly described as paternal alcoholism, with some noting Anorexia Nervosa in their mother or siblings (Sharp et al., 1994).

High Risk Occupations

Men in professions that necessitate weight restrictions, or are related to aesthetic appearance may have an increased vulnerability to body image issues and eating and exercise problems. Studies have found individuals in food and exercise related career paths to be at risk for disturbed dieting and exercise behaviors to the same or higher extent as the general population (Kinzl et al., 1999; McArthur & Howard, 2001; O'Dea & Abraham, 2001; Palmquist- Fredenberg et al., 1996; Worobey & Schoenfeld, 1999). They are exposed to similar socio-cultural pressures as other adults, yet their career paths are highly involved with food, eating and weight control, and may actually necessitate weight restrictions.

A preoccupation with food and exercise is also known to be characteristic of individuals with eating disorders (Larson, 1989; Worobey & Schoenfeld, 1999) and it has been suggested that this may cause them to gravitate towards careers that are food and exercise related (Crockett & Littrell, 1985; Reinstein et al., 1992; Sours, 1980). In addition, those suffering from exercise disorders have been known to seek employment in gyms and fitness centers despite holding higher qualifications to allow their own obsession with exercise and fitness to continue

In their study of 135 males at a Massachusetts general hospital, Carlat and colleagues (1997) found that of the 109 patients for which occupational data was available, 16 percent were categorized as being in potentially high risk jobs, such as those related to appearance (modeling), those traditionally held by women (nursing) and food-related jobs. It was also noted that in several cases, the disorder was clearly related to the occupation, for example one patient had reported taking appetite suppressant pills in order to remain slim for acting roles and then went on to develop binge eating and self-induced vomiting within a few months (Carlat et al., 1997).

Employment in the health and fitness industry is unique in that the knowledge and competence of staff is intentionally or subconsciously judged by their appearance. Male fitness leaders have been found to experience a professional need to project a certain image, and have made comments such as:

> "In this industry you have to look the part. I mean, there's no point in having someone who's overweight as a fitness leader. It's not the right image. You've got to look fit" (Phillips & Drummond, 2001, p 99).

Although the majority of fitness leaders in the aforementioned study were found to be satisfied with their appearance, this satisfaction was highly dependant upon their ability to complete strength exercises and to demonstrate a definite sense of control over their body weight and appearance.

High Risk Sports

Men who participate in certain sports and physical activity tend to engage in some disordered eating and exercise behaviors. At this stage, it is unknown whether certain sports and physical activity that necessitate weight restrictions and aesthetic appearance drive certain men to use disordered eating and exercise behaviors, or if men who suffer from eating disorders are attracted to certain sports due to their highly controlled personality and lifestyle (Drummond, 2002; Olivardia, Pope Jr, & Hudson, 2000). In a study at a New York eating disorder treatment facility between 1984 and 1987, 36.7 percent of the 51 males admitted stated that they were involved in an occupation or athletic team where performance relied on control of weight is (Braun et al., 1999). These sports included wrestling, weightlifting, running and team sports (Braun et al., 1999). The desire to achieve sporting success may then outweigh even the most pressing of health concerns. This can lead to potentially harmful weight loss or weight gain practices being used with no consideration of the effects on the body. Several studies have reported sub-clinical eating disorders and extreme dieting behaviors among both male and female athletes under pressure to achieve low body weights to qualify for or excel in their particular sport (Anderson, 2002; Fogelholm & Hilloskorpi, 1999; Thiel, Gottfried, & Hesse, 1993). Therefore high-risk behavioral practices such as dehydration, steroid use, excessive exercise (aerobic or strength) may be used in order to achieve personal and societal expectations of bodily perfection.

A recent study by the National Collegiate Athletic Association [NCAA] surveyed 1445 varsity athletes including 883 males. This study found one male to self reporting having anorexia nervosa; however the questionnaire used in the study identified 9.5 percent of male athletes to be “at risk” for anorexia nervosa and 38 percent “at risk” for bulimia nervosa (Johnson, Powers, & Dick, 1999). Similar numbers of male and female athletes (26.6 and 28.0 percent respectively) were found to report that they had engaged in binge eating at least once in their lifetime, and 8.4 percent of females and 8.6 percent of boys reported binge eating weekly (Johnson et al., 1999).

A study comparing the body dissatisfaction of football players and cross country runners identified significant body dissatisfaction in both sports, as 83 percent of cross country runners were dissatisfied with their current weight, and only five percent of footballers reported being satisfied with their current weight (McKay Parks & Read, 1997). The difference in the direction of this body dissatisfaction was then highly correlated with the demands of the sport they were participating in, with 43 percent of cross country runners wanting to increase, and 20 percent wanting to decrease their weight; while 80 percent of football players were wanting to increase and 15 percent were wanting to decrease their body weight (McKay Parks & Read, 1997). One limitation of this study was that there was no distinction between the desire for a change in body fat or muscularity, but based on previous reports (Collins & Plahn, 1988; Thompson & Tantleff, 1992) one can assume that the males desired loss of fat and increased muscle mass.

The prevalence of weight loss behaviors have not appeared to have changed despite significant variations in rules regarding weight cycling in wrestling in the USA (Oppliger,

Landry, Foster, & Lambrecht, 1993). In a large study of high school wrestlers, 48 percent stated that they would lose weight by the end of the wrestling season, four percent would vomit and two percent use diuretics or laxatives. The most frequent methods of weight loss reported were increased exercise, reported to be used daily by 41 percent or participants in the study, and heated wrestling rooms, which were used by 21 percent of participants daily (Kinningham & Gorenflo, 2001). In addition, this study was severely limited by a 35 percent response rate indicating the possibility of underreporting of weight loss and weight cycling behaviors.

Studies have found that competitive and recreational bodybuilders and men who train with weights desire a hyper-mesomorphic body shape and report feelings of anxiety, depression, isolation, and exhibit low self esteem, perfectionism and narcissism (Anderson, 2002; O'Sullivan & Tiggemann, 1997). This amounts to a similar psychological profile to women with eating disorders, in particular anorexia nervosa (Davis & Scott-Robertson, 2000), with the main difference being that a desire for muscularity and intense fear of being too small are present. They also tend to perceive themselves to be less muscular than they actually are (Loosemore & Moriarty, 1990; O'Sullivan & Tiggemann, 1997), which has further adverse effects on their self esteem and masculinity. Body builders had significantly higher levels of body dissatisfaction, bulimia, drive for leanness and drive for bulk when compared to men involved in martial arts and running (Blouin & Goldfield, 1995).

In an American study of 45 bodybuilders competing in a drug-free competition, 39 percent of competitors reported being always or often preoccupied with food during the body-building season. Techniques such as eating smaller meals (68 percent), calorie counting (56 percent), special diets (18 percent) and fasting (12 percent) were the most common methods used to lose weight. Amino acids (50 percent), eating extra meals (40 percent), protein powder (32 percent) and liquid supplements (26 percent) were reported methods of weight gain. Questionable sources of nutrition information and competition preparation were found to be used, including friends (27 percent), health club staff and former competitors (18 percent), magazines (16 percent) and books (7 percent) (Anderson et al., 1995).

Olivardia and his colleagues (2000) suggest that weight lifting in itself is not necessarily associated with a precursor to eating disorders or muscle dysmorphia. Rather it is the sociocultural, genetic and environmental influences as well as a vulnerable personality type that may lead to muscle dysmorphia, a mental illness that leads to excessive weight lifting in an effort to get bigger (Olivardia et al., 2000). A case-controlled study that separated normal weight lifters from those exhibiting signs of muscle dysmorphia found the groups to differ significantly. Those with muscle dysmorphia reported a greater period of time (three hours versus 41 minutes respectively) thinking about their muscularity and wanting to be bigger than the normal controls; and there was significant social impairment due to their perceived smallness. Weightlifters with muscle dysmorphia reported significant body dissatisfaction despite a greater fat free mass than the normal control group and 54 percent of muscle dysmorphic weight lifters reported 'little' or 'no' control over their compulsive weight lifting and dietary regimens (Olivardia et al., 2000)

Masculinity

In the past, men's esteem and success was based on their career, economic status and intelligence. Although this may still be the case, these factors have become closely linked to their appearance, to the point where an attractive muscular male exhibiting the ideal figure is assumed to possess certain social and personality characteristics such as intelligence, power, and social skills. Men's success is becoming more aesthetically oriented, to the point where it may even enable them more success in the workplace (Petrie & Rogers, 2001).

In addition, sport, exercise and endurance have significant cultural connotations of masculinity. In particular those sports and activities which promote culturally accepted masculine qualities such as strength, endurance, violence and aggression (Young, White, & McTeer, 1994).

Sexuality

Clinical studies conducted in eating disorder treatment facilities have shown a disproportionately high number of men to be homosexual or experiencing sexual conflict (Schneider & Agras, 1987; Siever, 1994). In a large study of males who had been treated for eating disorders, it was found that of the 122 males for which sexual orientation data was available, 41 percent were heterosexual, 27 percent were homosexual or bisexual and 32 percent were asexual (Carlat et al., 1997). One in three males with bulimia nervosa in a smaller clinical setting also identified as homosexual (Schneider & Agras, 1987).

Community samples including homosexual and heterosexual men show those identifying as homosexual have a higher incidence of body dissatisfaction and are more likely to engage in disordered eating (Siever, 1994). Gay men have been found to be similarly dissatisfied with their bodies as heterosexual and homosexual women, whereas heterosexual men were found to be significantly more satisfied (Beren, Hayden, Wilfley, & Grilo, 1996). Gay men have also been found to have significantly higher drive for thinness than other college subgroups (Yager, Kurtzman, Landsverk, & Wiesmeier, 1988), and a greater body dissatisfaction and increased presence of anorexic and bulimic symptoms (Connor & Grogan, 2004; Russell & Keel, 2002).

This has been attributed to the Western male homosexual subculture placing an exaggerated emphasis on youthfulness, thinness, attractiveness and a high value on appearance, while lesbian culture tends to de-emphasizes aesthetics (Carlat et al., 1997; Siever, 1994; Williamson, 1999). Gay men may also adhere to the centrality of physical appearance in attracting male partners as homosexual females (Siever, 1994; Williamson, 1999).

It is unknown as to whether these prevalence figures are representative only of those males who present for treatment, or those who volunteer to participate in studies about body image and eating behavior. It is known that men are typically reluctant to present for treatment (Anderson & Mickalide, 1983) and that women with eating disorders avoid completing questionnaires about body image and eating behavior (Beglin & Fairburn, 1992). Men who identify as homosexual or bisexual may be less concerned with the association of femininity and eating disorders.

Studies that refute the association between eating disorders and homosexual identity in males have been limited in sample size and generalizability (Anderson, 1984; Olivardia et al., 1995a) did not find correlation between sexuality and eating disorders in college men. However the statistical power of this group has been called into question (Russell & Keel, 2002). Recent studies have indicated that it may be gender role, rather than the sexual orientation that is related to disordered eating, with femininity appearing to be a specific risk factor, while masculinity is as a protective factor for eating disorder pathology (Meyer, Blissett, & Oldfield, 2001; Russell & Keel, 2002)

CREATINE AND SUPPLEMENT USE

The socially desirable, hyper-mesomorphic body shape for males is physiologically difficult to obtain without the use of dangerous eating or exercise behaviors, as well as supplements such as creatine, protein powders and anabolic steroids. Professional and recreational participation in sports and physical activity is known to predispose and then perpetuate athletes to engage in anabolic steroid use. A recent study of college males reported that 27 percent had used over the counter body building supplements such as creatine and ephedrine and/ or illicit drugs such as anabolic steroids to gain muscle or lose fat (Olivardia et al., 2004). These findings are believed to be underestimates due to fears of legal or personal consequences of using prohibited ergonomic aids.

Anabolic Steroids

Self reported use of anabolic steroids among males ranges from 0.6 to 72 percent in males, with variance attributed to the age and athletic pursuits of the participants (Drenowski et al., 1995; Loosemore & Moriarty, 1990). However these data are considered to be underestimates due to fears of legal or personal consequences of reporting steroid use. Drenowski and colleagues (1995) reported a 0.6 percent usage among 2088 athletes at freshman orientation at a large Midwestern University in the USA, where users were most likely to engage in basketball, weight training, swimming and running. In a small study of 43 recreational and competitive bodybuilders, 44.2 percent reported using steroids (Blouin & Goldfield, 1995) with "improved looks" and "increased size needed for competitive sport" cited as the major reasons for their use. In a Canadian study, 84 percent of body builders reported that they had considered and 72 percent reported that they had actually taken steroids; while only 16.6 percent of hockey players and 8 percent of the control subjects indicated that they had ever considered taking steroids (Loosemore & Moriarty, 1990). Men with muscle dysmorphia are known to be significantly more likely to use anabolic steroids, with 46 percent of men with muscle dysmorphia reporting the use of anabolic steroids compared to seven percent of the normal control men who lifted weights (Olivardia, Pope Jr, & Hudson, 2000). Many of the reported effects of anabolic steroids are anecdotal as clinical trials of the drug are not possible, however withdrawal and dependency disorders have been reported.

Creatine

Creatine is considered by recreational and professional athletes to be a safe and effective alternative to anabolic steroids (Smith & Dahm, 2000). It has been recommended as an ergogenic aid for athletes engaging in repeated bouts of brief, strenuous, high intensity maximal exercise (Feldman, 1999). However the scientific community has so far only been able to estimate the precise mechanism by which creatine improves performance, and the long term effects of its use are unknown (Juhn, O'Kane, & Vinci, 1999; Smith & Dahm, 2000). Side effects such as diarrhea, muscle cramps and loss of appetite have been reported (Juhn et al., 1999; Smith & Dahm, 2000), although these are largely anecdotal due to a substantial lack of clinical trials. Juhn and colleagues (1999) reported that although many of the athletes who reported taking creatine had also reported side effects, the perceived benefits of using it outweighed the possible risks.

Estimates of the use of creatine vary greatly. In professional athletes, the reported use of creatine includes between 25-75 percent of American professional football players, 40-45 percent of Norwegian power athletes aged 17-31 (Ronson, Sundgot-Borgen, & Maehlum, 1999). In a sample of 328 male high school athletes, 30 percent rarely, 35 percent weekly and 35 percent report daily use of creatine. In Canadian High school males, 9.9 percent stated that they would use creatine, 7.7 percent were currently using creatine and 55.5 percent of high school males reported that they would not use it (Bell, Dorsch, McCreary, & Hovey, 2004). Usage of creatine in young Australian males is estimated to be 9 percent in males 8-12 years, and 7 percent in males 12-18 years (O'Dea, 2003).

Perhaps more interesting than the variable prevalence of the use of creatine, is the lack of knowledge about it's performance enhancing ability and possible side effects by both the scientific community and the users themselves. In a recent study of creatine use among high school athletes, 75 percent of those currently using creatine were not aware of the dosage they were taking, or were taking higher doses than recommended (Smith & Dahm, 2000). Information about the use of creatine was predominantly obtained from friends, and a staggering 93 percent of current users wanted more information about the use of creatine (Smith & Dahm, 2000)

Supplements

There appears to be a high usage, yet low knowledge of the performance enhancing effects of nutritional supplements among adolescent males. In a study of 698 American High School students, 4.5 percent of boys trying to lose weight and 10.9 percent of boys trying to gain weight reported using powder mixes or food supplements (Rosen & Gross, 1987). Multivitamins and minerals were reported to currently be used by 42.4 percent of Canadian high school males, and 16.7 percent report that they were currently using protein supplements (Bell et al., 2004). The low level of knowledge was particularly apparent in this study as the boys stated that they believed multivitamins or minerals (55.7 percent), creatine (55.2 percent) and protein supplements (47.3 percent) to enhance performance (Bell et al., 2004). In addition, 35 percent of year 8 high school boys in Australia recommend that body building powders be used for weight gain (Nowak & Speare, 1996)

In a structured focus group study of 78 Australian High School students, it was found that 56.4 percent had consumed sports drinks, 48.7 percent sports drinks, and 48.7 had consumed vitamin or mineral supplements (O'Dea, 2003). Although many of the children could clearly articulate the perceived benefits of various forms of supplementation, they neglected to recognize any negative or potentially dangerous effects of the consumption of nutritional supplements; with an "energy boost", prevention of illness and taste were frequently mentioned as reasons for the consumption. When 8-12 year old males were compared with 12-18 year old males it was found that the boys were more likely than the adolescent men to consume sports drinks (53 percent versus 49 percent); vitamins and minerals (41 percent versus 36 percent); high protein milk supplements (32 percent versus 12 percent); and energy drinks (27 percent versus 24 percent) (O'Dea & Rawstorne, 2000).

ATTEMPTS AT PREVENTION OF EATING DISORDERS AND BODY IMAGE CONCERNS AMONG MALES

Early studies of eating disorder prevention tended to focus on teenaged females. Suggestions by eating disorder prevention theorists and researchers argued for the inclusion of boys (O'Dea & Abraham, 2000; Piran, 1995) for the benefit of the young male participants but also as a way of including young men in the feminist debate about the stereotyping of the slim female ideal. The early suggestions for the inclusion of male adolescents and fathers was seen as an influential way to reduce the reinforcement of the slim female stereotypes and thereby reduce the pressure placed on young females to seek the slim ideal body. More recently, (McCabe & Ricciardelli, 2004) quite sensibly suggest that preventive and intervention programs for body dissatisfaction and disordered eating be implemented among males before they become problems that require clinical interventions.

Table II presents a summary of all of the published randomized and controlled eating disorder prevention trials and body image improvement interventions to date that have included male school students.

The study of Smolak and her colleagues (1998) produced significant improvement in nutrition knowledge and knowledge of dieting among 9-10 year old students. The program did not affect behavior change but it did improve the student's attitudes towards fat people - a prejudice which underlies much of the teasing and bullying experienced by overweight children. A follow-up of the original students (Smolak & Levine, 2001) demonstrated a long-term maintenance of nutrition knowledge together with program participants reporting lesser usage of weight control techniques.

The later studies of O'Dea & Abraham (2000) and Varnardo-Sullivan et al, (2001) both produced significant improvements in the body image of male adolescents, supporting the inclusion of males in such prevention programs.

Future studies of eating disorder prevention and body image improvement should include males as well as females. Such interventions should incorporate design features that address issues pertinent to the specific body image concerns of males including issues of weight gain, muscularity and masculinity.

Table III presents a summary of body image improvement and disordered eating prevention programs that have included college males.

Table II. Summary of randomized & controlled eating disorder prevention programs and body image improvement interventions which have included male school students 1998-2004

Authors	Sample	Intervention	Results	Conclusions
(Smolak, Levine, & Schermer, 1998)	222 male and female 5th grade students aged 9-10 years in the USA	"Eating Smart, Eating for Me", a universal didactic psycho educational program that consisted of 10 classroom lessons about - Knowledge of nutrition, body fat and dieting - Attitudes about fat people and body esteem - Behaviors, eg healthy eating and exercise	-Improved knowledge of nutrition, effects of dieting and causes of body fat -Improved attitudes towards fat people	-Authors concluded that behavior change such as eating and exercise patterns, weight reduction attempts and teasing fat children was not changed by the program. -Was taught by classroom teachers who may have altered or omitted some lessons
(Buddeberg-Fischer, Klaghofer, Gnam, & Guddeberg, 1998)	314 male and female students 14-19 years in Switzerland who had scored relatively high on pre-test of disturbed eating	Didactic, targeted intervention of three health promotion lessons including material on: - Beauty ideals - Pubertal Development - Healthy eating and nutrition - Eating Disorders and their treatment	-No intervention effect in males or females for eating attitudes, physical distress or psychological impairment -Girls with highest eating disorders scores improved on physical impairment symptoms	-Recommendation that prevention programs address student's cognition, emotions and behavior
(O'Dea & Abraham, 2000)	470 Male and Female students aged 11-14 years in Australia	"Everybody's Different", a universal, interactive, self esteem based program consisting of 9 consecutive weekly lessons 50-80 minutes in duration including information on: - Stress management - Building positive sense of self - Analysis and rejection of cultural and media gender stereotypes - Building self esteem - No mention of food, eating or disorders	Intervention group: -Improved body satisfaction and decreased importance of social acceptance, physical appearance and athletic ability -Improved physical self esteem in females -Less weight loss and dieting in females -Improved body image, less drive for thinness and physical self esteem in the high risk students	-Self esteem development can improve body image in male and female adolescents -Involving parents, especially fathers, seems to help female students -Positive approach rather than negative, Problem based approach appears to be beneficial
(Varnado-Sullivan et al., 2001)	157 female and 130 male 6th and 7th grade private school students 12-13 years of age in the USA	"Body Logic" program 1was based on a universal, cognitive-behavioral model, and consisted of three sessions that included activities to: - improve body image - provide information about nutritional requirements - Increase resilience to teasing	-Females improved fear of fatness and avoidance of forbidden foods -Males improved on fear of fatness - Program 2 did not receive much interest from students and parents	-Recommend that parents and teachers undergo and are included in and provided with an intervention -Suggestion that lack of participation in program 2 may be because poor body image and disordered eating behaviors may be considered acceptable among these families.

Table II. Continued

Authors	Sample	Intervention	Results	Conclusions
		- Assist students in coping with the changes of puberty - Improve communication, self esteem and problem solving skills - And did not include educational information about eating disorders Program 2 was aimed at high risk students and involved an intensive family based intervention		
(Smolak & Levine 2001)	Original 9-11 year old boys and girls compared to an additional group of new controls in the USA	Long term effect of initial "Eating Smart, Eating for Me" program in 1998	-Participants had greater knowledge, used fewer weight control techniques -Original controls had scores "in-between" suggesting contamination of the original controls	-Girls benefited more than boys -Demonstrates long term impact -Spillover effect among controls suggests that children discussed what was learned in the program, demonstrating interest and relevance of the program
(Dalle Grave, De Luca, & Campello, 2001)	106 girls and boys 11-12 years old in Italy	Universal, interactive program consisting of 6 consecutive weekly sessions, each two hours in duration that attempted to: Increase knowledge of - Eating disorders - Effects of dieting - Pressures to be thin Avoid developing an eating disorder by: - reducing importance of appearance, shape and weight - accepting normal pubertal development - developing self acceptance - maintaining a healthy lifestyle	-Improved knowledge of intervention group -No effects for body dissatisfaction, dieting, negative effect or eating pathology	-Conclude that school-based programs can improve knowledge and some attitudes in young adolescents -Suggest that the intervention group may have influenced the control group as they were within the same school
(Kater, Rohwer, & Londre, 2002)	415 Boys and girls aged 9-13 years in the USA	The "Healthy body Image" program was an 11 week program taking a psycho-educational approach at prevention by providing information on - Pubertal changes - Genetic diversity - Hazards of dieting - Nutrition - Coping skills - Media analysis	-Intervention students improved on most scales but not controls -Modest improvement in knowledge and effect of the media	-Authors conclude that knowledge can be improved but not body image suggesting that young students should be included in future programs -Suggestion that adults and school administrators become involved

Table III. Summary of eating disorder prevention programs and body image improvement interventions in male and female college students 1990-2004

Authors	Sample	Intervention	Results	Conclusions
(Mitchell, 1990)	218 male (n=81) and female (n=196) undergraduate students at a West Coast American College.	182 students enrolled in the basic nutrition course (who were not dietetics majors) became the intervention group. Students from four other courses (n= 97) made up the control group. The basic nutrition course is aimed at the general student population and is not intended for those majoring in dietetics.	-Only 45% of all participants in the nutrition course stated that they had made changes to their diet specifically due to the intervention program. -Changes in the intervention group were described to be increased confidence in the students' diets, decreased supplement use, and increased use of low fat milk -The intervention also increased students concern about weight control and their intake of fats, sodium and cholesterol	-the authors concluded that a basic nutrition class may improve students' knowledge of nutrition and allow them to make some dietary changes
(Rabak-Wagener et al., 1998)	105 male and female undergraduate students in majors other than physical education who had elected to take a "healthful living" class at a medium sized Mid west university in the USA.	Four consecutive weekly classes of one hour and 35 minutes each in duration were given to the intervention group. Topics included: - Watching a video about "Slim hopes" - Critiquing fashion advertisements and stereotypes - Constructing magazine collages	-Women improved significantly in terms of beliefs and behaviors about body image -In men there was no change	-Authors concluded that this intervention was more effective with the women than the men -And that beliefs were altered more easily than behaviors
(Zabinski et al., 2001)	338 undergraduate students a at a West Coast American college	The "Fitness for Life" program was a 15 week semester course offered to seniors as a part of Project GRAD ("Graduates Ready for Activity Daily"). This involved a weekly one-hour lecture and one and a half hour small group behavior change lab. Topics of the lectures included: - body image issues - identification and rejection of cultural and media stereotypes - Realistic goal setting for exercise programs - Dangers of dieting and eating disorders The control group also met once a week, but discussed general health topics in a lecture format	-Had an adverse affect for women, as they showed a significant increase in drive for thinness without changes to BMI or body dissatisfaction. -Significant effects at posttest were found in three physical activity variables. These included Total energy expenditure, strength and flexibility exercises but not vigorous or moderate intensity exercise -There were no changes for men in terms of BMI, body dissatisfaction, drive for thinness or on any of the 5 physical activity variables	-Although there were no effects for men, the authors suggest further development of body image interventions including males -In regard to the increase in concerns of women, it is suggested that future interventions include assessment of potentially iatrogenic content.

The study by Mitchell (1990) aimed to improve nutrition knowledge and behaviors among university undergraduates. Although changes in knowledge of nutrition were observed in the intervention group, only 45 percent of participants reported making changes to their diet because of the program, and these changes were minimal, such as using reduced fat rather than full fat milk. A randomized controlled trial of a media literacy intervention implemented by (Rabak-Wagener, Eickhoff-Shemek, & Kelly-Vance, 1998) achieved positive attitudinal and behavioral change among women in terms of them feeling less pressured to resemble a fashion model in appearance and a decreased intention to diet and exercise to accomplish this goal. There were negligible results among the male participants with possible reasoning including a bias in the males who would have elected to take the healthful living course through which the intervention was delivered. In addition, the use of the "slim hopes" video, which is highly targeted towards women and the fact that the instructor was female may have led to limited results among the male participants. The intervention by (Zabinski, Calfas, Gehrman, Wilfley, & Sallis, 2001) aimed to increase the intent and frequency of physical activity and exercise. Once again, the measures used and intervention given were based around drive for thinness and body dissatisfaction, typical concerns for females but not for males. The results of the intervention showed no change for males on any of the variables; however the female participants demonstrated increased drive for thinness and concerns about their weight and eating habits.

Of the limited eating disorder prevention and body image improvement literature available that included males, only two of the studies were randomized controlled trials (Rabak-Wagener et al., 1998; Zabinski et al., 2001), and none achieved significant effects among the male participants. This may be attributed to the measures and intervention methods being used that have not specifically been designed to measure or address the body image concerns of males. It is suggested that future interventions utilize measures of drive for muscularity and incorporate activities that are relevant to men. In addition, it may be beneficial to use resources including men or male instructors in order to reduce the stigma of body image and eating problems being female problems and possibly increase men's reporting of behaviors.

A Current Intervention for College Males and Females

Despite evidence of an increasing prevalence of disordered eating and exercise behaviors, males have been essentially overlooked in the majority of body image improvement and eating disorder prevention programs and interventions in the college population. Those studies which have included males have used measures and activities that are largely oriented towards females and therefore largely irrelevant to males. Our current intervention aims to improve the body image, disordered eating and weight loss and weight gain practices among college students enrolled in physical education majors at the University of Sydney, Australia.

The control group consists of 65 males and females enrolled in their third year of a physical education major. This group will undergo their current training program, a didactic, lecture based presentation of anthropometry, body image, weight control and eating disorders. The following two year groups of 65 males and females enrolled in their third year of a physical education major will then form the intervention group. There is therefore limited opportunity for the contamination of the control group.

The intervention program will be aimed at a personal and professional level and take a cognitive-behavioral and self-esteem based approach. We aim are to improve the participants' personal body image and reduce the use of unhealthy weight loss and weight gain practices; as well as assist in developing appropriate knowledge and attitudes to enable them to present nutrition, body image and weight management information in a manner that will help prevent body image and disordered eating and exercise behaviors in male and female school students.

The pre-test, post-test and follow-up measures will include an anonymous questionnaire using validated measures of body mass index, body image, eating and exercise behavior and attitudes towards overweight. Measures that have been specifically included to address male body image and disordered eating and exercise behavior include the Drive for Muscularity questionnaire (McCreary & Sasse, 2000) and Obligatory Exercise Questionnaire (Pasman & Thompson, 1988).

CONCLUSION

Body image issues and eating disorders are considerable issues among young men in westernized countries. An ideal male figure comprising of a highly muscular body with exceptionally low levels of body fat has evolved. This ideal, is neither achievable by most men, nor is it required for optimal health (Labre, 2002). In fact, this ideal shape is physiologically difficult to acquire and is generally unattainable without the assistance of disordered eating and exercise behaviors including anabolic steroid use, all of which are accompanied by a myriad of damaging effects on physical and mental health. Yet it carries definite links to masculinity, power and success and is highly desired among adolescent and young men.

Reports of the clinical prevalence of eating disorders among males present various findings, with a general agreement that 5-10% of all individuals who experience eating disorders are male (Carlat & Carmargo, 1991; Lucas et al., 1991). This is coupled with a reluctance of male patients to seek diagnosis and treatment and therefore current prevalence rates are believed to be underestimates (Anderson & Holman, 1997). In addition, there is evidence to show a considerable amount of disordered eating and exercise behaviors and dangerous weight loss and weight gain practices being used among males that do not attract clinical diagnosis, but have a number of damaging physical, social and psychological side effects (O'Dea & Abraham, 2002).

In addition, there are many issues with the detection and diagnosis of disordered eating among males. Many males fail to attract attention to their disordered eating or exercise behaviors as they may not appear to lose large amounts of weight and dedication to an exercise program has become highly socially accepted and valued. Males may also be excluded for clinical diagnosis, as they do not experience amenorrhoea. Traditional scales designed to measure female body dissatisfaction and disordered eating are largely irrelevant to males as they tend to want greater muscularity and less body fat.

Those measures that have been developed for males have revealed emerging and established body dissatisfaction and disordered weight gain and weight loss practices being used by males across all ages in Westernized countries. Particular risk and contributing factors specific to men for both clinical and sub clinical disordered eating have been identified as training for and being employed in health and fitness related careers, participating in sports with an emphasis on weight, personal and family history of psychiatric illness, previous overweight and identifying as homosexual.

There have been limited prevention efforts for body dissatisfaction and eating disorders that have included males. In school students, only 6 randomized controlled trials including males have been identified, and only two among college men. Although included, the majority of these studies have still used measures that were designed for females and female-oriented programs and activities, rendering them ineffective in achieving attitudinal or behavioral change.

Current research to date suggests that the prevention of body image issues and eating disorders is important for males. The authors are currently developing an intervention for college males and females enrolled in physical activity majors that takes a personal and professional perspective towards the prevention of body image issues and eating disorders. This program aims to affect the personal body image and disordered eating and exercise behaviors of the participants while training them to effectively prevent body image issues and disordered eating among male and female school students.

These issues have been found to be important to adolescent and young men, and it is suggested that further research investigate the nature of male body image issues and eating disorders. It is also recommended that future school and college based prevention programs not only include males, but are designed to be specifically relevant to them.

REFERENCES

Agliata, D., & Tantleff-Dunn, S. (2004). The impact of media exposure on males' body image. *Journal of Social and Clinical Psychology*, 23(1), 7.

Anderson, A. E. (1984). Anorexia nervosa and bulimia in adolescent males. *Pediatric Annals,* 13, 901-907.

Anderson, A. E. (2002). Eating disorders in males. In C. G. Fairburn & K. D. Brownell (Eds.), Eating disorders and obesity: A comprehensive handbook (pp. 188-192). New York: *The Guilford Press.*

Anderson, A. E., Barlett, S. J., Morgan, G. D., & Brownell, K. D. (1995). Weight loss, psychological and nutritional patterns in competitive male body builders. International *Journal of Eating Disorders,* 18(1), 49-57.

Anderson, A. E., & DiDomenico, L. (1992). Diet vs. shape content of popular male and female magazines: A dose-response relationship to the incidence of eating disorders? International *Journal of Eating Disorders,* 11(3), 283-187.

Anderson, A. E., & Holman, J. E. (1997). Males with eating disorders: Challenges for treatment and research. *Psychopharmacology bulletin,* 33(3), 391-397.

Anderson, A. E., & Mickalide, A. E. (1983). Anorexia nervosa in the male: An underdiagnosed disorder. *Psychosomatics,* 24, 1066-1074.

Barbarich, N. (2002). Lifetime prevalence of eating disorders among professionals in the field. *Eating Disorders,* 10, 305-312.

Barthel, D. (1992). When men put on appearances: Advertising and the social construction of masculinity. In S. Craig (Ed.), Men, Masculinity and the media (Vol. 1). Thousand Oaks, CA: *Sage Publications.*

Beglin, S., & Fairburn, C. (1992). Women who choose not to participate in surveys on eating disorders. *International Journal of Eating Disorders,* 12, 113-116.

Bell, A., Dorsch, K. D., McCreary, D., & Hovey, R. (2004). A look at nutritional supplement use in adolescents. *Journal of Adolescent Health,* 34, 508-516.

Beren, S., Hayden, H., Wilfley, D., & Grilo, C. (1996). The influence of sexual orientation on body dissatisfaction in adult men and women. *International Journal of Eating Disorders,* 20(2), 135-141.

Beumont, P. J. V., Bearwood, C. J., & Russell, G. F. M. (1972). The occurrence of the syndrome of anorexia nervosa in male subjects. *Psychological medicine,* 2, 216-231.

Bloomgarden, A., Gerstein, F., & Moss, C. (2003). The last word: A "recovered enough" therapist. *Eating Disorders,* 11, 163-167.

Blouin, A. G., & Goldfield, G. S. (1995). Body image and steroid use in male bodybuilders. *International Journal of Eating Disorders,* 18(2), 159-165.

Bramon-Bosch, E., Troop, N., & Treasure, J. (2000). Eating disorders in males: A comparison with female patients. *European Eating Disorders Review,* 8, 321-328.

Braun, D. L., Sunday, S. R., Huang, A., & Halmi, K. A. (1999). More males seek treatment for eating disorders. *International Journal of Eating Disorders,* 25, 415-424.

Buddeberg-Fischer, B., Klaghofer, R., Gnam, G., & Guddeberg, C. (1998). Prevention of disturbed eating behaviour: A prospective intervention study in 14-to19year old Swiss Students. *Acta Psychiatrica Scandinavica,* 98(2), 146-155.

Cafri, G., Roehrig, M., & Thompson, K. J. (2004). Reliability assessment of the somatomorphic matrix. *International Journal of Eating Disorders,* 35, 597-600.

Cafri, G., & Thompson, J. K. (2004). Measuring male body image: A review of current methodology. Psychology of men and masculinity, 5(1), 18-29.

Carlat, D. J., & Carmargo, C. A. (1991). Review of Bulimia Nervosa in males. *American Journal of Psychiatry,* 148, 831-843.

Carlat, D. J., Carmargo, C. A., & Herzog, D. B. (1997). Eating disorders in males: A report on 135 patients. *American Journal of Psychiatry,* 154, 1127-1132.

Cohane, G., & Pope, H. G. (2001). Body image in boys: A review of the literature. *International Journal of Eating Disorders,* 29, 373-379.

Collins, J. K., & Plahn, M. R. (1988). Recognition accuracy, stereotypic preference, aversion, and subjective judgement of body appearance in adolescents and young adults. *Journal of Youth and Adolescence,* 17, 317-334.

Connor, M., & Grogan, S. (2004). Gender, sexuality, body image and eating behaviours. *Journal of Health Psychology,* 9(4), 505-515.

Connor-Greene, P. A. (1988). Gender differences in body weight perception and weight-loss strategies of college students. *Women and Health,* 14(2), 27-43.

Crisp, A. H., & Toms, D. A. (1972). Primary anorexia nervosa or weight phobia in the male: A report on 13 cases. *British Medical Journal,* 1, 334-338.

Crockett, S. J., & Littrell, J. M. (1985). Comparison of eating patterns between dietetic and other college students. *Journal of Nutrition Education,* 17, 47-50.

Dalle Grave, R., De Luca, L., & Campello, G. (2001). Middle school promary prevention program for eating disorders: A controlled study with a twelve-month follow up. *Eating Disorders,* 9, 327-337.

Davis, C., & Scott-Robertson, L. (2000). A psychological comparison of females with anorexia nervosa and competitive male bodybuilders: Body shape ideals in the extreme. *Eating Behaviors,* 1, 33-46.

Drenowski, A., Kurth, C., & Krahn, D. (1995). Effects of body image on dieting, exercise, and anabolic steroid use in adolescent males. *International Journal of Eating Disorders,* 17(4), 381-386.

Drenowski, A., & Yee, D. K. (1987). Men and body image: Are males satisfied with their body weight? *Psychosomatic Medicine,* 49, 626-634.

Drummond, M. (1999). Life as a male 'anorexic'. *Australian Journal of Primary Health-Interchange,* 5(2), 80-89.

Drummond, M. (2002). Men, body image and eating disorders. *International Journal of Men's Health,* 1, 79-93.

Dwyer, J. T., Feldman, J., Seltzer, C., & Mayer, J. (1969). Body image in adolescents: Attitudes towards weight and perception of appearance. *American Journal of Clinical Nutrition,* 20, 1045-1056.

Fairburn, C. G., & Beglin, S. J. (1990). Studies of the epidemiology of bulimia nervosa. *American Journal of Psychiatry,* 147, 401-408.

Fallon, A. E., & Rozin, P. (1985). Sex differences in perceptions of desirable body shape. *Journal of Abnormal Psychology,* 94, 102-105.

Feldman, J. (1999). Creatine: A dietary supplement and ergogenic aid. *Nutrition Reviews,* 57(2), 45-50.

Field, A. E., Camargo, C. A., Taylor, C. B., Berkey, C. S., Roberts, S. B., & Colditz, G. A. (2001). Peer, parent and media influences on the development of weight concerns and frequent dieting among preadolescent and adolescnt girls and boys. *Pediatrics,* 107, 54-60.

Field, A. E., Carmargo, C. A., Barr Taylor, C., Berkey, C. S., Frazier, L., Gillman, M. W., et al. (1999). Overweight, weight concerns and bulimic behaviors among girls and boys. *Journal of the American Academy of Child and Adolescent Psychiatry,* 38(6), 754-755.

Fogelholm, M., & Hilloskorpi, H. (1999). Weight and diet concerns in finnish female and male athletes. *Medicine and Science in Sports and Exercise,* 31, 229-135.

Furnham, A., & Calnan, A. (1998). Eating disturbance, self esteem, reasons for exercising and body weight dissatisfaction in adolescent males. *European Eating Disorders Review,* 6, 58-72.

Garman, J. F., Hayduk, D. M., Crider, D. A., & DHodel, M. M. (2004). Occurrence of exercise dependence in a college-aged population. *Journal of American College Health,* 52(5), 221-228.

Garner, D. M., Olmstead, M. A., & Polivy, J. (1983). Development and validation of a multidimensional eating disorder inventory for anorexia and bulimia. *International Journal of Eating Disorders,* 2, 15-34.

Gull, W. W. (1874). Anorexia nervosa (apepsia hysterica, anorexia hysterica). *Transactions of the clinical society of London,* 7, 22-28.

Gustafson-Larson, A. M., & Terry, R. D. (1992). Weight related behaviors and concerns of fourth-grade children. *Journal of the American Dietetic Association,* 92, 818-822.

Halmi, K. A., Falk, J. R., & Schwartz, E. (1981). Binge eating and vomiting: A survey of a college population. *Psychological Medicine,* 11, 697-706.

Hausenblas, H. A., Janelle, C. M., Gardner, R. E., & Hagan, A. L. (2002). Effects of exposure to physique slides on the emotional responses of men and women. *Sex Roles,* 47(11/12), 569-574.

Humphreys, P., & Paxton, S. (2004). Impact of exposure to idealised male images on adolescent boys' body image. *Body Image,* 1, 253-266.

Johnson, C., Powers, P. S., & Dick, R. (1999). Athletes and eating disorders: The National Collegiate Athletic Association Study. *International Journal of Eating Disorders,* 26, 179-188.

Juhn, M. S., O'Kane, J. W., & Vinci, D. M. (1999). Oral creatine supplementation in male collegiate athletes: A survey of dosing habits and side effects. *Journal of the American Dietetic Association,* 99(5), 593-595.

Kater, K. J., Rohwer, J., & Londre, K. (2002). Evaluation of an upper elementary school program to prevent body image, eating and weight concerns. *Journal of School Health,* 72(5), 199-204.

Katzman, M. A., Wolchik, S. A., & Braver, S. L. (1984). The prevalence of frequent binge eating and bulimia in a nonclinical college sample. *International Journal of Eating Disorders,* 3(3), 53-62.

Kearney-Cooke, A., & Steichen-Asch, P. (1990). Men, body image and eating disorders. In A. E. Anderson (Ed.), Males with eating disorders (pp. 54-74). New York: *Brunner/Mazel.*

Kinningham, R. B., & Gorenflo, D. W. (2001). Weight loss methods of high school wrestlers. *Medicine and Science in Sports and Exercise,* 810-813.

Kinzl, J., Traweger, C., Trefalt, E., Mangweth, B., & Biebl, W. (1999). Dieticians: Are they a risk group for eating disorders? *European Eating Disorders Review,* 7, 62-67.

Labre, M. P. (2002). Adolescent boys and the muscular male body ideal. *Journal of Adolescent Health,* 30, 233-242.

Larson, B. (1989). The new epidemic: Ethical implications for nutrition educators. *Journal of Nutrition Education,* 21, 101-103.

Leit, R. A., Gray, J. J., & Pope Jr, H. G. (2002). The media's representation of the ideal male body: A cause for muscle dysmorphia? *International Journal of Eating Disorders,* 31, 334-338.

Leit, R. A., Pope Jr, H. G., & Gray, J. J. (2001). Cultural expectations of masculinity in men: The evolution of Playgirl centrefolds. *International Journal of Eating Disorders,* 29, 90-93.

Loosemore, D., & Moriarty, D. (1990). Body dissatisfaction and body image distortion in selected groups of males. *Canadian Association of Health, Physical Education and Recreation Journal,* November / December, 11-15.

Lucas, A. R., Beard, M., O'Fallon, W. M., & Kurland, L. T. (1991). 50-year trends in the incidence of Anorexia Nervosa in Rochester, Minn: A population-based study. *American Journal of Psychiatry,* 148, 917-922.

Mangweth, B., Hausmann, A., Walch, T., Hotter, A., Rupp, C. I., Biebl, W., et al. (2004). Body fat perception in eating-disordered men. *International Journal of Eating Disorders,* 35, 102-108.

McArthur, A., & Howard, A. (2001). Dietetics majors' weight-reduction beliefs, behaviours, and information sources. *Journal of American College Health,* 49, 175-184.

McCabe, M. P., & Ricciardelli, L. A. (2003). Body image and strategies to lose weight and increase muscle among boys and girls. *Health Psychology,* 22(1), 39-46.

McCabe, M. P., & Ricciardelli, L. A. (2004). Body image dissatisfaction among males accross the lifespan: A review of past literature. *Journal of Psychosomatic Research,* 56, 675-685.

McCreary, D., & Sasse, D. (2000). An exploration of the drive for muscularity in adolescent boys and girls. *Journal of American College Health,* 48(6), 297-304.

McKay Parks, P. S., & Read, M. H. (1997). Adolescent male athletes: Body image, diet, and exercise. *Adolescence,* 32(127), 593-602.

Meyer, C., Blissett, J., & Oldfield, C. (2001). Sexual orientation and eating psychopathology: The role of masculinity and femininity. *International Journal of Eating Disorders,* 29, 314-318.

Mishkind, M. E., Rodin, J., Silberstein, L. R., & Striegel-Moore, R. (1986). The embodiment of masculinity. *American Behavioral Scientist,* 29(5), 545-562.

Mitchell, S. (1990). Changes after taking a college basic nutrition course. *Journal of the American Dietetic Association,* 90(7), 955-963.

Morrison, T. G., Morrison, M. A., & Hopkins, C. (2003). Striving for bodily perfection? An Exploration of the drive for muscularity in Canadian men. *Psychology of Men & Masculinity,* 4(2), 111-120.

Morton, R. (1694). Phthisologia- or a treatise of consumptions. London: *Smith & Walford.*

Murray, S., Touyz, S. W., & Beumont, P. J. V. (1996). Awareness and percieved influence of body ideals in the media: A comparison of eating disorder patients and the general community. Eating Disorders: *The journal of treatment and prevention,* 4(1), 33-46.

Nemeroff, C. J., Stein, R. I., Diehl, N. S., & Smilack, K. M. (1994). From the Cleavers to the Clintons: Role choices and body orientation as reflected in magazine article content. *International Journal of Eating Disorders,* 16(2), 167-176.

Neumark-Sztainer, D., & Hannan, P. (2000). Weight-related behaviors among adolescent girls and boys: Results from a national survey. *Archives of Pediatrics & Adolescent Medicine,* 154(6), 569-577.

Neumark-Sztainer, D., Story, M., Faulkner, N., Beuhring, T., & Resnick, M. (1999). Sociodemographic and personal characteristics of adolescents engaged in weight loss and weight/muscle gain behaviors: Who is doing what? *Preventive Medicine,* 28, 40-50.

Nowak, M., & Speare, R. (1996). Gender differences in food related concerns, beliefs and behaviours of North Queensland adolescents. *Journal of Paediatrics and Child Health,* 32(5), 424-427.

O'Dea, J. (1999). Cross-cultural, body weight and gender differences in the body size perceptions and body ideals of university students. *Australian Journal of Nutrition and Dietetics,* 56, 144-150.

O'Dea, J. (2000). School based interventions to prevent eating problems: First do no harm. *Eating Disorders,* 8, 123-130.

O'Dea, J. (2002). Can body image education programs be harmful to adolescent females? *Eating Disorders,* 10, 1-13.

O'Dea, J. (2003). Consumption of nutritional supplements among adolescents: Usage and percieved benefits. *Health Education Research,* 18(1), 98-107.

O'Dea, J., & Abraham, S. (1999). Onset of disordered eating attitudes and behaviors in early adolescence: Interplay of pubertal status, gender, weight and age. *Adolescence,* 34(136), 671-679.

O'Dea, J., Abraham, S., & Heard, R. (1996). Food habits, body image and weight control practices of young male and female adolescents. *Australian Journal of Nutrition and Dietetics,* 52, 32-38.

O'Dea, J., & Abraham, S. F. (2000). Improving the body image, eating attitudes, and behaviours of young male and female adolescents: A new educational approach that focuses on self esteem. *International Journal of Eating Disorders,* 28, 43-57.

O'Dea, J., & Abraham, S. F. (2001). Knowledge, beliefs, attitudes and behaviours related to weight control, eating disorders, and body image in Australian trainee home economics and physical education teachers. *Journal of Nutrition Education,* 33, 332-340.

O'Dea, J., & Abraham, S. F. (2002). Eating and Exercise Disorders in Young College men. *Journal of American College Health,* 50, 273-278.

O'Dea, J., & Rawstorne, P. (2000). Consumption of dietary supplements and energy drinks by schoolchildren. *Medical Journal of Australia,* 173(2), 389.

O'Dea, J., & Rawstorne, P. (2001). Male adolescents identify their weight gain practices, reasons for desired weight gain and sources of weight gain information. *Journal of the American Dietetic Association,* 11, 105-107.

O'Dea, J. A., & Caputi, P. (2001). Association between socioeconomic status, weight, age and gender, and the body image and weight control practices of 6-to19-year-old children and adolescents. *Health Education Research,* 16(5), 521-532.

Offer, D., Schonert-Reichl, K. A., & Boxer, A. M. (Eds.). (1996). Normal adolescent development: Empirical research findings. Baltimore: *Williams & Wilkins.*

Ogden, J., Veale, D., & Summers, Z. (1997). The development and validation of the Exercise Dependence Questionaire. *Addiction Research,* 5(4), 343-356.

Olivardia, R., Pope, j., Harrison G., Mangweth, B., & Hudson, J. I. (1995a). Eating diosorders in college men. *American Journal of Psychiatry,* 152(9), 1279-1285.

Olivardia, R., Pope, j., Harrison G., Mangweth, B., & Hudson, J. I. (1995b). Eating disorders in college men. *American Journal of Psychiatry,* 152(9), 1279-1285.

Olivardia, R., Pope Jr, H. G., Borowiecki, J. J., & Cohane, G. (2004). Biceps and body image: The relationship between muscularity and self-esteem, depression, and eating disorder symptoms. *Psychology of Men & Masculinity,* 5(2), 112-120.

Olivardia, R., Pope Jr, H. G., & Hudson, J. I. (2000). Muscle dysmorphia in male weightlifters: A case-control study. *The American Journal of Psychiatry,* 157(8), 1291-1296.

Olivardia, R., Pope Jr, H. G., & Hudson, J. I. (2000). Muscle Dysmorphia in weightlifters: A Case-control study. *American Journal of Psychiatry,* 157(8), 1291-1296.

Oppliger, R. A., Landry, G. L., Foster, S. W., & Lambrecht, A. C. (1993). Bulimic behaviors among interscholastic wrestlers: A statewide survey. Pediatrics, 91, 826-831.

O'Sullivan, G. A., & Tiggemann, M. (1997). Body dissatisfaction and body image distortion in men who train with weights. *Journal of Gender, Culture, and Health,* 2, 321-329.

Palmquist- Fredenberg, J., Berglund, P., & Dieken, H. (1996). Incidence of eating disorders among selected female university students. *Journal of the American Dietetic association,* 96, 64-66.

Pasman, L., & Thompson, K. J. (1988). Body image and eating disturbance in obligatory runners, obligatory weightlifters, and sedentary individuals. *International Journal of Eating Disorders,* 7, 759-769.

Paxton, S. J., Wertheim, E. H., Gibbons, K., Szmukler, G. I., Hillier, L., & Petrovich, J. C. (1991). Body image satisfaction, dieting beliefs and weight loss behaviours in adolescent girls and boys. *Journal of Youth and Adolescence,* 20, 361-379.

Pederson Mussel, M., Binford, R. B., & Fulkerson, J. (2000). Eating Disorders: Summary of risk factors, prevention programming, and prevention research. *Counseling psychologist,* 28, 764-796.

Petrie, T. A., & Rogers, R. (2001). Extending the discussion of eating disorders to men and athletes. *The Counseling Psychologist,* 29(5), 743-753.

Piran, N. (1995). Prevention: Can early lessons lead to a delineation of an alternative model? A critical look at prevention with schoolchildren. *Eating Disorders,* 3(1), 28-36.

Pope, H., Jr., Gruber, A. J., Mangweth, B., Bureau, B., deCol, C., Jouvent, R., et al. (2000). Body image perception among men in three countries. *The American Journal of Psychiatry,* 157(8), 1297-1301.

Pope, H. G., Gruber, A. J., Choi, P., Olivardia, R., & Phillips, K. (1997). Muscle Dysmorphia: An underrecognized form of body dysmorphic disorder. *Psychosomatics,* 38, 548-557.

Pope, H. G., Katz, D. L., & Hudson, J. I. (1993). Anorexia and 'reverse anorexia' among 108 male bodybuilders. *Comprehensive Psychiatry,* 34, 406-409.

Pope, H. G. J., Olivardia, R., Gruber, A. J., & Borowiecki, J. J. (1999). Evolving ideals of male body image as seen through action toys. *International Journal of Eating Disorders,* 26, 65-72.

Pope, J., Harrison G, Hudson, J. I., & Jonas, J. M. (1986). Bulimia in men: A series of fifteen cases. *The Journal of Nervous and Mental Disease,* 174(2), 117-119.

Pope, j., Harrison G., Gruber, A. J., Mangweth, B., Bureau, B., deCol, C., Jouvent, R., et al. (2000). Body image perception among men in three countries. *The American Journal of Psychiatry,* 157(8), 1297-1301.

Pyle, R. L., Halvorson, P. A., Neuman, P. A., & Mitchell, J. E. (1986). The increasing prevalence of bulimia in freshman college students. *International Journal of Eating Disorders,* 5(631-647).

Rabak-Wagener, J., Eickhoff-Shemek, J., & Kelly-Vance, L. (1998). The effect of media analysis on attitudes and behaviors regarding body image among college students. *Journal of American College Health,* 47(1), 29-35.

Reinstein, N., Koszewski, W., Chamberlain, B., & Smith-Johnson, C. (1992). Prevalence of eating disorders among dietetics students: does nutrition education make a difference? *Journal of the American dietetic association,* 92, 949-954.

Robinson, T. N., Chang, J. Y., Haydel, K. F., & Killen, J. (2000). Overweight concerns and body dissatisfaction among third-grade children: The impacts of ethnicity and socioeconomic status. *The Journal of Pediatrics,* 138, 181-187.

Rohlinger, D. A. (2002). Eroticizing men: Cultural influences on advertising and male objectification. *Sex Roles,* 46(3/4), 61.

Ronson, O., Sundgot-Borgen, J., & Maehlum, S. (1999). Supplement use and nutritional habits in norwegian elite athletes. *Scandinavian Journal of Medicine and Science in Sports,* 9, 28-35.

Rosen, J. C., & Gross, J. (1987). Prevalence of weight reducing and weight gaining in adolescent girls and boys. *Health Psychology,* 6(2), 131-147.

Russell, C. J., & Keel, P. K. (2002). Homosexuality as a specific risk factor for eating disorders in men. *International Journal of Eating Disorders,* 31, 300-306.

Rutz, S. (1993). Nutrition educators should practice what they teach. *Journal of Nutrition education,* 25(2), 87-88.

Schneider, J., & Agras, W. (1987). Bulimia in males. A matched comparison with females. *International Journal of Eating Disorders,* 6, 235-242.

Sharp, C. W., Clark, S. A., Dunan, J. R., Blackwood, D. H. R., & Shapiro, C. M. (1994). Clinical presentation of anorexia nervosa in males: 24 new cases. *International Journal of Eating Disorders,* 15(2), 125-134.

Siever, M. D. (1994). Sexual orientation and gender as factors in socioculturally acquired vulnerability to body dissatisfaction and eatinig disorders. *Journal of Counseling and Clinical Psychology,* 62(2), 252-260.

Silberstein, L. R., Striegel-Moore, R., Timko, C., & Rodin, J. (1988). Behavioural and psychological implications of body dissatisfaction: Do men and women differ? *Sex Roles: A journal of Research,* 19 (3/4), 219-232.

Smith, J., & Dahm, D. (2000). Creatine use among a select population of high school athletes. *Paper presented at the Mayo Clinic Proceedings.*

Smith, J., & Dahm, D. L. (2000). Creatine use among a select population of high school athletes. *Mayo Clinic Proceedings,* 75, 1257-1263.

Smolak, L., & Levine, M. (2001). A two-year followup of a primary prevention program for negative body image and unhealthy weight reduction. *Eating Disorders,* 9(4), 313-325.

Smolak, L., Levine, M., & Schermer, F. (1998). A controlled intervention of an elementary school primary prevention program for eating problems. *Journal of Psychosomatic Research,* 44, 339-353.

Sours, J. (1980). Starving to death in a sea of objects: The anorexia nervosa syndrome. New York: *J Aronson.*

Spitzer, B. L., Henderson, K. A., & Zivian, M. T. (1999). Gender differences in population versus media body sizes: A comparison over four decades. *Sex Roles*, 40(7-8), 545-555.

Stewart, A. (1998). Experience with a school - based eating disorders prevention program. In W. Vandereycken & G. Noordenbos (Eds.), The prevention of eating disorders. London: *The Athlone Press.*

Stice, E. (2002). Risk and maintenance factors for eating pathology: A meta-analytic review. *Psychological Bulletin,* 128(5), 825-848.

Striegel-Moore, R., Garvin, V., Dohm, F.-A., & Rosenheck, R. (1999). Psychiatric comorbidity of eating disorders in men: A national study of hospitalised veterans. *International Journal of Eating Disorders,* 25, 399-404.

Stunkard, A., Sorenson, T., & Schulsinger, F. (1980). Use of the Danish adoption register for the study of obesity and thinness: *Raven Press.*

Taraldson, K. W., Eriksen, L., & Gunner Gotestam, K. (1996). Prevalence of eating disorders among Norwegian women and men in a psychiatric outpatient unit. *International Journal of Eating Disorders,* 20(2), 185-190.

Thiel, A., Gottfried, H., & Hesse, F. (1993). Subclinical eating disorders in male athletes. *Acta Psychiatrica Scandinavica,* 88, 259-265.

Thompson, J. K., & Tantleff, S. (1992). Female and male ratings of upper torso: Actual, ideal and stereotypical conceptions. *Journal of social behaviour and Personality,* 7, 342-354.

Tiggemann, M. (1994). Gender differences in the interrelationships between weight dissatisfaction, restraint, and self esteem. Sex Roles: *A journal of Research,* 30, 319-331.

Touyz, S. W., Kopec-Schrader, E. M., & Beumont, P. J. V. (1993). Anorexia Nervosa in males: A report of 12 cases. *Australian and New Zealand Journal of Psychiatry,* 27, 512-517.

Turnbull, J. D., Freeman, C., & Barry, F. (1987). Physical and psychological characteristics of five male bulimics. *British Journal of Psychiatry,* 150, 25-29.

Varnado-Sullivan, P. J., Zucker, N., Williamson, D., Reas, D., Thaw, J., & Netemeyer, R. G. (2001). Development and implementation of the Body Logic program for adolescents: A two-stage prevention program for eating disorders. *Cognitive and Behavioral Practice,* 8, 248-259.

Wang, M. Q., & Yesalis, C. E. (1994). Desire for weight gain and potential risks of adolescent males using anabolic steroids. *Perceptual and Motor Skills,* 78, 267-274.

Williamson, I. (1999). Why are gay men a high risk group for eating disturbance? *European Eating Disorders Review,* 7, 1-4.

Woodside, B. D., Garfinkel, P. E., Lin, E., Goering, P., Kaplan, A. S., Goldbloom, D. S., et al. (2001). Comparisons of men with full or partial eating disorders, men without eating disorders and women with eating disorders in the community. *American Journal of Psychiatry,* 158, 570-574.

Worobey, J., & Schoenfeld, D. (1999). Eating disordered behaviour in dietetics students and students in other majors. *Journal of the American Dietetic Association,* 99, 100-104.

Yager, J., Kurtzman, F., Landsverk, J., & Wiesmeier, E. (1988). Behaviors and attitudes related to eating disorders in homosexual male college students. *The American Journal of Psychiatry,* 145(4), 495-306.

Yates, A. (1991). Compulsive exercise and the eating disorders : toward an integrated theory of activity. New York, N.Y.: *Brunner/Mazel.*

Young, K., White, P., & McTeer, W. (1994). Body talk: Male athletes reflect on sport, injury and pain. *Sociology of Sport Journal,* 11, 175-194.

Zabinski, M. F., Calfas, K. J., Gehrman, C. A., Wilfley, D. E., & Sallis, J. F. (2001). Effects of a physical activity intervention on body image in university seniors: Project GRAD. *Annals of Behavioral Medicine,* 23(4), 247-252.

Zmijewski, C. F., & Howard, M. O. (2003). Exercise dependence and attitudes toward eating among young adults. *Eating Behaviors,* 4, 181-195.

Zuckerman, D. M., Colby, A., Ware, N. C., & Lazerson, J. S. (1986). The prevalence of bulimia among college students. *American Journal of Public Health,* 76(9), 1135-1137.

In: New Developments in Eating Disorders Research
Editor: Pamela I. Swain, pp. 37-63
ISBN 1-59454-542-1

Chapter 2

GENDER-RELATED ASPECTS OF EATING DISORDERS: A PSYCHOSOCIAL VIEW

Rosa Behar*

University of Valpraiso, Valpraiso, Chile

ABSTRACT

Various biological, psychological, and sociocultural factors have been considered in the attempt to understand the etiology of eating pathologies such as anorexia nervosa and bulimia nervosa. Psychosexual issues are neither sufficient nor necessary for the development of an eating disorder in a young person, and it should be considered as only one factor in the multidimensional, multifactorial framework needed to clarify this complex and still poorly understood set of disorders (Fornari and Dancyger, 2003).

In particular, gender roles and sociocultural expectations appear strongly implicated in the development of eating disorders, since anorexia nervosa and bulimia nervosa occur predominantly among women (Garfinfel and Garner 1982; Hsu 1990). This is frequently attributed to the continued emphasis on physical attractiveness and a thin physique for women (Polivy *et al*, 1986). In consequence, women reportedly express greater dissatisfaction about their bodies (Fallon and Rozin 1985), more concern with appearance and body weight (Pliner *et al*, 1990), and more frequently engage in weight-control efforts (Herman and Polivy 1980; Polivy and Herman 1983).

Since at least 90 per cent of eating disordered patients are females, then it would therefore seem plausible to suggest that the female role might play a part in the genesis of these pathologies. This fact strongly supports that the meaning of femininity in Western society has some relationship with the development of eating problems (Garfinkel and Garner, 1982; Garner *et al*, 1983; Garner *et al*, 1985).

Eating disorders are common, serious illnesses that present major challenges to physicians and other health care professionals. Sociocultural body norms for ideal size and shape may be reinforced by participation in activities, sports, or membership in groups that promotes weight loss and shape change. Eating disorders are furthermore reinforced when high status individuals (e.g. parents, teachers, coaches, doctors) encourage a susceptible individual to diet. Studies indicate that a complex combination of

* Professor of the Department of Psychiatry, University of Valparaiso, Mailbox 92-V, Valparaiso, CHILE.

genetic and sociocultural-developmental factors is responsible for the onset of these illnesses (Andersen, 1999).

Society and Eating Disorders

Eating disorders can also be regarded as a cultural phenomenon and a social problem, and may illuminate the influence of culture on psychopathology better than other disorders. Nevertheless, the role of sociocultural factors continues to be underemphasized in the theoretical and empirical literature and the meaning of sociocultural influences needs to be closely examined.

Culture has been identified as one of the etiological factors leading to the development of these syndromes. Rates of these pathologies appear to vary among different cultures and to change across time as cultures evolve. Additionally, eating disorders appear to be more widespread among contemporary cultural groups than was previously believed. It seems likely that the sociocultural factors that have occurred across time and throughout different contemporary societies play a role in the emergence of these disorders. In many non Western societies, plumpness is considered attractive and desirable, and may be associated with prosperity, fertility, success and economic security (Nassar, 1988). In such cultures, eating disorders are found much less commonly than in Western nations. Anorexia nervosa has been described as a possible "culture-bound syndrome", with roots in Western cultural values and conflicts (Prince, 1983).

Cultures in which female social roles are restricted appear to have lower rates of eating disorders, reminiscent of the lower rates observed during historical eras in which women lacked choices. For example, some modern affluent Muslim societies limit the social behavior of women according to male dictates; in such societies, eating disorders are virtually unknown. This supports the notion that freedom for women, as well as affluence, are sociocultural factors that may predispose to the development of eating disorders (Bemporad, 1997).

Eating disorders may, in fact, be more prevalent within various cultural groups than previously recognized, as Western values are becoming more widely accepted. Historical and cross-cultural experiences suggest that cultural change, itself, may be associated with increased vulnerability to eating disorders, especially when values about physical aesthetics are involved. Such change may occur across time within a given society, or on an individual level, as when an immigrant moves into a new culture. In addition, cultural factors such as affluence and freedom of choice for women may play a role in the development of these pathologies (Bemporad, 1997; Miller and Pumariega, 2001).

Contrary to the biological determinism perspective, the sociocultural view of gender roles states that gender roles and stereotypes develop within a culture and are then perpetuated by that culture. Individuals within the culture are expected to conform to these norms, and are socialized in manners which constantly reinforce the beliefs and behaviors which are prescribed and presupposed for them.

The biological view of gender roles states that the differentiated gender roles which exist in our society are the products of our evolution, and are inextricably linked with abilities predominant in one gender or the other which are biologically determined. The roles prescribed for each sex are based on physical abilities and properties of that sex, such as intelligence, brain lateralization, and differing hormone levels. Implicit within this view is the belief that these roles are both desirable and immutable (Singleton, 1987).

The assumption that sex roles are biological, and therefore unchanging, can be refuted by the simple observable fact that sex roles, even within our society, have changed and are in the process of changing. Thus far, the focus of gender eating-disorders research has been on gender role adoption. However, being female means more than adopting a particular gender role. It also implies that certain experiences, particularly involving objectification of the body, become more likely (Bordo, 1993). Women have been shown to be significantly less satisfied with their bodies, due to a gender role which states that they must be beautiful and slender in order to attract a man, which should be of paramount importance in their lives. Even women of low body weight commonly diet, believing themselves fat. This becomes a problem when it is shown that these feelings of inadequacy about one's own body are linked to eating disorders, low self-esteem, depression, and lowered or insufficient use of contraceptives (Mintz and Betz, 1986). The role of sociocultural factors continues to be underemphasized in the theoretical and empirical literature and that the role of sociocultural influences needs to be closely examined.

Sex Roles and Gender Identity

Sex roles can be defined as a set of behaviors and characteristics that are standard for each gender in a society. Sex role stereotypes are widely-held beliefs about those behaviors and characteristics. Society forces people to adopt certain roles simply by expecting that those roles are proper and enforcing them.

Empirical findings support the view that sex roles are flexible and may be influenced by life situations and demands (Rewal and Kapur 1991). In general, the roles prevalent in modern Western society prescribe that men should be domineering, aggressive, and superior at mathematics and sciences, should become successful in their careers, and should control and suppress their feelings. Women, on the other hand, should be submissive, nurturing, gentle, better at languages and the humanities, emotional, and desirous of nothing more than a happy family and a husband to provide for her, while she remains at home and tends the house. These sex-typed roles are perpetuated and reinforced by the mass media and society in general in many ways, some obvious and others more subtle. Research conducted in the 1970s demonstrated that male and female psychologists listed the same ideal characteristics for a healthy "person" and a healthy "male", whereas their conception of a mature female was antithetical to their description of a healthy "person" (Broverman *et al*, 1972).

As described above, sex or gender roles are characteristics, behaviors and interests defined by a society or culture as appropriate for members of each sex. Many objective studies have found evidence linking gender traits to both problem eating and body dissatisfaction. Researchers have studied women with eating disorders, community and students samples consisting of young adult women and men, and adolescent girls and boys (Murnen and Smolak, 1997). However, other kinds of relationships have also been found. Some empirical data suggest a relationship between low masculinity scores, problem eating, and body dissatisfaction (Holleran *et al*, 1988; Johnson *et al* 1996; Klingenspor, 1994). Some evidence supports that higher masculinity is associated with higher levels of problem eating (Cantrell and Ellis 1991; Silverstein *et al*, 1990). One study found that an undifferentiated gender personality, low feminine and low masculinity, was associated with problem eating in a clinical sample (Lewis and Johnson, 1985). Finally, another finding pointed out that lower femininity was associated with body dissatisfaction among a premenstrual group of adolescent girls whereas higher masculinity was associated with body dissatisfaction for menstrual girls (Usmiani and Daniluk, 1997)

EATING DISORDERS AND GENDER

Gender Differences and Disordered Eating

Women are remarkably more likely to develop eating disorders and their associated symptoms than men are (American Psychiatric Association, 2000). A variety of strong empirical evidence conducted since 1970 confirms that women perceive slenderness to be the most important aspect of physical attractiveness (Garner *et al*, 1985). The fact that young girls, but not young boys, have such precocious concerns about attractiveness is compelling evidence for the power of sex-role socialization and the potency of the diet message (Brumberg, 1988).

The onset of adolescence — the period of transition between childhood and adulthood — is usually accompanied by dramatic and often difficult changes in the life of a young person. Biological, cognitive, social, and environmental factors all contribute to influence an adolescent's personal development and self-esteem. Studies have shown that adolescent girls tend to have lower self-esteem and more negative assessments of their physical characteristics and intellectual abilities than boys have. These findings may explain why the incidence of suicide attempts, depression, and eating disorders is substantially higher in girls. Future research on methods for promoting self-esteem may help reduce the negative feelings of adolescent girls, as well as the problems that stem from them (Kearney-Cooke A, 1999).

In a large number of male and female college students, for males, the current ideal and attractive figures were near identical, and each was significantly more rounded than the average male figure preferred by women. That is, in general men misperceive the shape that appeals to women in a manner that reconciles it with their perception of their current shape and their ideal shape for themselves. It is very plausible that this "distortion" serves to maintain self-esteem (Lewinsohn *et al*, 1980). What a college woman thinks is attractive to men, however, is actually significantly thinner than the shape preferred by those men. Most important is the sad fact that the woman's ideal shape is even thinner than her misperception of the shape ideally attractive to men — in other words — it is the thinnest of all the ratings. Women's magazines may be particularly influential in the glorification of thinness, certainly contributing to the objectification of women, and to the reigning misbelief that to be fit is to be thin and *vice versa* (Garner *et al*, 1985).

The cultural deification of thinness has placed pressure on women to diet in order to conform to an unrealistic standard for feminine beauty. In puberty and adolescence a major portion of a young woman's weight gain derives from fat rather than muscle. While boys are developing muscles as a consequence of biological development, girls experience an increase in adiposity, particularly in their breasts and hips. In our fat phobic society, where female self-worth is so intimately tied to a slim figure, these biological differences have critical and distinctive emotional consequences. For adolescent boys, growing larger is frequently a source of pleasure and power; for girls, an increase in size is often confusing, awkward, and stressful. This distaste is expressed by many young girls through the wish to be thin; they no longer want to eat, they constantly watch their weight. In this sense, normal maturation in our society sets up young women for anorexia nervosa and/or bulimia nervosa.

Males and females are dissatisfied with different parts of their bodies. Most females are distressed about the areas below their waists, whereas males are more likely to be displeased with their upper bodies. More males that females would accept a normal body weight for age and height if they could choose a stereotypical male body image. Females, on the other hand, are more often motivated to attain a low body weight independent of shape. For most women raised in Western, industrialized nations, dieting is initiated as a result of a cultural endorsement of thinness (Vandereycken, 1992). In contrast, males who develop eating disorders begin dieting, in the majority of cases, (1) to avoid childhood teasing for being overweight; (2) to improve athletic performance; (3) to avoid developing medical illnesses associated with weight problems; and (4) to improve a homosexual relationship (Andersen and Holman, 1997). Unlike males, young women diet because of a common belief that weighing less is inherently good. In addition, males may also suffer from a relatively unknown form of eating disorder, "reverse anorexia", characterized by a fear of being thin and a drive for bulking up (Pope, 1993).

Moreover, Drewnowski and Yee (1987), Andersen and Holman (1997) have documented substantial gender differences with regard to perception of actual body weight as a percentage of a reference norm for age and height. According to these studies, adult women consider themselves thin at less than 87% of a healthy weight. Men however consider themselves thin up to 105% of a reference weight norm. The perception of being overweight is, therefore, highly dependent on gender. Furthermore, girls and young women appear to be more dedicated to the ideal of slimness than any religious, moral, or other social norm, whereas most males do not demonstrate a comparable preoccupation with body image.

It appears that gender differences emerge by middle school and possibly in elementary school (Smolak and Levine, 1994). Such gender differences have led theorists to attempt to tie gender role adoption to eating disorders. Hilde Bruch (1978) for example, suggested that anorexics might be trying to avoid female adulthood, particularly the reproductive and sexual aspects. Similarly, others have argued that bulimics are trying to reject the feminine, maternal roles ambivalently embraced by their stay-at-home-mothers (Silverstein and Perdue 1988).

On the other hand, Boskind-Lodahl (1976) proposed that women suffering from eating disorders were high in passivity, dependence, and need for approval from others (Morawsky, 1992). Steiner-Adair argued that the discrepancy between ideal and self-perceived masculine characteristics forms a basis for eating problems. More specifically, young women perceive that society values masculine characteristics, and so wish to possess them but fear they do not. They develop eating problems as a way of meeting the social demands for thinness, controlling their own bodies, and coping with the stress of their self-doubts. Thus, theoretical approaches vary dramatically in postulating relationships between traditionally defined gender roles (i.e., gender roles as measured by the Bem Sex Role Inventory (BSRI), Bem (1974) or the Personal Attributes Questionnaire (PAQ), (Spence and Helmreich, 1978) and eating disorders, especially anorexia nervosa and bulimia nervosa.

Sexual Orientation

Whereas male homosexuality is a risk factor for developing an eating disorder, lesbian orientation may be a protective factor, although this remains controversial (Siever, 1994). Approximately 20% of males suffering from eating disorders are homosexuals (Herzog *et al*, 1990). Gay men, who represent 3% to 5% of the total male population, exhibit a prevalence of eating disorders that is roughly four times greater than the total frequency of eating disorders. Male homosexuality is a risk factor for developing an eating disorder because of the increased value placed on thinness in the gay community compared with heterosexual environments (Siever, 1994).

One hundred university students (40 homosexual; 60 heterosexual) completed the Bem Sex Role Inventory and the Eating Attitudes Test. For the group as a whole, there were links between femininity and high levels of eating psychopathology, whereas masculinity was associated with relatively healthy eating-related attitudes and behaviours. When considering the role of sexual orientation, these links were specific to homosexual men and women. In relation to homosexual men and women, the results support a model where femininity might be seen as a specific risk factor for eating disorders, whereas masculinity is likely to be a protective factor (Meyer *et al*, 2001).

Siever (1994) confirmed the hypothesis that gay men and heterosexual women are dissatisfied with their bodies and vulnerable to eating disorders because of a shared emphasis on physical attractiveness and thinness, that is sustained on a desire to attract and please men. Although men place priority on physical attractiveness in evaluating potential partners, women place greater emphasis on other factors, such as personality, status, power, and income. Hence, lesbians and heterosexual men are less concerned with their own physical attractiveness and, consequently, less dissatisfied with their bodies and less vulnerable to eating disorders (Siever, 1994).

Femininity and Eating Disorders

In a meta-analytical review the relationship between femininity and eating disorders was based in 22 studies. Although the effect size was small it was significant, and showed that eating disordered women reported higher levels of femininity than non eating disordered women did (Murnen and Smolak, 1997). The largest effect size was found in the group of women diagnosed with anorexia nervosa. Eating disordered people had lower masculinity scores than did controls.

Females suffering from eating disorders are more likely to refuse traditional concepts of the female gender role, especially a traditional concept of motherhood (Henning K and Strauss B, 2003). When Steiner-Adair (1986), described “superwoman”, a woman who achieves in both masculine (e.g., career, assertiveness) and feminine (e.g., family, nurturance) realms, and who is attractive while doing all of this, high schools girls who endorsed this image demonstrated greater eating pathology (Steiner Adair, 1986, 1989). Thorton and Leo (1991) reported similar findings for college women. Thus, “superwoman” may be a form of feminine gender role adoption which constitutes a risk factor for eating problems.

Silverstein and Perlick (1995) have suggested that it is the mismatch between an adolescent’s modern gender role and her parents’ traditional gender expectations that sets the stage for eating disorders. Thus far, the focus of gender eating disorders research has been on gender role adoption. However, being female means more than adopting a particular gender role. It also means that certain experiences, particularly involving objectification of the body, become more likely (Bordo, 1993). These experiences, including sexual harassment and sexual abuse, may be direct contributors to eating disorder (Wooley, 1994). Such experiences, especially when combined with society's sexual double standard, may leave young women confused about their sexual identity. Such confusion over society's messages and one's ability to control a sexual situation may lead to a sense of vulnerability, which may play out as an eating problem. The common finding that women suffering from bulimia nervosa are often promiscuous while those suffering from anorexia nervosa may appear to fear or be repulsed by sex suggests that sexual and eating issues are both body concerns for many women (Murnen and Smolak, 1997). Some developmentalists have suggested that early adolescence is a time of gender role shifts and gender intensification (e.g., Brown and Gilligan 1992). This is precisely the time that it appears to begin an intensification of eating problems in white American girls (Murnen and Smolak, 1997).

Relationship Between Eating Disorders and Gender Identity

The relationship between gender role and eating dysfunction is complex and requires multidimensional conceptualizations (Cantrell and Ellis, 1991).

Sociocultural pressures are divided into 3 categories; the thin ideal body for women, the centrality of appearance in the female gender role, and the importance of appearance for societal success. This model delineates probable carriers of cultural messages (peer, family, and media influences), examines relations between societal pressures and eating pathology, and considers the moderating role of internalizing societal pressures and of body dissatisfaction, restrained eating, negative affect, self-esteem and identity confusion, weight, social learning, coping skills, and impulsivity (Stice, 1994).

Internalization of sociocultural pressures mediate the adverse effects of the thin ideal. Stice *et al* (1994), found that our culture places a higher value on physical beauty in the evaluation of females than males. Garner *et al* (1980), have found that the average size of idealized woman (as portrayed by models), has become progressively thinner and has stabilized at 13% to19% below physically expected weight. Rodin *et al* (1984), suggest that this thin ideal is unachievable for most women and is likely to lead to feelings of self-devaluation, feelings of dysphoria (depression), and helplessness.

Feminine Gender Identity

Researchers and clinicians assert that there is an association between femininity and eating disorders, particularly anorexia nervosa and bulimia nervosa (Lancelot *et al*, 1994).

At present the relationship between eating disorders and feminine biology or sex role identity remains unclear; anorexia nervosa and bulimia have been variously associated with a rejection of femininity (Crisp, 1980), a confused acceptance of femininity (Boskind-White and White, 1983), and a rebellious redefinition of femininity (Orbach, 1985). These discrepancies in theory should not, however, obscure the obvious: the extreme sex difference in the prevalence of eating disorders means that the nature of femininity in our culture is a significant risk factor in the development of anorexia nervosa and bulimia.

Streigel-Moore *et al* (1986) discuss the relationship between eating disorders and many issues in the psychology of femininity, for example, the connections among physical attractiveness, pleasing and serving others, and self-esteem.

College women with bulimic behaviors tend to be more traditionally feminine in their sex-role identity and ideology than their nonbulimic peers (Brown *et al*, 1990). In a research, Szymanski and Chrisler (1990-91), observed that subjects that qualified in the feminine category on the Bem Sexual Role Inventory, ranged significantly higher on the Eating Disorders Inventory (EDI) (Garner *et al*, 1983) Bulimia subscale. Brown *et al* (1990), administering the Attitudes Scale and Personal Attributes Questionnaire, determined that a group of students with bulimic behaviors tended to be more traditionally feminine regarding her identity and ideology linked to sexual role than their non bulimic peers.

One of the explanations proposed for the "femininity hypothesis" is that the identification with characteristics typically labeled as "feminine", reflects a need of approval from others and lower self-esteem (Boskind-Lodahl, 1976; Paxton and Sculpthorpe, 1991). Data from sufferers of anorexia nervosa and bulimia nervosa are consistent with the presence of submissive behaviours and perceived low social rank (e.g. low self-esteem, helplessness, and feelings of shame). In a study, patients with eating disorders reported significantly higher levels of submissive behaviour and a more unfavourable social comparison than did student controls. Furthermore, levels of submissive behaviour and unfavourable social comparison were significantly related to severity of eating disorder symptoms, even after taking into account of depressive symptoms and other psychopathology (Troop *et al*, 2003).

Consequently, individuals who demonstrate higher levels of femininity are viewed as being more susceptible to the development of problem eating. Another possibility is that the relationship between femininity and problem eating for girls becomes more pronounced after adolescence and the onset of puberty. With the onset of puberty, girls experience a normative increase in body fat, which inevitably moves them further away from societal's ideal body shape for a woman. Therefore it is not surprising that several studies have found puberal development to be associated with higher levels of body dissatisfaction and disordered eating for girls (Attie and Brooks-Gunn, 1989; Swarr and Richards, 1996). In addition, during puberty adolescents receive greater pressures to conform to adult and gender roles (Alfieri *et al*, 1996; Basow 1992; Usmiani and Daniluk, 1997). Stereotypic behaviors and attitudes as reflected by gender traits are likely to play a more important role in determining psychological adjustment and problem eating. Further research is needed to examine how the development of puberty may moderate the relationship between femininity and disordered eating among adolescent girls. (Thomas and Ricciardelli, 2000)

Overall, the array of findings suggests that there may be more than one dimension underlying the relationship between gender traits, problem eating, and body dissatisfaction (Davis *et al*, 1996). Therefore, further research is needed to help us clarify the nature and the development of the relationship.

PSYCHOSOCIAL PROFILE OF EATING DISORDERED WOMEN

Current theorists have also suggested that gender role orientation, self-esteem, and dependence on others' approval are associated with disordered eating. Those who have addressed gender role orientation have claimed that either extreme femininity (Boskind-Lodahl 1976; Boskind-White and White, 1983; Bruch, 1978) or rejection of femininity (Chernin 1985; Orbach 1978; Thomä, 1967) is found in disordered eating. Related to the need for approval is the suggestion that both anorexics (Crisp, 1980) and bulimics (Boskind-Lodahl, *et al*, 1978; Hawkins and Clement, 1984) exhibit low self-confidence and self-esteem. A uniform picture has emerged of the eating disordered woman as a dependent, immature, "good girl" with an "abnormal" gender role identity (Beren and Chrisler, 1990).

Wilson, White (1946) and Crisp (1967, 1977) concluded that immaturity is integrally related to the eating disorder. Some researchers suggest that bulimics are "hyperfeminine" (Boskind-Lodhal 1976; Boskind-Lodhal *et al*, 1978) or they are more likely than non disordered eaters to endorse the traditional feminine role (Rost *et al*, 1982). Lewis and Johnson (1985) compared scores on the Bem Sex Roles Inventory for a group of bulimic women and a non-disordered control group and found that a significant number of bulimics were classified as undifferentiated. The authors conclude that bulimics may not have a clearly defined sense of self and suggest that this undifferentiated orientation may reflect a different type of feminine identification, as women have traditionally been socialized away from self-identification through others. These results support Chernin's (1985) theory that eating disordered women lack a sense of identity. A significant number of eating disordered women did describe themselves as childlike on the Bem Sex Role Inventory; a finding that may actually relate to the eating disordered women's lack of self-esteem, in that they do not perceive themselves as capable and adult-like because they are not confident in their abilities. In our society men are judged by the qualities of their minds, women are judged by the qualities of their bodies (Freedman 1986; Greenspan 1983). Women think that they must be attractive, and, today that means being thin. Eating disordered women, with their low self-confidence and self-esteem, would be especially susceptible to these sociocultural pressures. Because of this lack of self-esteem, thinness may assume a key importance as they overemphasize its necessity and believe that once they become thin (and hence attractive) that they will also be happy, successful, and confident (Boskind-White and White, 1983).

Boskind-White and White (1983), point out that these young women are generally bright, energetic, talented, interesting, and privileged. But this potential only seems to contribute to a strong feeling of being trapped between a dedication to traditional feminine values and an overpowering sense that they must compete with men and women in developing a successful career. To maintain the balance of power in favor of men or some vague conception of the *status quo*, this resistant majority has perverted the feminist demands for equality of opportunity into an unrealistic insistence that women reconcile the traditional and contradictory masculine and feminine roles into a "super" identity (Boskind-White, 1983). This identity retains many features of the established feminine role, for example, an obsession with the body, sensitivity to others, and dependence on male approval, but redefines the substance and style of femininity to emphasize thinness, youth, ambition, self-control, and self-sufficiency (Boskind-White, 1985).

Moreover, it is likely that rejection of the stereotypical feminine role with its images of a soft, rounded, and self-effacing mother contributes in some way to our cultural obsession with thinness (Garner *et al*, 1983). The other side of the new coin may be the need to look younger and more masculine, that is, thinner, in order to compete and gain respect in the essentially masculine world of business. Or both motives can be condensed into a single need, to compete with other women over who is the thinnest and most virtuous at the dinner table. The new, slender style is not a true symbol of liberation, but simply a newer badge of subjugation, this time to a god of thinness that is much more dangerous than whalebone corsets or stiletto heels (Boskind-White, 1985).

Steiner-Adair found that of all the girls attending a private high school, a group at risk for eating disorders, was quite aware of the "superwoman" ideal. These girls were able to describe themselves as thin, attractive, smart, active, independent, autonomous, and dominant within relationships, and somehow perfectly successful in establishing a career, being an exciting wife, and raising a family. Sixty percent of the girls seemed to understand that pursuing this myth would jeopardize the sense of interpersonal connectedness around which girls, as opposed to boys, tend to build their identities (Gilligan C, 1982). Forty percent wholeheartedly embraced this contradictory vision of interdependent autonomy, seeing no internal inconsistencies and no dissonance between the intense pressure to be separate *versus* their socialization to value relationship above complete individuation. Of the girls who saw through the superwoman myth and rejected it, not one had an Eating Attitudes Test (EAT) (Garner *et al*, 1982) score in the eating disorder range. Of the girls who identified themselves with the superwoman, 85% had scores in the eating disorder range and another one was borderline. Levine (1987) assumes that the work of Boskind-White and Steiner-Adair provides strong support for the belief that complex transformations in the feminine role constitute a sociocultural factor in the proliferation of eating disorders.

Maternal Identification

Very few of today's women feel that their mothers like their own bodies. Additionally, a woman's negative attitude toward her own body is highly correlated with the perception that both the mother and the father are or were critical of her body shape. Levine (1987) and Wooley and Wooley (1985) point out that the mothers of today's teenage girls are the first cohort of women to experience generalized dissatisfaction with their weight and themselves as a result of fashion propaganda, the changing roles of women, and our culture's increasing emphasis on youth. When these girls reach puberty, or even before, their body shape may become a projective surface for their mother's unfulfilled wishes and uncertainties and for the daughter's needs to act like a woman (mother) while becoming her own, "better" woman (not mother). In this emotionally charged interaction, dieting may serve simultaneously as identification, differentiation, revenge, and penance. Perhaps the hostile purification of the anorexic and the uncontrollable gorging and purging of the bulimic represent a culturally supported lack of respect for the normal female body and a need to escape the choices posed by the dilemma of maternal *versus* paternal identification.

The Role of the Feminist Movement

The proliferation of eating disorders has coincided, not only with feminism and increasing pressures for thinness, but also with an explosion of violence against women in the streets, at home, on films, and in literature. Surely such denigration does nothing to help girls and women learn how to respect their bodies and themselves. Furthermore, women are socialized to deny anger or keep it to themselves. Both these factors increase the likelihood that eating disorders are in part self-directed expressions of rage that also serve to mock the very same dependency, objectification, and idealization of thinness that many anorexics and bulimics cannot refrain from embodying. Now many vulnerable people, young women, convert powerful new conflicts between internal needs (to "be in control" and to "be someone") and external properties ("being thin" and "feminine") into eating disorders.

Wooley and Wooley (1985) propose three facts that clearly connect eating disorders with changes in the feminine sex role. First, the upsurge of eating disorders coincides with the increased impact of the feminist movement and the resultant expansion of the feminine sex role to include contradictory demands for autonomous and interdependent behaviors. Second, most anorexics and bulimics are female who develop their eating disorders during adolescence, a time of life in which issues of identity and intimacy are paramount in personal development. Third, the research by Steiner-Adair demonstrates a correlation between identification with the "super-thin superwoman" ideal and anorexic-like attitudes and behaviors. At present we do not know precisely how these confusing and oppressive changes in the feminine sex role combine with the traditional feminine investment in personal appearance to set the stage for eating disorders. It is very likely, however that the relentless pursuit of thinness reflects numerous themes, including identification with current ideals of youthful beauty, rejection of traditional feminine shapes and limitations, and the struggle for control of something concrete – weight and shape – in a world of abstract ambiguities. (Wooley and Wooley, 1985; Orbach, 1985; Boskind-White, 1985).

Schwartz *et al* (1982) believe that rather the association between the feminist movement and eating disorders, this fact may indicate "if one lives in a culture where the roles of women are complex, conflicting, and in change, and these pressures exist in a milieu which emphasizes a high positive value on slimness and negative value on obesity, one is at greater risk for anorexia (and bulimia).

A Feminist View

The emphasis on feminine attractiveness has continued despite the changing social roles, expectations, and opportunities for women that have occurred in the past 30 years or so. Moreover, these social changes have contributed to increase stress for women resulting from conflict between many of the competing role demands, facing them in both personal and professional aspects of their lives (Emmett 1985; Orbach 1978, 1986; Palazzoli, 1978). Feminists see the expectation that a woman be physically attractive and capable of being an effective wife, mother, and working woman as an ideal that many women attempt to achieve, yet frequently find to be unrealistic, unattainable, undesirable, and oppressive (Orbach, 1978).

According to Orbach (1978), being fat or eating compulsively is a directed conscious or unconscious challenge to sex-role stereotyping and the culturally defined experience of womanhood. In other words, a woman is expected by society to market herself as being available to men, marriage and motherhood. In the face of this pressure, exploited by advertising and the media, her desire to realize her potential as a person becomes of secondary importance in relation to her public image as an attractive female package. For some women compulsive eating develops as a way to avoid being "marketed" in this way, a way to avoid competition with other women, and possibly the only way for a woman to defend herself against the powerlessness of her position in society *vis-à-vis* men (Gilbert S, 1986).

It is suggested that disordered eating reflects women's response to the stress of these multiple pressures and conflicting demands (Orbach, 1978; Palazzoli, 1978). Thus, in a culture in which women's roles are complex and frequently conflicting, and the emphasis placed on appearance and thinness results in unrealistic body image and body dissatisfaction, conditions exist for heightened chronic stress and reduced self-esteem that may contribute to increased risk among women of developing an eating disorder (Schwartz *et al*, 1985).

There is the argument, on the one hand, that the female role makes women vulnerable to coercion, whereas on the other, it is seen as the source of women's personal conflict. A feminist perspective tends to emphasize the coercive elements in the female role. Women, it is argued, generally have much less control over their lives than men, and they are also subject to the quite explicit expectation that they should conform to a stereotypical body shape. The requirement is that they should be thin. This expectation is coercive, for the cost of failing to conform to conventional standards of slimness is to be made to feel unacceptable. There are many who are likely to be particularly vulnerable to such pressures during adolescence. There is the rather more subtle idea that emaciation and obesity are alternative strategies which enable women to escape from the demands of their role. By being either too fat or too thin a woman avoids being an object of sexual attraction. Being "outside the status of sex object" the anorexic is thus refusing to fit in with the expectation that she should be passive, decorative and dependent, and in so doing she is daring to define herself. The anorexic's modification of her body shape, like that of the obese woman, is an attempt to establish her existence as an individual independent of her female role, in so far as the emaciation in the anorexic will eventually produce physical weakness and with this a state of greater ineffectiveness and so dependence (Orbach S, 1978).

Feminists, often therapists, avoid casting the eating disordered behaviour as pathological. Instead, they seek to demonstrate that these disorders are an inevitable consequence of a misogynistic society that demeans women by devaluing female experience and women's values, by objectifying their bodies, and by discrediting vast areas of women's past and present achievements. Both overeating and noneating are a "protest against the way in which women are regarded in our society as objects of adornment and pleasure" (Orbach, 1986).

Boskind-White and White (1983) and Boskind-Lodahl (1976) suggest that the most appropriate treatment for anorexia nervosa and bulimia should include feminist therapy, which emphasizes the sociocultural influences which shape eating disorders and which recognizes the importance of increasing the disordered eaters' self-esteem, self-control, and feelings of empowerment.

The Influence of Gender Role in the Development

Some degree of conflict is inherent in the female roles. All the child needs to develop an adequate role concept that comes from experience of the wider culture. At a wider social and cultural level the girl is confronted with a scale that stresses the worth and importance of assertiveness, independence, intellectual prowess, the ability to be productive, and other attributes of this kind which are aligned far more with the role requirements for boys than with those for her own sex. They are attributes that have a positive value in general social terms, but a negative value for the girl in terms of her female role. This requires that she should be passive, yielding and dependent, decorative rather than productive, and helpless rather than competent. Such attributes as these conflicts rather than coincide with wider social values. Then, it is not surprising, that even at quite an early age there is evidence that the self esteem of boys is markedly higher than the self-esteem of girls (Kohlberg, 1966).

Although the educational system ostensibly prepares and encourages men and women equally for higher education and careers, these are really limited by both social and psychological pressures to men. While decrying the loss of female potential in both economic and personal terms, society provides little, if any, positive encouragement for women to be interested in pursuing a career. The culturally prevalent view is that femininity and individual achievement are mutually exclusive ends. Female students clearly associate unusual academic excellence in women with loss of femininity, social rejection and "personal and societal destruction". Some have stressed that it means that a woman could be unhappy, aggressive, and unmarried. It is at puberty that the "motive to avoid success" emerges, when there is an increased awareness of gender roles and the tendency to be particularly vulnerable to social ostracism. From this time onwards a girl is likely to experience anxiety in relation to her role. Anxiety is also experienced most frequently when women compete with men in traditionally male-dominated areas. It is believed that fear of success is largely responsible for the substantial under representation of women in higher education. Certainly some women do overcome many of the pressures and pursue a career, but few manage this without feeling guilty, anxious, unfeminine, and selfish (Slade, 1984).

From earliest childhood men learn that their role is to be active, intelligent, dominant, rational, and assertive. Women learn at a similarly early age that assertiveness on their part is inappropriate; taking initiative is not their task. Their concern is with caring and nurturing, with being receptive to the feelings of those around them, with being sensitive and supportive in their response to human needs. Not only does this strength and competence often go unrecognized and unacknowledged but, it is all too likely to be systematically devalued. And at best it is represented as feminine weakness, and at worst as female pathology. Women all too often fulfill the demands of their female role to the best of their ability, deriving meanwhile precious little self-esteem from their endeavours. Furthermore, the particular concerns that their role assigns to them gives them greater experience generally in human development and personal relationships. Women, learn to judge themselves in the same way as they are judged by the dominant culture. This contributes to her sense of unworthiness and to her feeling that she is being given help and resources that she does not deserve, and often which the family cannot easily afford (Slade, 1984).

The Influence of the Family as Predisposing Factor

The eating disordered patients, particularly the anorexic feels she is under strong pressure to succeed educationally, and to pursue a career. Her family is all the more pleased when her career is one that carries high status, which often means that she is competing, or preparing to compete, in male-dominated professions.

The anorexic shares with her family a powerful ethic of individual effort and self-improvement. Anorexic's families are generally concerned with social position, respectability, and financial security. Success is important to them. In this context being emotional and expressing feelings is far from a priority. There is less demand upon women to control or repress their feelings. As a consequence they, far more than men, become familiar with their feelings and obtain openness in dealing with them. The fact which is generally overlooked in psychological accounts of anorexia nervosa is that this kind of emotionally supportive response is entirely compatible with the requirements of the female role. The anorexic's response to her parents' needs may indicate her "abnormal considerateness", even her "over submissiveness". It is this receptivity to human needs as a characteristic of the female role that provides the link between the anorexic and the values and experiences of her family. As a result of her upbringing – in the widest possible sense – the anorexic becomes attuned to responding to the needs of those around her: to being sensitive, compliant, supportive, and making others feel at ease; she is so attuned because she is female. Moreover, receptivity is a personal attribute which she herself values (Slade, 1984).

Gender roles indicate to the individual a way of ordering priorities. The anorexic is quite unable to decide, however, whether being sensitive to others should take precedence over the performance of the task, or *vice versa*. The anorexic cannot easily order her priorities because she feels obliged to respond both in a way that is generally considered socially desirable for males, and in a way that is considered socially desirable for females. It is, paradoxically, because of her female receptivity that she feels obliged take on the male tasks of being a good performer and achiever of success. Her family's values create the obligation for its members to respond in ways that are valued for males, but this is only possible, and can only be maintained, through their being aware and receptive in a way that is valued for females.

What is in fact taking place between the anorexic and her family is a skewed transaction. Her parents see her as developing intellectual potential and as being given every encouragement to make something of herself, and, having her best interests at heart, they provide her with opportunities that they probably had to strive for, and which her grandparents may never have had. The anorexic, meanwhile, being sensitive to her parents' values and attitudes, knows that achievement will please them and sees it as her task to be successful, even though she feels unequal to this. Through her success and her loyalty in this respect, she helps to underpin her family's sense of establishment and well-being. However, she places no particular value for herself on what is involved in doing good. Her family praises her for her success, but they fail to acknowledge this contribution to their feeling of well-being for the service that it is. The praises the girl receives she feels are empty, for being told how good she is for doing something she does not value does nothing to increase her own sense of worth. As in all such skewed transactions the anorexic is left with the overall feeling that she is "bad" (Slade, 1984).

SANDRA BEM AND SEX ROLES CATEGORIES

The Concept of Androgyny

As previously mentioned, there is a consensus on the stereotyped roles for the average man or woman. The traits in these stereotypes fall into two separate groups. The first expresses competence and independence, while the second focuses on warmth and expressiveness. Men are seen as having the competence, while women are seen as more expressive. Some of these traits are: feminine (tactful, quiet, aware of feelings of others, need for security, easily express tender feeling), masculine (aggressive, independent, dominant, competitive, active, ambitious, make decisions easily). Competence (masculine) traits are valued more in Western societies; in contrast expressive (feminine) traits are viewed negatively.

Sandra Lipsitz Bem, a Stanford University psychologist, introduced the concept of androgyny (1977) that seeks to indicate the degree to which a person is culturally influenced by gender roles. This word comes from the Greek: *andro* for male and *gyne* for female referring to a blending of what are usually agreed as positive characteristics of both sexes. The androgynous individual possesses flexibility. S/he can be assertive, independent, and self-reliant as well as relate to others, be sensitive to others' needs, and is able to depend on others for emotional support. Androgyny allows an individual to be independent and tender, assertive and yielding, masculine and feminine. Thus androgyny greatly expands the range of behavior open to everyone, permitting people to cope more effectively with diverse situations as well as assimilate the understanding necessary to develop mature, lasting relationships. The androgynous person is high in both masculine and feminine traits. Bem hypothesized that psychological androgyny with equally high levels of feminine and masculine traits constitute optimal mental health for both men and women. She also argued that masculinity and femininity were independent dimensions, with the possibility of both sets of characteristics co-existing in the one individual. Androgynous people can be aggressive or yielding, forceful or gentle, sensitive or assertive, as the particular situation requires. Likewise, feminine women have trouble being independent and assertive, even when independence and assertiveness are needed. In contrast, choosing from a wider range of behaviors, truly androgynous people are able to modify their responses, according to their needs and the needs of the situation. Bem believed that androgynous people are freer, more adaptable, and more emotionally healthy than those who restrict their behavior to traditional sex roles.

Bem Sex Role Inventory (Bem 1974) consists of 60 self-descriptive, personality-characteristic adjectives designed to measure psychological masculinity and femininity as two independent variables. All adjectives are designed to be positive toned, or socially desirable. This scale is measuring the cultural, not biological influences on gender roles. Twenty items assess masculinity, 20 assess femininity, the others are neutral. Each adjective is ranked on a Likert scale where 1= 'never or almost never true' and 7= 'always or almost always true'. Scores on each dimension can range from 20 to 140. Individuals are classified on the basis of median splits as 'masculine' (high masculinity, low femininity), 'feminine' (high femininity, low masculinity), 'androgynous' (high masculinity and femininity), or 'undifferentiated' (low masculinity and femininity) and contains a 10-item masculinity and a 10 item femininity scale. In determining a person's sex-role on this scale, the medians of masculinity and femininity scales are derived. Individuals who score above both medians are androgynous, while people scoring below both medians are considered undifferentiated. A man who scores above the median on the masculinity scale and below the median on the femininity scale is a traditional male, and a woman who scores below the masculinity but above the femininity median display a traditional feminine sex-role.

Gender Stereotyped Traits in Eating Disordered Patients

Gender traits, typically referred to as "masculinity and "femininity", provide one of the ways for studying the sociocultural context underlying many of our attitudes and behaviors. Specifically gender traits reflect stereotypes about the beliefs and behaviors typically attributed to men and women, which are acquired as they learn about the world and their roles in it (Basow, 1992; Deux and Major, 1987).

The presence of sex role stereotypes in the population as a whole has been demonstrated many times (Slade, 1984). The author describes one study in which a large sample of men and women was presented with a list of personal characteristics and asked how desirable they, as individuals, felt it was for men and for women in society to have these characteristics. Both men and women decided that certain characteristics — such as forceful, analytical, ambitious — were socially desirable for men, whereas other characteristics — such as affectionate, yielding, sensitive to the needs of others — were socially desirable for women. Other characteristics such as truthful and happy were judged to be equally desirable for men and women, and were therefore placed in a neutral category that make possible to identify individuals who accept that they have characteristics that are socially desirable for males and for females. Anorexics were generally more satisfied with themselves in relation to stereotypically female characteristics than stereotypically male characteristics; they were more satisfied particularly in relation to those female characteristics associated with sensitivity to other people. The socially desirable characteristics for females that they considered important to decision making were loyalty, sympathy, sensitivity to the needs of others, and understanding. They rejected all other feminine characteristics, and this included such attributes as warm, yielding, affectionate, and tender. Of those traits socially desirable for males, they accepted analytical, independent, self-reliant and, for obvious reasons, the ability to make decisions easily, as being important to this task. Among the other male-valued characteristics that they rejected were such attributes as aggressive, competitive, having a strong personality, and willingness to take a stand. Many neutral qualities were accepted as important to decision making as both male and female qualities together. In other words, faced with the problem of having to make up her mind what to do in any situation, the anorexic is the more likely to attempt to be adaptable, sincere, helpful, reliable, truthful, and conscientious; thus choosing to avoid, where possible, gender type characteristics. Likewise the anorexic values certain aspects of the female role whilst strenuously rejecting others. Sympathy, sensitivity, and understanding are most important to her, but the openness and spontaneity of feeling that are usually accepted as accompanying these qualities, and as essential to their normal expression, are given no part in her life. The emotionality that is implicit in such female characteristics as tender, warm, affectionate, love for children, she has learned to reject. Thus, within the female role too she is taking on the task of being sensitive and responding to the needs of those around her without assuming those aspects of the role that will enable her to perform those tasks more fully and with greater personal satisfaction. She is acutely sensitive to other people's feelings; she is also utterly convinced that she must keep her own feelings to herself. Her sense of failure and accumulating feelings of inadequacy are aspects of her life that she must not burden anyone with, least of all members of her family. Anorexic's families generally maintain the inherent contradiction of negating the value of feelings while demanding sensitivity to the need for loyalty and cohesion; the situation is further complicated by their ambivalence towards other kinds of behaviour which conventionally belong to the female role (Slade, 1984; Behar, 1992).

Behar *et al* (2001) compared female eating disordered patients *versus* female university students without eating problems and confirmed that the feminine condition emerges as the main category of gender identity in the formers, whilst healthy students were mainly identified with androgyny category. Eating disordered patients displayed the following profile on BSRI: childlike, moody, willing to take a stand, unpredictable, jealous, conventional, and inefficient. These traits are according with clinical characteristics widely seen among anorexics and bulimics. In contrast, female students without eating dysfunctions were more sympathetic, happy, self-reliant, independent, and assertive, made decisions easily, self-sufficient, helpful, conscientious, truthful, gentle, and tactful. These predominant neutral traits are protective, beneficial, adaptable, favorable, and determinant to obtain a desirable and ideal biopsychosocial welfare. Feminine characteristics such as loyalty, femininity, understanding, sensitivity to other's needs, were sociably desirable for eating disordered subjects; masculine traits such as defends own beliefs, willing to take a stand, analytical, and independent, were more valued by them, and among neutral features, they preferred to be reliable, sincere, friendly, and secretive. In this research, a 42.9% of the patients, in contrast with the 23.8% of the students were classified within the Feminine category. Contrary, a 31.7% and a 42.9% of the latter was qualified as Androgynous and Undifferentiated *versus* the 19% and 27% of the patients respectively. There were significant differences between patients and students in 22 items of the BSRI ($p < 0.01$). Both groups rejected and were identified with some feminine, masculine and neutral qualities (Table 1).

In another analyses, Behar *et al* (2002) confronted female eating disordered patients *versus* non clinical populations of female and male subjects without eating problems corroborating their earlier results and demonstrating that female subjects without eating disorders showed more drive for thinness and displayed more body dissatisfaction than their male peers (Tables 2 and 3).

Additionally, they found (2003) the highest percentage of feminine category on the BSRI among restricted anorexics, and simultaneously they ranked higher on the EDI Maturity fears subscale. Again, femininity emerged as the main trait of gender identity in patients suffering from an eating pathology, in contrast to androgyny showed by female subjects without eating disorders (Figure 1). Restrictive anorectics displayed more femininity than the others eating disorders subtypes. Compulsive.purgative anorectics showed more level of severity within the eating disorder spectrum, and more drive for thinness, perfectionism and interpersonal distrust. Restrictive anorectics exhibited more maturity fears and purgative bulimics more bulimic behaviours, body dissatisfaction, ineffectiveness and interoceptive awareness (Figures 2 and 3).

Table 1. Comparison of answers on the BRSI between groups TCA (N= 63) y C (N= 63)

Item	Category	ED Group	E Group	p Value	X-DE	X-DE
Cheerful(B5)	Feminine	5,0	(1,6) (1,7)	5,9	(0,8)	<0,001*
Sympathetic (B23)	Feminine	5,0	(1,8) (1,8)	6,2	(0,6)	<0,001*
Childlike (B50)	Feminine	4,3	(1,7)	3,0	(1,4)	<0,001*
Self-reliant (B1)	Masculine	4,4	(1,7)	6,0	(0,9)	<0,001*
Independent (B7)	Masculine	5,0	(1,8)	5,9	(1,0)	<0,001*
Assertive (B13)	Masculine	4,6	(1,8)	5,6	(0,9)	<0,001*
Analytical (B22)	Masculine	5,3	(1,9)	6,0	(1,0)	<0,008*
Makes decisions easily (B31)	Masculine	3,8	(1,7)	5,1	(1,2)	<0,001*
Self-sufficient (B34)	Masculine	4,6	(1,7)	5,8	(1,0)	<0,001*00
Willing to take a position (B43)	Masculine	5,6	(1,8)	4,0	(1,7)	<0,001*
Helpful (B3)	Neutral	4,8	(1,5)	6,0	(0,9)	<0,001*
Moody (B6)	Neutral	5,3	(1,7)	3,7	(1,9)	<0,001*
Conscientious (B9)	Neutral	5,4	(1,8)	6,3	(1,0)	<0,001*
Happy (B15)	Neutral	4,2	(1,8)	6,0	(0,9)	<0,001*
Unpredictable (B18)	Neutral	4,7	(1,7)	3,7	(1,6)	<0,001*
Jealous (B24)	Neutral	5,0	(1,1)	4,4	(1,8)	<0,047*
Truthful (B27)	Neutral	5,4	(1,2)	6,2	(0,7)	<0,001*
Sincere (B33)	Neutral	6,1	(1,7)	6,4	(0,6)	<0,021*
Likable (B39)	Neutral	5,4	(1,6)	5,9	(0,7)	<0,003*
Solemn (B42)	Neutral	4,3	(1,8)	3,3	(1,4)	<0,001*
Inefficient (B48)	Neutral	2,9		1,9	(1,1)	<0,001*
Tactful (B57)	Neutral	5,1		5,7	(0,8)	<0,017*

X= Mean
ED group= Eating disordered patients
DE= Standard deviation
E Group= Students without eating problems
*= Statistically significant difference

Table 2. Comparison of variables between groups TCA (n= 119) y F (n= 63)

Variable	ED Group	F Group	p Value	X-DE	X-DE
Present weight	54,9	(10,7)	55,8	(5,8)	NS
Height	157,7	(21,4)	161,3	(5,3)	NS
Ideal weight	50,5	(5,7)	53,5	(4,7)	<0,001*
EAT-40	51,6	(21,4)	10,4	(6,4)	<0,001*
EDI	87,6	(31,6)	23,3	(18,2)	<0,001*
Drive for thinness	14,4	(6,3)	2,4	(3,9)	<0,001*
Interoceptive awareness	13,3	(6,9)	1,1	(2,6)	<0,001*
Bulimia	8,8	(5,8)	2,5	(1,9)	<0,001*
Body dissatisfaction	15,8	(8,1)	5,1	(6,6)	<0,001*
Ineffectiveness	9,0	(7,6)	0,9	(2,0)	<0,001*
Maturity fears	11,1	(6,1)	3,9	(4,2)	<0,001*
Perfectionism	9,2	(4,3)	6,2	(4,4)	<0,001*
Interpersonal distrust	6,0	(5,2)	1,3	(2,0)	<0,001*

X= Mean
ED group= Eating disordered subjects
DE= Standard deviation
F group= Female students without
*= Statistically significant difference eating problems
NS= No significant difference

Table 3. Comparison of variables between M (n= 89) and F (n= 63) groups

Variable	*M Group*	F Group	p Value	X-DE	X-DE
Present weight	73,7	(9,7)	55,8	(6,0)	<0,001*
Height	176,2	(7,1)	161,3	(5,3)	<0,001*
Ideal weight	72,6	(8,4)	53,5	(4,7)	<0,001*
EAT-40	10,7	(5,8)	10,4	(6,4)	NS
EDI	21,7	(11,6)	23,3	(18,3)	NS
Drive for thinness	0,9	(2,1)	2,4	(3,9)	<0,003*
Interoceptive awareness	1,2	(1,8)	1,1	(2,6)	NS
Bulimia	2,4	(1,7)	2,5	(1,9)	NS
Body dissatisfaction	2,8	(3,9)	5,1	(6,6)	<0,009*
Ineffectiveness	0,6	(1,4)	0,9	(2,0)	NS
Maturity fears	3,9	(3,9)	3,9	(4,2)	NS
Perfectionism	7,7	(3,5)	6,2	(4,4)	<0,020*
Interpersonal distrust	2,3	(2,4)	1,3	(2,0)	<0,008*

X= Mean
ED group= Eating disordered subjects
DE= Standard deviation
F group= Male students without
* = Statistically significant difference eating problems
NS= No significant difference

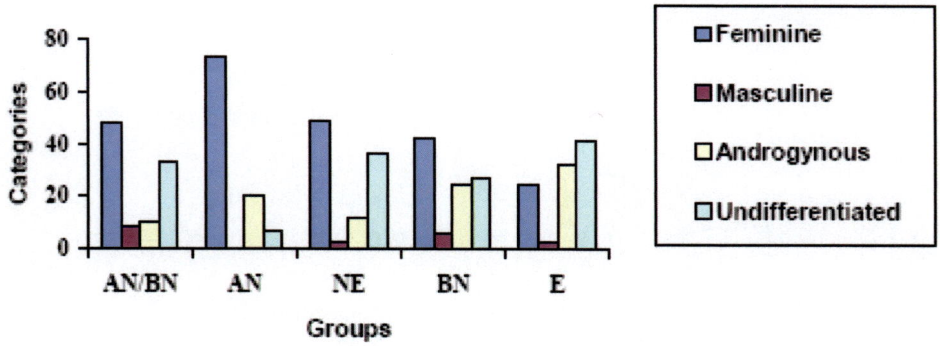

Figure 1. Gender identity categories on the BRSI and its difference among groups

The distinction between anorexia nervosa and bulimia is often not well defined, they frequently co-occur, and both may be symptomatic of common antecedents (Hsu, 1990). Related to the need for approval is the suggestion that both anorexics (Crisp, 1980) and bulimics (Boskind-Lodahl, Sirlin and White, 1978; Hawkins and Clement, 1984) have low self-confidence and self- esteem. People classified as undifferentiated on the Bem Sex Role Inventory have also been found to report significantly lower self-esteem, as measured by the Texas Social Behavior Inventory, than androgynous, masculine, or feminine subjects (Bem, 1977; Lewis and Johnson, 1985, Spence, Helmreich and Stapp, 1975). Lewis and Johnson (1985) reported bulimics to be less feminine than control subjects; Katzman and Wolchik (1984), however, reported no differences in femininity or masculinity between bulimics and controls. Anorexics, on the other hand, reportedly do not differ from control subjects on femininity, but are less masculine than controls (Sitnick and Katz, 1984). Murnen and Smolak

(1996) in their meta-analysis, found the largest effect size in the group of women diagnosed with anorexia nervosa that were likely to score higher on the gender role assures compared to control groups. In nineteen of the studies, eating disordered people had lower masculinity scores than did controls (Murnen and Smolak, 1996).

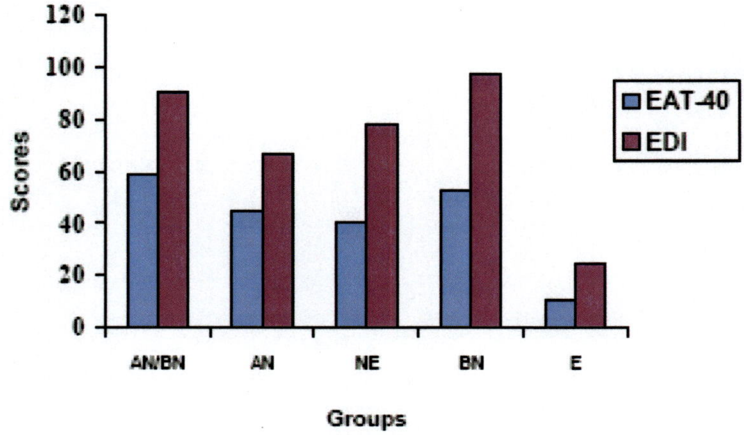

Figure 2. EAT-40 and EDI scores among groups

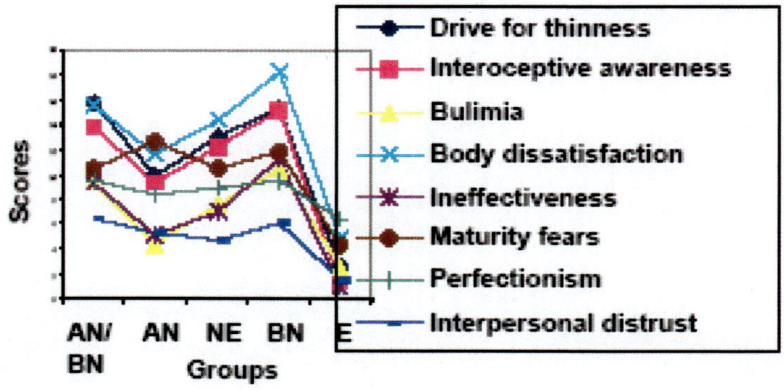

Figure 3. EDI scores and its items among groups

Evidence About Androgyny

There is a growing evidence in the literature regarding androgynous traits.

Androgynous approaches promise increased independent thinking, action, and self-esteem, (Bradley, 1993; Shimonaka *et al*, 1994) and androgynous people prefer other androgynous people (Orlofsky, 1982; Pursell, *et al*, 1981).

Throughout life span of both sexes, it has been found that there is a relationship between androgyny and successful adaptation. Self-esteem and subjective health seems to be the most effective predictors of adaptation. (Shimonaka *et al*, 1997) In fact, scores on a measure of androgyny are predictive of those on an index of empathy in medical students and residents (Yarnold *et al*, 1993).

On the other hand, Napholz (1994) observed that subjects who were undifferentiated in sex role orientation had significantly higher depression scores, lower self-esteem scores, and lower life satisfaction scores than the androgynous and cross-typed groups. Androgyny is an instance of a more general situational flexibility (Vonk and Ashmore, 1993), and is associated with more liberal attitudes toward sexual expression (Johnson, 1989). In a study, participants high on androgyny reported less same sex and opposite sex touch avoidance than did subjects low on androgyny (Crawford, 1994); is predictive of greater life satisfaction than an undifferentiated orientation (Dean and Gilroy, 1993), is related to characteristics that enhance the development and maintenance of close friendships, such as a communal orientation and positive conceptions of friends (Jones *et al*, 1990). On the other hand, androgynous profiles are rated as more desirable across occupations (Arkkelin and O'Connor, 1992). Androgynous nurses reported lower depression and vocational stress than their undifferentiated counterparts (Steenbarger and Greenberg, 1990).

Androgynous and undifferentiated women may possess specific characteristics that enable them to cope effectively with the different and conflicting demands of masculine and feminine roles. In addition (Root, 1990) notes certain other "protective factors" with regard to disordered eating (high self-esteem, emotional stability, low self-consciousness, and an emphasis on healthy body rather than appearance) that may be more characteristic of androgynous women; for instance, androgynous individuals have the highest levels of self-esteem among the four gender categories and undifferentiated individuals typically have the lowest self-esteem (Bem 1977; Spence and Helmreich, 1978) as well as generally lower achievement motivation (Spence, Helmreich, 1978)

Hypothesis concerning the relationship of sex role flexibility (androgyny) to mental health have been supported for females in both college and psychiatric populations (Burchardt and Serbin, 1982). Highly feminine women are more likely to have weak body boundaries than more androgynous women (Ricards and McAlister, 1994). In light of a society not yet gender schematic, psychological androgyny is invoked as the development ideal (Mead and Ignico, 1992).

Finally, Skoe (1995) described that high levels of care-based moral reasoning, i.e., a balanced concern for the welfare of self and others, was related to androgyny for women. According to this author, women in particular relinquishing the stereotyped sex role definition and becoming more androgynous are important for their ego identity as well as care-based moral development.

References

Alfieri T, Ruble D, Higgins E. Gender stereotypes during adolescence: Developmental changes and the transition to junior high school. *Developmental Psychology* 1996; 32: 1129-1137.

American Psychiatric association. Practice guideline for the treatment of patients with eating disorders (Revision). *Am J Psychiatry* 2000; 157 (Suppl 1): 1-39.

Andersen A, Holman J. Males with eating disorders: Challenges for treatment and research. *Psychopharmacol Bull* 1997; 33 (3): 391-397.

Andersen A. Gender-related aspects of eating disorders: A guide to practice. *The Journal of Gender-Specific Medicine* 1999; 2(1): 47-54.

Arkkelin D, O'Connor R. The "good" professional: Effect of sex profile gender type, androgyny, and likableness on impressions of incumbents of sex typed occupations. *Sex Roles* 1992; 27 (9-10): 517-532.

Attie I, Brooks-Gunn J. Development of eating problems in adolescent girls: A longitudinal study. *Developmental Psychology* 1989; 25: 70-79.

Basow S. Gender stereotypes and roles. California: Brooks/Cole, 1992.

Behar R. Gender roles and anorexia nervosa. *Acta Psiquiát Psicol Am Lat* 1992; 38 (2): 119-22.

Behar R, De la Barrera M, Michelotti J. Gender identity and eating disorders. *Rev Méd Chile* 2001; 129: 1003-1011.

Behar R, De la Barrera M, Michelotti J. Gender differences in attitudes towards eating behaviors. *Rev Méd Chile* 2002; 130: 964-975.

Behar R, De la Barrera M, Michelotti J. Clinical features and gender identity among eating disordered patient's subtypes. *Rev Méd Chile* 2003; 131: 748-758.

Bem S. The measurement of psychological androgyny. Journal of *Consulting and Clinical psychology* 1974; 42: 155-162.

Bem S. On the utility of alternative procedures for assessing psychological androgyny. *Journal of Consulting and Clinical Psychology* 1977; 45: 196-205.

Bemporad J. Cultural and historical aspects of eating disorders. *Theor Med* 1997; 18: 401-420.

Beren S, Chrisler J. Gender role, need for approval, childness, and self-esteem: markers of disordered eating? *Research Communications in Psychology, Psychiatry and Behavior* 1990; 15(4): 183-198.

Bordo S. *Unbearable weight: Feminism, Western culture, and the body.* Berkeley: University of California Press, 1993.

Boskind-Lodahl M. Cinderella's stepsisters: A feminist perspective on anorexia nervosa and bulimia. *Journal of Women in Culture and Society* 1976; 2: 342-355.

Boskind-Lodahl M, Sirlin J, White WC. The definition and treatment of bulimarexia in college women: A pilot study. *Journal of the American College Health Association* 1978; 27: 84-86.

Boskind-White M, White W. *Bulimarexia: The binge/ purge cycle.* New York: WW Norton, 1983.

Boskind-White M. Bulimarexia: A sociocultural perspective. In: Emmett S, editor. *Theory and treatment of anorexia nervosa and bulimia: Biomedical, sociocultural, and psychological perspectives.* New York: Brunner/Mazel, 1985. p. 113-26.

Bradley J. Autonomy through androgyny. *Nurs Manage* 1993; 24 (10): 64J, 64N-64.

Broverman I et al. Sex role stereotypes: A current appraisal. *Journal of Social Issues* 1972; 28: 59-78.

Brown J, Cross H, Nelson J. Sex role identity and sex role ideology in college women with bulimic behaviour. *Int J Eat Disord* 1990; 9 (5): 571-575.

Brown L, Gilligan C. *Meeting at the crossroads: Women's psychology and girls' development.* New York: Ballantine Books, 1992.

Bruch H. *The golden cage: The enigma of anorexia nervosa.* Cambridge MA: Harvard University Press, 1978.

Brumberg J. *Fasting girls. The emergence of anorexia nervosa as a modern disease.* Cambridge: Harvard University Press, 1988.

Burchardt C, Serbin L. Psychological androgyny and personality adjustment in college and psychiatric populations. *Sex Roles* 1982; 8(8): 835-851.

Cantrell P, Ellis J. Gender role and risk patterns for eating disorders in men and women. *J Clin Psychol* 1991; 47(1): 53-7.

Cauwels J. *Bulimia: The binge-purge compulsion.* New York: Doubleday, 1983.

Crawford C. Effects of sex and sex roles on avoidance of same and opposite sex touch. *Percept Mot Skills* 1994; 79 (1 Pt 1): 107-112.

Crisp A. Anorexia Nervosa. *Hospital Medicine* 1967; 1: 713-718.

Crisp A. Differential diagnosis of anorexia nervosa. *Proc R Soc Med* 1977; 70:686-690.

Crisp A. *Anorexia nervosa. Let me be.* London: Academic Press, 1980.

Chernin K. *The hungry self.* New York: Harper and Row, 1985.

Davis C, Dianne M, Lazarus L. Gender-role orientation and body image in women and men: The moderating influence of neuroticism. *Sex Roles* 1996; 34: 493-505.

Dean C, Gilroy F. Relation of sex-role orientation to life satisfaction in a healthy elderly sample. *Journal of Social Behavior and Personality* 1993; 8(1): 133-140.

Deux K, Major B. Putting gender into context: An interactive model of gender related behaviour. *Psychological Review* 1987; 94: 369-389.

Drewnowski A, Yee D. Men and body image: Are males satisfied with their body weight? *Psychosomatic Medicine* 1987; 49: 626-634.

Emmett S. Future trends. In: Emmett S, editor. *Theory and treatment of anorexia nervosa and bulimia: Biomedical, sociocultural and psychological perspectives.* New York: Brunnel/Mazel, 1985.p. 73-94.

Fallon A, Rozin P. Sex differences in the perception of body shape. *J Abnorm Psychol* 1985; 94: 102-5.

Fornari V, Dancyger IF. Psychosexual development and eating disorders. *Adolesc Med* 2003 ;14(1):61-75.

Freedman R. *Beauty bound.* Lexington MA: Lexington Books, 1986.

Freedman R. *Body Image: Learning to like our looks and ourselves.* New York: Harper and Row, 1988.

Garfinkel P, Garner D. *Anorexia nervosa: A multidimensional perspective.* New York: Brunner/Mazel, 1982.

Garner D, Garfinkel P, Schwartz D, Thompson M. Cultural expectation of thinness in women. *Psychological Reports* 1980; 47: 483-491.

Garner D, Olmstead M, Bohr I, Garfinfel P. The eating attitudes test: Psychometric features and clinical correlates. *Psychological Med* 1982; 12: 671-8.

Garner D, Garkinfel P, Olmsted M. An overview of sociocultural factors in the development of anorexia nervosa. In: Darby P and others, editors. *Anorexia nervosa: Recent developments in research.* New York: AR Liss. 1983. p. 65-82.

Garner D, Olmstead M, Polivy J. Development and validation of a multidimensional eating disorder inventory for anorexia nervosa and bulimia. *Int J Eat Disord* 1983; 2: 151-34.

Garner D, Rockert W, Johnson C. Psychoeducational principles of bulimia and anorexia nervosa. In: Garner D, Garfinkel P, editors. *Handbook of psychotherapy for anorexia nervosa and bulimia*. New York: Guilford Press, 1985. p. 513-72.

Gilbert S. *Pathology of eating. Psychology and treatment. Social and psychological aspects of medical practice*. London and New York: Routledge & Kegan Paul, 1986.

Gilligan C. *In a different voice: Psychological theory and women's development*. Cambridge: Harvard University Press, 1982.

Greenspan M. *A New Approach to women & therapy*. New York: McGraw-Hill, 1983.

Herman C, Polivy J. Restrained eating. In: Stunkard A, editor. *Obesity*. Philadelphia: Saunders, 1980. p. 208-225.

Herzog D, Bradburn I, Newman K. Sexuality in males with eating disorders. In: Andersen A, editor. *Males with eating disorders*. New York: Brunner/Mazel, 1990. p. 40-53.

Holleran P, Pascale J, Fraley J. Personality correlates of college age bulimics. *Journal of Counselling and Development* 1988; 66: 378-381.

Hawkins R, Clement P. Binge eating syndrome: The measurement problem and a conceptual model. In: Hawkins R, Fremouw W, Clement P, editors. *Binge-eating: Theory, research and treatment*. New York: Springer, 1984. p. 229-251.

Henning K, Strauss B. Personal child-related motives and attitudes in females with eating disorders--indicators for gender role conflicts? *Psychother Psychosom Med Psychol* 2003 ;53(1):23-8.

Hsu L. *Eating disorders*. New York: Guilford Press, 1990.

Johnson M. Sex role orientation and attitudes toward sexual expression. *Psychological Reports* 1989; 64(3, Pt 2): 1064.

Johnson M, Brems C, Fischer P. Sex role conflict, social desirability, and eating disorder attitudes and behaviors. *The Journal of General Psychology* 1996; 123: 75-87.

Jones D, Bloys N, Wood M. Sex roles and friendship patterns. *Sex Roles* 1990; 23 (3-4): 133-45.

Katzman MA, Wolchick SA. Bulimia and binge eating in college women: A comparison of personality and behavioral characteristics. *Journal of Consulting and Clinical Psychology* 1984; 52: 428-523.

Kearney-Cooke A. Gender differences and self-esteem. *J Gend Specif Med* 1999; 2(3):46-52.

Klingenspor B. Gender identity and bulimic eating behavior. *Sex Roles* 1994; 31: 407-431.

Kohlberg L. A cognitive developmental analysis of children's sex role concepts and attitudes. In: Maccoby E, editor. *The development of sex differences*. Stanford: Stanford University Press, 1966. p. 82-193

Lancelot C, Kaslow J. Sex role orientation and disordered eating in women: A review. *Clinical Psychology Review* 1994; 14 (2): 139-157.

Levine M. *How schools can help combat student eating disorders: Anorexia nervosa and bulimia*. Washington DC: National Education Association, 1987.

Lewinsohn P, Mischel W, Chaplin W, Barton R. Social competence and depression: The role of illusory self-perceptions. *J of Abnormal Psychol* 1980; 89: 203-12.

Lewis L, Johnson C. A comparison of sex role orientation between women with bulimia and normal controls. *Int J Eat Disord* 1985; 4: 247-257.

Mead B, Ignico A. Children's gender typed perceptions of physical activity: Consequences and implications. *Percept Mot Skills* 1992; 75: (3 Pt 2): 1035-42.

Meyer C, Blissett J, Oldfield C. Sexual orientation and eating psychopathology: The role of masculinity and femininity. *Int J Eat Disord* 2001; 29(3):314-8.

Miller M, Pumariega A. Culture and eating disorders: A historical and cross-cultural review. *Psychiatry* 2001; 64 (2): 93-110.

Mintz L, Betz N. Sex differences in the nature, realism, and correlates of body image. *Sex Roles* 1986; 15: 185-195.

Morawski J. The measurement of masculinity and femininity: Engendering categorical realities. In: Bohan J, editor. *Seldom seen, rarely heard: Woman's place in psychology.* Boulder: Westview Press, 1992. p. 199-226.

Murnen S, Smolak L. Femininity, masculinity, and disordered eating: A meta-analytic review. *Int J Eat Disord* 1997; 22: 231-242.

Napholz L. Indices if psychological well-being and sex role orientation among working women. *Health Care Women Int* 1994; 15 (4): 307-16.

Nassar M. Eating disorders: The cultural dimension. *Soc Psychiatry Psychiatr Epidemiol* 1988; 23: 184-187.

Orbach S. *Fat is a feminine issue. The anti-diet guide to permanent weight loss.* New York: Paddington Press, 1978.

Orbach S. Visibility/Invisibility: Social considerations in anorexia nervosa (A feminist perspective. In: Emmett S, editor. *Theory and treatment of anorexia nervosa and bulimia: Biomedical, sociocultural, and psychological perspectives.* New York: Brunner/Mazel, 1985. p. 127-38.

Orbach S. *Hunger strike. The anorectic's struggle as a metaphor for our age.* New York: Faber and Faber, 1986.

Orlofsky J. Psychological androgyny, sex-typing, and sex-role ideology as predictors of male-female interpersonal attraction. *Sex Roles* 1982; 8: 1057 - 1073.

Palazzoli M. *Self-starvation. From individual to family therapy in the treatment of anorexia nervosa.* New York: Jason Aronson, 1978.

Paxton S, Sculthorpe A. Disordered eating and sex role characteristics in young women: Implications for sociocultural theories of disturbed eating. *Sex Roles* 1991; 24: 587-598.

Pliner P, Chaiken S, Flett G. Gender differences in concern with body weight and physical appearance over the life span. *Personality and Social Psychology Bulletin* 1990; 16: 263-273.

Polivy J, Herman P. *Breaking the diet habit.* New York: Basic Books, 1983.

Polivy J, Garner D, Garfinkel P. Causes and consequences of the current preference for thin female physics. In: Herman C, Zanna M, Higgins E, editors. *Physical appearance, stigma, and social behavior: The third Ontario symposium in personality and social psychology.* New Jersey: Erlbaum, 1986. p. 89-112.

Pope K, Hudson J. Anorexia nervosa and "reverse anorexia" among 108 male bodybuilders. *Compr Psychiatry* 1993; 34 (6): 406-409.

Prince R. The concept of culture-bound-syndromes: Anorexia nervosa and brain-fag. *Soc Sc Med* 1985; 21: 197-203.

Pursell S, Banikiotes P, Sebastian R. Androgyny and the perception of marital roles. *Sex Roles* 1981; 7: 201-215.

Rewal V, Kapur V. Sex roles: Masculinity, femininity and androgyny as a function of age, sex and city. *Journal of Personality and Clinical Studies* 1991; 7(1): 67-72.

Ricards L, McAlister L. Female submissiveness, nonverbal behavior, and body boundary definition. *J Psychol* 1994; 128 (4): 419-24.

Rodin J, Silberstein L, Striegel-Moore R. Women and weight: A normative discontent. In: Sonderegger T, editor. *Nebraska Symposium on Motivation, 1984: Psychology and gender.* Lincoln: University of Nebraska, 1985. p. 267-308.

Root P. Disordered eating in women of color. *Sex Roles* 1990; 22: 525-536.

Rost H, Neuhaus M, Florin O. Bulimia nervosa: Sex role attitudes, sex role behavior, and sex role related locus of control in bulimarexic women. *Journal of Psychosomatic Research* 1982; 26: 240-244.

Schwartz D, Thompson M, Johnson C. Eating disorders and the culture. In: Anorexia nervosa and bulimia: The sociocultural context. *Int J Eat Disord* 1982; 1: 20-36.

Siever M. Sexual orientation and gender as factors in socioculturally acquired vulnerability to body dissatisfaction and eating disorders. *J Consult Clin Psychol* 1994; 62(2): 252-60.

Silverstein B, Perdue L, Wolf C, Pizzolo C. Binging, purging, and estimates of parental attitudes regarding female achievement. *Sex Roles* 1988; 19: 723-733.

Silverstein B, Carpman S, Perlick D, Perdue L. Nontraditional sex role aspirations, gender identity conflict, and disordered eating among college women. *Sex Roles* 1990; 23: 687-695.

Silverstein B, Perlick D. *The cost of competence: Why inequality causes depression, eating disorders, and illness in women.* New York: Oxford University Press, 1995.

Singleton C. Biological and social explanations of sex-role stereotyping. In: Hargreaves D, Colley A, editors. *The Psychology of sex roles.* Cambridge: Hemisphere, 1987. p. 3-26.

Shimonaka Y, Nakazato K, Marushima R. Androgyny and psychological well-being among older and younger Japanese adults. *Aging Milano* 1994; 6(1): 43-8.

Shimonaka Y, Nakazato K, Kawaai C, Sato S. Androgyny and successful adaptation across the life span among Japanese adults. *J Genet Psychol* 1997; 158 (4): 389-400.

Skoe E. Sex role orientation and its relationship to the development of identity and moral thought. *Scand J Psychol* 1995; 36 (3): 235-45.

Slade R. *The anorexia nervosa reference book.* London: Harper & Row, Publishers, 1984.

Smolak L, Levine M. Toward an empirical basis for primary prevention of eating problems with elementary school children. Eating disorders: *Journal of Treatment and prevention* 1994; 4: 293-307.

Spence J, Helmreich R, Stapp J. Ratings of self and peers on sex roles attributes and their relations to self-esteem and conceptions of masculinity and femininity. *Journal of Personality and Social Psychology* 1975; 32: 29-39.

Spence J, Helmreich R. *Masculinity and femininity: Their psychological dimensions, correlates and antecedents.* Austin: University of Texas Press, 1978.

Steenbarger B, Greenberg R. Sex roles, stress, and distress: A study of person by situation contingency. *Sex Roles* 1990; 22(1-2): 59-68.

Steiner-Adair C. The body politic: Normal female adolescent development and the development of eating disorders. *Journal of the American Academy of Psychoanalysis* 1986; 14: 95-114.

Steiner-Adair C. Developing the voice of the wise woman: College students and bulimia. *Journal of College Student Psychotherapy* 1989; 3: 151-165.

Stice E. Review of the evidence for a sociocultural model of bulimia nervosa and an exploration of the mechanisms of action. *Clinical Psychology Review* 1994; 14(7): 633-661.

Stice E, Schupak E, Shaw H, Stein R. Relation of media exposure to eating disorder symptomatology: An examination of mediating mechanisms. *J Abnorm Psychol* 1994; 103 (4): 836-40.

Striegel-Moore R, Silberstein L, Rodin J. Towards an understanding of risk factors for bulimia. *American Psychologist* 1986; 41: 246-63.

Swarr A, Richards M. Longitudinal Effects of Adolescent Girls. Pubertal Development, Perceptions of Pubertal Timing, and Parental Relations on Eating Problems. *Developmental Psychology* 1996; 32: 636-646.

Szymanski L, Chrisler J. Eating disorders, gender role and athletic activity. Special issue: Special Recognition to Dr. Russell N. Cassel. *Psychology a Journal of Human Behaviour* 1990-91; 27 (4) – 28 (1): 20-29.

Thomä H. *Anorexia nervosa*. New York: International University Press, 1967.

Thomas K, Ricciardelli L. Gender traits and self-concept: Indicators of problem eating and body dissatisfaction among children. *Sex Roles* 2000;

Thornton B, Leo R, Alberg K. Gender role typing, the superwoman ideal, and the potential for eating disorders. *Sex Roles* 1991; 25: 469-484.

Troop NA, Allan S, Treasure JL, Katzman M. Social comparison and submissive behaviour in eating disorder patients. *Psychol Psychother* 2003; 76(Pt 3):237-49.

Usmiani S, Daniluk J. Mothers and their adolescent daughters: Relationship between self-esteem, gender role identity and body image. *Journal of Youth and Adolescence* 1997; 26(1), 45-61.

Vandereycken W, Hoek H. Are eating disorders culture-bound syndrome? In: Halmi K, editor. *Psychobiology and treatment of anorexia nervosa and bulimia nervosa.* Washington DC: American Psychiatric Association, 1992. p. 19-38.

Vonk R, Ashmore R. The multifaceted self: Androgyny reassessed by open ended self descriptions. *Social Psychology Quarterly* 1993; 56(4): 278-287.

Wooley S, Wooley O. Intensive outpatient and residential treatment for bulimia. In: Garner D, Garfinkel P, editors. *Handbook of psychotherapy for anorexia nervosa and bulimia.* New York: Guilford Press, 1985. p. 391-430.

Wooley S. Sexual abuse and eating disorders: The concealed debate. In: Fallon P, Katzman M, Wooley S, editors. *Feminine perspectives on eating disorders.* New York: Guilford Press, 1994. p. 171.211.

Yarnold P, Martin G, Soltysik R, Nightingale S. Androgyny predicts empathy for trainees in medicine. *Percept Mot Skills* 1993; 77(2): 576-8.

In: New Developments in Eating Disorders Research
Editor: Pamela I. Swain, pp. 65-91

ISBN 1-59454-542-1

Chapter 3

CULTURAL DIFFERENCES IN WESTERN, INDIAN AND OMANI ADOLESCENTS TO EATING, WEIGHT AND BODY IMAGE ATTITUDES

***Samir Al-Adawi*[*1,4], *Atsu S. S. Dorvlo*[2]; *Rodger G. Martin*[1], *Kazuhiro Yoishiuchi*[3], *Hiroaki Kumano*[3], and *Tomifusa Kuboki*[3]**

[1]Department of Behavioral Medicine, College of Medicine and Health Sciences, Sultan Qaboos University, P.O. Box 35, Al-Khoudh 123, Muscat, Sultanate of Oman.
[2]Department of Mathematics and Statistics, Sultan Qaboos University, P.O. Box 36, Al-Khoudh 123, Muscat, Sultanate of Oman
[3] Department of Psychosomatic Medicine, Graduate School of Medicine, The University of Tokyo, 7-3-1 Hongo, Bunkyo-ku, Tokyo 113, Japan.

ABSTRACT

Previous studies into the role that culture plays in shaping attitude and behavior to food and weight have provided limited insight as most of the research is cross-national. The present study compared Omani, Indian and western adolescent schoolchildren attending three schools in Muscat, Oman. Assessment with cross-cultural valid measures such as *Eating Attitude Test-26*, subscale of *Eating Disorder Inventory* to gauge the presence of fat-phobia and Bradford *Somatic Inventory* to elicit presence of somatization were used. Significant differences in attitudes to eating, body image and somatization between the western and non western children were found. This paper suggests trajectories of eating disorder such body image disturbance as expressed in fat-phobia and somatization tend to vary from culture to culture and underscores the view that some of the health related behavior among adolescent needs to be examined within socio-cultural context.

* Department of Psychosomatic Medicine, The University of Tokyo Hospital; 7-3-1 Hongo, Bunkyo-ku, Tokyo 113-8655; JAPAN; Telefax: +81 3-5800-9737; Telephone: +81 3-5800-9764; E-mail: adawi-kty@umin0ac.jp

INTRODUCTION

Dysfunctional eating behaviors and unhealthy weight loss practices leading to eating disorders that include anorexia nervosa, bulimia and their variants are now being recognized as a 'silent epidemic' among adolescents in industrial countries of the West, Japan as well as other parts of the world (Kuboki et al., 1996; Becker et al., 2002; Gordon, 2004; Kiriike et al., 1998; Serrano et al., 2004; Shroff & Thompson, 2004), including the Arab world (Abou-Saleh, Younis & Karim, 1998; Al-Adawi et al., 2002B; Rasheed, 1998; Al-Subaie, 2000; Hoek & van Hoeken, 2003; Edman &, Yates, 2004). Although thought to be generally benign and an integral part of adolescent behavior, empirical evidence suggests that a preoccupation with body image and weight-loss behavior increases the risk of clinical eating disorder (Braun, Sunday & Halmi, 1994; Agras et al., 2004; Pike, 1998; Godart et al., 2003; Stacher, 2003; Keel et al., 2003). Deliberate food restriction coupled with the psychopathology of anorexia nervosa affects normal bodily function and may lead to other medical complications and death. With the increase of anorexia in different parts of the world (Yates, Edman & Aruguete, 2004) there is an urgent need to understand the socio-cultural factors underlying eating behavior in young people.

There is debate about whether anorexia nervosa has similar manifestations in different cultures and whether eating disorder constitutes a culture-bound or culture-reactive phenomenon. Although there are suggestions that susceptibility to weight loss behavior is linked to a traditional rather than a Westernized cultural orientation (Mumford & Whitehouse, 1994), there are suggestions that ethnicity, coupled with exposure to western culture's ideal of beauty and the 'medicalization' (Germov &, Williams, 1996; Thompson & Heinberg, 1999; Paquette & Raine, 2004) and stigma (Geier, Schwartz & Brownell, 2003; Wang, Brownell & Wadden, 2004; Friedman, 2004) of overweight have denigrated traditional features of body preference. Studies of adolescents exposed to westernization in developing countries are affected by eating disorders, which were already evident in their counterparts in the industrialized world (Nasser, 1988; Brewis & McGarvey, 2000; Cachelin et al., 2000; Sjostedt, Schumaker & Nathawat, 1998; Gupta et al., 2001; Yates, Edman & Aruguete, 2004; Pina & Silverman, 2004; Szabo, 1999). Al-Adawi et al. (2000) have shown the presence of eating disorder and abnormal eating attitudes in school children in Oman that are largely absent among an older generation of Omanis. However despite the abundance of studies of this nature, most of them tend to compare western and non-western populations in different countries or settings. One of the aims of this study is to address such a deficiency with the convenient sub-cultural groups in Oman.

In the Diagnostic and Statistical Manual of Mental Disorders- Fourth Edition (American Psychiatric Association, 1994), anorexia nervosa is characterized by significant weight loss, amenorrhea, distorted body image and a relentless pursuit of thinness. However results emerging from cross-cultural studies on the nature and expression of eating disorder, question the validity of current diagnostic criteria for eating disorders. Studies conducted in various parts of the world suggest that preoccupation with fear of fatness, a core feature in current diagnosis, presents in complex ways which are often inconsistent with how it is conceptualized in current western nosology (Lee, Ho & Hsu, 1993; Lee, 1994; Hebebrand et al., 2004). The orthogonal manifestation to 'fat aversion' in eating disorders (Drewnowski, Pierce & Halmi, 1988) is characterized by lack of exaggerated dread of fatness and but still with marked reduction in body mass index (Rieger et al., 2001). In western populations, manifestations of fat-phobia have been shown to vary among various ethnic grouping (Altabe, 1998; Contento, Basch & Zybert, 2003; Rubin, Fitts & Becker, 2003), with notably low incidence among African-Americans in some studies but not in others (Bagley, Character & Shelton, 2003; Jennifer et al., 2001; Williamson, 1998; James, Phelps & Bross, 2001; Duncan & Robinson, 2004). In western populations, the lack of exaggerated dread of fatness is found in 15% to 20% of patients with eating disorders, thus challenging the view that the presence of 'non-fat phobia' constitutes an 'exotic' cross-cultural aberration of eating pathology (Ramacciotti et al., 2002). Similarly, emerging evidence from many parts of Asia suggest a high presence (estimated to be 59%) of anorexic patients with lack of fear of obesity (Lee, 1994; Ngai, Lee &, Lee, 2000) however other studies suggest the level of fat-phobia to be similar to Euro-American population (Nishizono-Maher, Miyake & Nakane, 2003). Comparative studies are needed to examine whether the lower drive for thinness as one of the indices of non-fat phobia is found in other non-western ethnic groups. As many studies have examined the presence or absence of fat-phobia in clinical populations (Lee, 1994; Ngai, Lee &, Lee, 2000), community studies are needed to examine the presence of such body image disturbance or fat-phobia in the community.

Lee, Ho & Hsu (1993) have suggested that non-fat phobia anorexic patients were predominantly characterized with somatic complaints such as epigastric pain and gastritis, others have commented on their diminished appetite, hunger for food, or inability to consume adequate amounts of food (Rieger et al., 2001). This view echoes the original observation of Lesegue (1997) in anorexia nervosa who talked of 'afflictions of the stomach (p. 495). As non-fat-phobics tended to have a more benign prognosis and less severe forms of psychopathology they have been described as 'atypical' (Watson & Andersen, 2003; Strober, Freeman &, Morrell, 1999; Turner & Bryant-Waugh, 2004; Lee, Chan & Hsu, 2003). Uncertainty remains whether presentation of non-fat phobic anorexia reflects how different sociocultural groups use different 'languages of distress' in communicating their suffering to others (Helman, 1990). In various ethnic groups, numerous studies have suggested that some patients tend to use "somatopsychic" idioms of distress rather than verbalize their distress in psychological concepts (Leff, 1977; Kleinman, 1987). For example, Nakao et al. (1998) examined consecutive clinical features of patients attending urban tertiary centers in Japan and found that the majority of the patients had somatoform disorders that are likely to be considered 'atypical' in Euro-American diagnostic criteria. Other reports are congruent with such views (Al Lawati et al., 2000; Pina & Silverman, 2003; Mumford, 1996; Nakao, Yamanaka & Kuboki, 2001). This suggests that somatic presentations are valid idioms of distress and neither abnormal or more primitive. Somatopsychic presentations are likely to merely reflect a different way of living in which the individual is conditioned to obey the traditional laws as represented in the norms of both the nuclear and extended family. These subjects "endorse somatization as powerful metaphor for orchestrating the social response to illness" (Lee 1995 p. 27) However, to our knowledge, there are no studies examining whether variations in the tendency for a somatic idiom of distress may be related to the tendency of 'concealment' or 'denial' found in non fat-phobia patients of certain ethnic groups (Casper, 1998). It is worthwhile to note that the 'geography' of somatopsychic culture appears to be related to those ethnic groups that have been suggested to have a lack of fat-phobia (Chan & Parker, 2004). Although other forms of somatoform disorders have been explored in the context of anorexia nervosa (e.g. Nijenhuis et al., 1999; Grant & Phillips, 2004; Waller et al.,

2003), to our knowledge, studies using assessment measures that directly elicit a tendency to a somatopsychic idiom of distress are lacking. One aim of this paper, albeit directly, is to examine whether there is ethnic variations among age group that is vulnerable to eating pathology in endorsing attitude and behavior central to somatopsychic idiom of distress. Theoretically, such undertaking would help to tease out whether the lack of fat-phobia is a variant of eating disorder or a continuum of a diverse characteristic of anorexia nervosa that has so far been largely neglected in current diagnosis.

The population of Oman is composed of assorted ethnicities/nationalities that provide a natural setting for studying cross-cultural differences in health behavior, this study aims to compare the performance of Omani, Indian and European students on indices of (i) eating attitude and behavior, (ii) fat phobia and (iii) somatic distress.

METHODS

Subjects

The present study involved three groups – Omani, European and American and Indian students. These students differed in terms of ethnicity and culture. A sample of Omani students was recruited from three state schools in the Muscat metropolitan area, the nation capital. These schools were selected because they drew students from a cross section of Omani society. The second group consisted of 'Westerners' (here dubbed as Euro-American i.e. American, British and Western European adolescents). A third group consisted of Indian adolescents who, like their Euro-American counterparts, were residing with their parents, who worked in various multinational companies and government agencies in Oman. The rationale for choosing these cohorts was described elsewhere (Al-Adawi et al., 2002A).

For all participants, a brief explanation of the study was given and participants were assured that the data would be confidential, and then their oral consent was taken. The students were interviewed during class time, and instead of a lecture, they were asked to give their time towards this study. The home-room teacher at the selected lecture helped supervise the dispensing of the assessment measures to the students. It was explicitly stated that their responses would have no influence on their academic performance. To steer clear of peer influence, the students were asked not to discuss the questionnaire among themselves.

ASSESSMENT MEASURES

1. Eating Attitude and Behaviour

The Eating Attitude Test, EAT-26, is a 26 item self-report questionnaire that measures symptoms associated with anorexia nervosa (Garner & Garfinkel, 1979). Participants rated the frequency with which they experienced each statement on dieting, bulimic behaviors, and self-control of eating behavior, using a six-point scale. The statements were scored as 3 for the extreme response in the directions of high risk towards anorexia nervosa. Adjacent alternatives were scored 2, 1 and 0.

Various authors have reported that the EAT-26 is effective for assessing a wide range of attitudes and behaviors characteristic of eating disorders and is capable of identifying individuals with eating disturbances (Nasser, 1994; Al Subaie et al., 1996; Stephens et al., 1999; Perez-Gaspar et al., 2000). While high scores on the EAT-26 do not necessarily equate with clinical eating disorders, many of the characteristics represented are the same as those found in anorexia nervosa. The EAT-26 is considered to be an appropriate screening device for eating disorders and has been widely translated (Lee, Lee & Leung 1998). In a majority of studies, its performance has been found to be acceptable in the Arab part of the world (Nasser, 1986; Al-Subaie et al., 1996).

EAT-26 was scored using the Al Subaie et al. (1996) system in which the three categories at the non-anorexic end of the six-point Likert scale scored zero; the other categories scored 1, 2 and 3 for each question. The scores on the individual questions were summed up to obtain a composite score. Subjects who scored 20 or greater on the composite score, as established elsewhere in many cross-cultural studies including the Arab part of the world (Nasser, 1994; Al-Adawi et al., 1999), were considered to have a tendency towards disturbed weight and dieting behavior.

2. Presence of Fat-Phobia: The Drive for Thinness

A subscale derived from one of the most widely used assessment measures of eating disorder; the Eating Disorder Inventory (EDI; Garner, Olmstead, & Polivy, 1983) was used to measure fat phobia or a 'drive for thinness'. The EDI is a self-report measure, validated on both clinical and non-clinical populations (Garner, 1991; Garner, Olmsted & Polivy, 1983). It has valid and reliable psychometric properties that were established in various ethnic groups (Lee, Lee & Leung, 1998; O'Keefe & Lovell, 1999; Garcia-Garcia et al., 2003; Shimura et al., 2003; Yates, Edman & Aruguete, 2004) including the Arab part of the world (Al-Subaie et al., 1996).

The subscale utilized here contains seven items that elicit the drive for thinness (Table 8). Higher scores indicate greater levels of eating pathology, with score of 15 or more suggesting a preoccupation with weight and/or body shape, or demonstration of a morbid fear of weight gain, an excessive concern with dieting or a strong desire for thinness.

3. Somatization

Bradford Somatic Inventory (BSI; Mumford et al., 1991) is a 44-item inventory for psychosomatically expressed psychological distress. The BSI is an instrument that is reported to be relatively free of cultural bias. This has been substantiated in studies carried out in Great Britain, Pakistan, India, Nepal, and Russia (Mumford et al., 1995; Havenaar et al., 1996). The BSI enquires about a wide range of somatic symptoms during the previous month, and whether or not the subject has experienced a particular symptom, on more or fewer than 15 days during the month (scoring 1 or 2 respectively). For the present purpose, 12 items derived from BSI were employed (Table 10). These items covered the parts of the body that are likely to be affected by eating and body image due to preoccupation with food. The scoring was based on Mumford et al. (2000) where a higher score suggested somatoform disorder. The psychometric property of BSI has been established for Arabic speaking population (Zahid Motaal & Razik, 2001).

All of the above-mentioned assessment measures were translated by experienced staff members into Arabic using a method of back-translation suggested by Ko and Cohen (1998). Efforts were made to make certain that all items of these measures fulfilled conceptual, semantic and technical equivalence to the original versions. The translated measures were only given the Omani subjects. The other participants, Euro-American and Indian subjects, were given the original English versions of the screening instrument. These two cohorts were attending schools where the medium of instruction was English.

STATISTICAL ANALYSIS

The statistical packages SPSS and StatXact were used for the analysis. Summary statistics, chi-square tests for independence, logistics regression, and both parametric and non-parametric analyses of variance were some of the procedures used.

The study was approved by both the 'Ethic Committee for Human and Clinical Research' and the 'Medical Research Committee' (Project No. 96) of the College of Medicine, Sultan Qaboos University, Oman.

RESULT

(I) Demographic and Anthropomorphic Variables

There were 378 students in the sample. There were 130 Indian teenagers (34.4%), 135 Omani teenagers (35.7%), and 113 Euro-American teenagers. The groups comprised 164 males and 214 females (Table 1).

Table 1. Distribution of students by nationality and gender

Nationality	Male	Female	Total
Indian	51	79	130
Omani	72	63	135
Euro-American	41	72	113
Total	164	214	378

Table 2 summarizes the age, height, weight and BMI of the students by nationality. The students were aged between 14 to 17 years. The average age was 15.4 years with a standard deviation equal to 0.9 years. They weighed between 30 and 94 kgs. There was a simple linear relationship between the current weight of the students and the most they had weighed at the current height ($r = 0.94$). Both parametric and nonparametric tests show that the Indian students (15.6 years) were older than the Omani students (15.4 years), who were older than the Euro-American students (15.1 years) ($F=11.9$, p-value <0.001). The students were not statistically different with regards to their height, weight and BMI (Table 2).

Table 2. Summary statistics of demographic and anthropomorphic variables

	Ethnicity	n	Mean ± std	Min.	Median	Max.	F(p-value)
Age	Indian	127	15.61 ± 1.02	14	16	17	11.93(0.000)
	Omani	134	15.37 ± 0.80	14	15	17	
	Euro-American	113	15.06 ± 0.77	14	15	17	
	Total	374	15.36 ± 0.90	14	15	17	
Height(cm)	Indian	123	163.41 ± 8.53	127	165	178	0.94(0.392)
	Omani	132	163.17 ± 9.84	127	167	179	
	Euro-American	106	161.82 ± 9.68	141	160	201	
	Total	361	162.86 ± 9.36	127	164	201	
Weight(kg)	Indian	127	57.79 ± 11.99	30	57	92	0.35(0.705)
	Omani	127	59.08 ± 12.49	32	57	92	
	Euro-American	105	58.30 ± 12.66	36	56	94	
	Total	361	58.39 ± 12.34	30	57	94	
Most ever weighed (kg)	Indian	130	61.03 ± 11.87	33	59	92	0.34(0.715)
	Omani	135	62.17 ± 12.69	33	59	92	
	Euro-American	105	61.00 ± 14.73	42	60	99	
	Total	370	61.44 ± 13.01	33	59	99	
Body Mass Index (kg/m^2)	Indian	123	21.53 ± 4.69	10.98	20.66	35.96	1.15(0.317)
	Omani	126	22.38 ± 5.20	10.69	20.74	37.78	
	Euro-American	100	22.21 ± 3.65	14.87	21.46	34.21	
	Total	347	22.04 ± 4.62	10.69	20.83	37.78	

The average weight was 58.4 ± 12.3 kg. The average height of all the students was 1.63 ± 0.09m. The average body mass index (BMI) was 22.0 ± 4.6. The BMI ranged between 10.7 and 37.8. On average, 66% of this sample was classified as normal on the BMI scale. A good proportion, 16%, were classified as under-weight while another 8% (28) were classified as over-weight and a further 10% (33) were classified as obese on the BMI scale. The distribution of the students based on obese classification is reported in Table 3. Based on the Kruskal-Wallis test of identical distributions the three nationalities were dissimilar (Chi=5.35, p-value=0.07).

Table 3. Distribution of students by body mass Index (BMI) classification*

Nationality	Underweight	Normal	Overweight	Obese	Total	Chi square (p-value)
Indian	30	71	14	7	122	5.35 (0.07)
Omani	23	75	10	17	125	
Euro-American	4	83	4	9	100	
Total	57	229	28	33	347	

* BMI Categories: underweight = <18.5; normal weight = 18.5-24.9; overweight = 25-29.9; Obesity = BMI of 30 or greater

(II) Behaviour and Attitudes Towards Eating

The second aim of this study was to elucidate the hypothesis that disordered eating differs between ethnic groups. The questions on EAT correlated well with each other as measured by Cronbach's alpha of 0.87. The composite scores for the twenty-six items ranged from 0 to 57. It is noted that the maximum possible was 78. Two Omani and two Indian students scored 57; whereas the highest score for the Euro-American students was only 30. About 89% of the students scored less than 20, with 11% indicating possible caseness for anorexia nervosa. The average composite EAT-26 for the entire sample was only 9.1 ± 10.1. The summary of the composite score by nationality is given in Table 4. The average composite scores are low when compared with the threshold score, 20. The group with the highest score was the Indian students (11.8 ± 12.7) and the group with the lowest average was the Euro-American group (5.59 ± 7.29). The average scores are significantly different (F=9.0, p-value < 0.001) for the three groups. Bonferroni's multiple comparison test indicated that the Indian and Euro-American students had significantly different averages (Table 4). The Omani and Euro-American students also had significantly different averages.

Table 4. Summary of composite scores of Eating Attitude by nationality and Bonferroni's multiple correction tests

	n	Mean ± std	Minimum	Median	Maximum
Indian	112	11.82 ± 12.74	0	8	57
Omani	121	9.17 ± 9.34	0	6	57
Euro-American	86	5.59 ± 7.29	0	4	30
Total	319	9.10 ± 10.48	0	6	57
	Mean Difference		**Standard Error**		**p-value**
Indian-Omani	2.76		1.34		0.122
Indian-Euro-American	6.23		1.47		0.000
Omani-Euro-American	3.47		1.44		0.050

The summary scores by gender are given in Table 5. There was a significant difference between the male and female students (F=11.7, p-value=0.001) with the female teenagers scoring significantly higher.

Table 5. Summary of composite scores by gender by Eating Attitude Test

	n	Mean ± std	Minimum	Median	Maximum	F(p-value)
Males	150	7.00 ± 6.82	0	6	36	11.73(0.001)
Females	169	10.96 ± 12.62	0	6	57	
Total	319	9.10 ± 10.48	0	6	57	

(III) Presence of Fear of Fat

The questions on fear of fatness that was elicited by the drive for thinness, derived from Eating Disorder Inventory, correlated well with each other as measured by Cronbach's alpha of 0.78. The composite scores for the seven items ranged from 0 to 17 out of a maximum possible 21. The Euro-American teenagers scored significantly greater than the Indian and Omani teenagers. The highest composite score of an Indian teenager was 8 out of the possible 21. Seven Omanis out of 135 scored more than 8 while 38 out of the 112 Euro-American teenagers scored 8 or less.

The average composite score for the entire sample was only 4.91 ± 4.23. The summary of the composite score by nationality is given in Table 6. The average composite scores are low when compared with the threshold score, 8, except for the average score of the Euro-American teenagers. They scored on average 9.62 ± 3.58 and the group with the lowest average was the Indian teenagers (2.80 ± 2.06). The average scores are significantly different (F=207, p-value < 0.001) for the three groups. Bonferroni's multiple comparison test indicated that the Indian and Euro-American students and Omani and Euro-American students had significantly different averages (Table 6).

Table 6. Summary of composite scores of fear of fatness by nationality and Bonferroni's multiple correction tests

	n	Mean ± std	Minimum	Median	Maximum
Indian	130	2.80 ± 2.06	0	3	8
Omani	135	3.04 ± 3.00	0	2	17
Euro-American	112	9.62 ± 3.58	2	11	15
Total	377	4.91 ±4.23	0	4	17
	Mean Difference		Standard Error		p-value
Indian-Omani	-0.24		0.33		1.000
Indian-Euro-American	-6.82		0.34		0.000
Omani-Euro-American	-6.57		0.34		0.000

The summary scores by gender are given in Table 7. There was a significant difference between the male and female students (F=14.0, p-value=0.001).

Table 7. Summary of Composite scores by gender by fear of fatness

	n	Mean ± std	Minimum	Median	Maximum	F(p-value)
Males	164	4.00 ± 4.02	0	3	15	14.00(0.000)
Females	213	5.62 ± 4.26	0	4	17	
Total	377	4.91 ± 4.23	0	3	17	

Logistic regression analysis showed that age, height and weight did not affect the indicators of fat-phobia. The odds ratios of these parameters were mostly close to unity. There were significant differences between the Euro-American teenagers and the other two groups of teenagers since the odds ratios were significantly different from unity except in one case (Table 8).

Table 8. Logistic regressions showing the effect of age, height and weight by nationality of fat phobia

				95% bounds on Odds Ratio	
		Odds Ratio	p-value	Lower bound	Upper bound
I think about thinness	Age	1.38	0.115	0.92	2.07
	Height	1.02	0.190	1.00	1.06
	Weight	1.01	0.370	0.98	1.04
	Indian	60.14	0.000	23.72	152.48
	Omani	25.87	0.000	12.39	54.02
	Euro-American				
I am afraid of getting fat	Age	0.831	0.201	0.625	1.104
	Height	1.030	0.37	1.002	1.059
	Weight	1.010	0.329	0.990	1.031
	Indian	1.569	0.194	0.795	3.093
	Omani	3.141	0.000	1.665	5.928
	Euro-American				
I care too much about my weight	Age	0.768	0.121	0.551	1.072
	Height	1.090	0.000	1.055	1.126
	Weight	0.976	0.053	0.952	1.000
	Indian	7.915	0.000	3.958	15.826
	Omani	9.029	0.000	4.556	17.894
	Euro-American				
I think about getting thinner	Age	0.967	0.819	0.728	1.285
	Height	0.996	0.755	0.969	1.023
	Weight	1.038	0.001	1.015	1.061
	Indian	6.981	0.000	3.700	13.171
	Omani	5.278	0.000	2.910	9.575
	Euro-American				
If I gain a pound, I worry that I will keep gaining	Age	0.834	0.187	0.637	1.092
	Height	1.022	0.107	0.995	1.048
	Weight	1.022	0.033	1.002	1.042
	Indian	3.456	0.000	1.793	6.663
	Omani	3.672	0.000	1.944	6.935
	Euro-American				
I get upset when I eat sweets	Age	0.984	0.969	0.451	2.15
	Height	1.024	0.478	0.959	1.092
	Weight	1.020	0.485	0.966	1.077
	Indian	*	*	*	*
	Omani	*	*	*	*
	Euro-American				
I feel sorry after eating too much food	Age	0.966	0.984	0.003	29.362
	Height	1.363	0.432	0.630	2.948
	Weight	1.777	0.422	0.437	7.225
	Indian	*	*	*	*
	Omani	*	*	*	*
	Euro-American				

NB: Euro-American is redundant in the equations.

* Possibly quasi-complete separation. Model fit uncertain.

Table 9. Distribution of fear of fatness score over Eating Attitude Test

			95% Confidence	
	n	Mean ± SD	Lower bound	Upper bound
EAT score less than 20	282	4.98 ± 4.33	4.4709	5.49
EAT score 20 or more	36	3.25 ± 3.44	2.09	4.41
Total	318	4.78 ± 4.27	4.31	5.25

Table 10. Perception of fat phobia by nationality

	Indian*		Omani		Euro-American		
	Never	At least Once	Never	At least Once	Never	At least Once	Chi-square (p-vale)
I think about thinness	123	7	113	22	22	91	180.7 (0.000)
	94.6%	5.4%	83.7%	16.3%	19.5%	80.5%	
I am afraid of getting fat	41	89	55	80	21	92	14.2 (0.001)
	31.5%	68.5%	40.7%	59.3%	18.6%	81.4%	
I care too much about my weight	109	21	114	21	45	68	75.5(0.000)
	83.8%	16.2%	84.4%	15.6%	39.8%	60.2%	
I think about getting thinner	100	30	94	41	41	72	47.42 (0.000)
	76.9%	23.1%	69.6%	30.4%	36.3%	63.7%	
If I gain a pound, I worry that I will keep gaining	60	70	59	76	22	91	22.1 (0.000)
	46.2%	53.8%	43.7%	56.3%	19.5%	80.5%	
I get upset when I eat sweets	130	0	134	1	15	96	305.6 (0.000)
	100%	0%	99.3%	0.7%	13.3%	86.7%	
I feel sorry after eating too much food	130	0	134	1	0	113	373.2 (0.000)
	100%	0%	99.3%	0.7%	0	0	

Those who scored less than 20 on the EAT scale scored significantly higher on the fear of fatness scale than those who scored 20 or more on the EAT scale (F=5.3, p-value=0.022) (Table 9). Among the nationalities, it was only among the Indian teenagers that the score on the fear of fatness scale was significantly higher for those who score less than 20 on the EAT scale (Table 10).

(IV) Present of Somatization

Twelve selected questions from the Bradford Somatic Inventory were used to elicit psychosomatically expressed distress in the three nationalities. The questions were internally stable (Cronbach's alpha = 0.96). The composite scores for the twelve items ranged from 0 to the maximum possible 24. The average composite score for the entire sample was only 1.66 ± 4.75. The summary of the composite scores by nationality is given in Table 11. The Indian and Omani teenagers scored the highest composite scores. The Euro-American teenagers scored significantly lower than the Indian and Omani teenagers (F = 9.22, p-value<0.001). The highest composite score of a Euro-American teenager was only 4.

Table 11. Summary of composite scores by somatization by nationality and using Bonferroni's multiple correction tests

	n	Mean ± std	Minimum	Median	Maximum
Indian	130	2.35 ± 5.72	0	0	24
Omani	135	2.32 ± 5.37	0	0	24
Euro-American	113	0.09 ± 0.51	0	0	4
Total	378	1.66 ± 4.75	0	0	24
	Mean Difference		**Standard Error**		**p-value**
Indian-Omani	0.03		0.57		1.000
Indian-Euro-American	2.26*		0.60		0.001
Omani-Euro-American	2.23*		0.60		0.001

*Statistical difference

Only one Euro-American teenager had a throat discomfort and was unable to consume adequate amounts of liquid. Whereas 13 Omani and 20 Indian teenagers had this discomfort. 13 Indian and 12 Omani teenagers and only one Euro-American teenager had a burning sensation in their stomach and were unable to consume adequate amounts of food. In response to all twelve questions on somatopsychic presentations, only three out of 112 Euro-American teenagers responded positively to having these symptoms (Table 12). The present data unequivocally suggests that Indian and Omani teens significantly differed from the Euro-American teens in their endorsement of items eliciting a tendency towards psychosomatically expressed distress, with Euro-American having lower scores than their counterpart Indian and Omani teens. The summary scores by gender, as shown in Table 13, suggest that there were no significant differences between genders in terms of expression of somatopsychic distress.

Those who scored less than 20 on the EAT scale scored significantly lower on the somatization scale than those who scored 20 or more on the EAT scale (F=143.6, p-value < 0.001) (Table 14). Among the nationalities, the score on the somatization scale was significantly lower for those who score less than 20 on the EAT scale for the Indian (F=94.9, p-value<0.001) and Omani (F=75.1, p-value< 0.001) (Table 15). However although lower the difference was not significant for the Euro-American teenagers (F=3.6, p-value=0.06).

The average composite scores were the same for the Indian and Omani teenagers. However their scores were much higher than the score for the Euro-American teenagers

(Table 11). There were no gender differences in the response to the twelve questions on the somatic disorders (Table 13).

Table 12. Distribution of indices of somatization

	Indian		Omani		Euro-American		Chi-square (p-vale)
	Absent	Present	Absent	Present	Absent	Present	
Throat discomfort unable to consume adequate amounts of food	110	20	122	13	112	1	16.5 (0.002)
A burning sensation in my stomach: unable to consume adequate amounts of food	117	13	123	12	112	1	10.7 (0.028)
I have been suffering ache or discomfort in the abdomen	116	14	126	9	110	3	8.3 (0.083)
I have fluttering or a feeling of something moving in my stomach?	116	13	122	13	112	1	11.6 (0.020)
I suffer from indigestion	118	12	123	12	113	0	11.2 (0.024)
I have diminished hunger for food renders me to unable to consume adequate amounts of food	114	16	123	12	113	0	17.2 (0.002)
I feel my stomach is swollen or bloated	117	13	118	17	113	0	16.8 (0.002)
I feel sick in the stomach (nausea)	115	15	125	10	113	0	14.7 (0.005)
I am troubled by constipation	109	21	120	15	113	0	30.8 (0.000)
I have a bitter taste in my mouth	108	22	123	12	113	0	23.8 (0.000)
I have suffered from excessive wind (gas) or belching?	113	17	108	27	112	1	31.4 (0.000)
I have diminished appetite for food: renders me unable to consume adequate amounts of food	114	16	113	22	112	1	40.8 (0.000)

Age, height and weight did not directly affect whether the somatic disorders were present or not. The odds ratios for the different parameters were not statistically different from unity. However, the responses were different for the ethnic groups. For example, our sample suggested that Indian teenagers were 22 times and Omani teenagers were 12 time more likely to suffer from throat discomfort that made them unable to consume adequate amounts of food.

Table 13. Summary of composite scores by gender by indices of somatization

	n	Mean ± std	Minimum	Median	Maximum	F(p-value)
Males	164	1.43 ± 4.12	0	0	24	0.71(0.401)
Females	214	1.84 ± 5.18	0	0	24	
Total	378	1.66 ± 4.75	0	0	24	

Table 14. Distribution of indices of somatization score over Eating Attitude Test

	n	Mean ± SD	95% Confidence	
			Lower bound	Upper bound
EAT score less than 20	283	0.88 ± 2.42	0.60	1.16
EAT score 20 or more	36	9.89 ± 10.78	6.24	13.54
Total	319	1.90 ± 5.11	1.33	2.46

Table 15. Logistic regressions showing the effect of age, height and weight by nationality of somatic attribution

		Odds Ratio	P-value	95% Confidence	
				Lower bound	Upper bound
Throat discomfort unable to consume adequate amounts of food	Age	0.750	0.187	0.489	1.150
	Height	1.023	0.345	0.976	1.072
	Weight	0.902	0.000	0.859	0.947
	Indian	22.204	0.003	2.796	176.328
	Omani	13.413	0.015	1.662	108.226
A burning sensation in my stomach: unable to consume adequate amounts of food	Age	0.748	0.294	0.435	1.287
	Height	1.004	0.900	0.948	1.062
	Weight	0.832	0.000	0.773	0.895
	Indian	11.844	0.026	1.349	103.972
	Omani	15.228	0.013	1.770	130.984
I have been suffering ache or discomfort in the abdomen	Age	0.877	0.594	0.541	1.421
	Height	1.057	0.079	0.994	1.125
	Weight	0.870	0.000	0.820	0.922
	Indian	3.347	0.092	0.823	13.619
	Omani	2.229	0.279	0.522	9.511
I have fluttering or a feeling of something moving in by stomach?	Age	1.112	0.669	0.683	1.813
	Height	1.025	0.387	0.969	1.084
	Weight	0.874	0.000	0.825	0.926
	Indian	9.076	0.043	1.073	76.807
	Omani	12.601	0.019	1.521	104.378

Table 15. Continued

		Odds Ratio	P-value	95% Confidence	
				Lower bound	Upper bound
I suffer from indigestion	Age	0.516	0.021	0.295	0.905
	Height	1.041	0.193	0.980	1.105
	Weight	0.851	0.000	0.792	0.914
	Indian	*	*	*	*
	Omani	*	*	*	*
I have diminished hunger for food: renders me unable to consume adequate amounts of food	Age	0.637	0.075	0.388	1.046
	Height	1.064	0.050	1.000	1.132
	Weight	0.854	0.000	0.798	0.913
	Indian	*	*	*	*
	Omani	*	*	*	*
I feel my stomach is swollen or bloated	Age	0.945	0.818	0.585	1.527
	Height	1.080	0.015	1.015	1.149
	Weight	0.887	0.000	0.838	0.938
	Indian	*	*	*	*
	Omani	*	*	*	*
I feel sick in the stomach (nausea)	Age	0.626	0.080	0.370	1.057
	Height	1.057	0.090	0.991	1.127
	Weight	0.845	0.000	0.787	0.908
	Indian	*	*	*	*
	Omani	*	*	*	*
I am troubled by constipation	Age	1.033	0.879	0.678	1.574
	Height	1.035	0.181	0.984	1.088
	Weight	0.913	0.000	0.872	0.956
	Indian	*	*	*	*
	Omani	*	*	*	*
I have a bitter taste in my mouth	Age	0.677	0.082	0.435	1.051
	Height	1.029	0.260	0.979	1.080
	Weight	0.889	0.000	0.843	0.938
	Indian	*	*	*	*
	Omani	*	*	*	*
I have suffered from excessive wind (gas) or belching?	Age	0.624	0.022	0.417	0.936
	Height	1.068	0.005	1.020	1.119
	Weight	0.929	0.000	0.895	0.965
	Indian	15.923	0.009	2.015	125.354
	Omani	29.827	0.001	3.879	229.321
I have diminished appetite for food: renders me unable to consume adequate amounts of food	Age	0.659	0.059	0.428	1.015
	Height	1.019	0.393	0.976	1.063
	Weight	0.901	0.000	0.859	0.945
	Indian	17.780	0.007	2.219	142.442
	Omani	25.197	0.002	3.202	198.302

* Possibly quasi-complete separation. Model fit uncertain.
Euro-American group redundant in the equation

DISCUSSION

This exploratory study aims to address questions about weight and eating attitudes among teenagers residing in Oman which sheds light on whether such adjustment disorder are culture-bound or culture-reactive phenomenon. Recent acculturation, modernization and the discovery of hydrocarbons have attracted large numbers of foreign workers to work in the commercial and industrial sectors of Oman. Oman lies at the Southeast border of the Arabian Peninsula with approximately 2.5 million people of which about 30-40% are foreign nationals (Longuenesse, 1985; Omran & Roudi, 1993; Peterson, 2004). This assortment of ethnicities in Oman allows for the study the cross-cultural differences in weight and eating variation. The native population of Oman, in the second phase of a demographic transition, is structured like a pyramid with the majority of the population in the adolescent age group (Sulaiman et al., 2001; Al Riyami, Afifi & Mabry, 2004; Russell, 2004). This age group, in the midst of prevailing modernization and acculturation, is considered to be more vulnerable to adjustment disorders (Zaidan et al., 2002) including eating disorders. In traditional Omani society, the standard of female beauty is metaphorically equated with the shape of an egg, suggesting a preference for a voluptuous female form. In some parts of Oman, prior to marriage, prospective brides are sent to a 'fattening factory' so as to achieve plumpish figure. A large ethnic group residing in Oman is Indian nationals. Although there is no evidence to suggest that plumpness is more favored as an expression of beauty in traditional Indian culture, Gupta et al. (2001) have reported that some part of the body like ankles, wrists and the breast were equated with eroticism and were venerated aspects of women. Do such conceptions of beauty, that appear to be diametrically in contrast to western notions of beauty, serve as protective factors against developing eating disorder? It would be theoretically and clinical relevant to compare these divergent cultural group on indices of weight and eating with a western group living in Oman.

The first aim of this study was to compare the performance among heterogeneous ethnicities residing in Oman on indices of eating attitude and behavior. Previous cross-national research have compared the performance of eating indices on adolescence living in two difference settings, often Euro-American children and their counterparts in developing countries (Sjostedt, Schumaker & Nathawat, 1998; Gupta et al., 2001; Yates, Edman & Aruguete, 2004; Pina & Silverman, 2004; Szabo, 1999; Abdollahi &, Mann, 2001; Lippincott & Hwang, 1999). Similarly, some studies have compared the performance of eating indices on non-western children living in western countries (Davis &, Katzman, 1999; Furnham & Husain, 1999; Barnett, Keel & Conoscenti, 2001; Mumford, Whitehouse & Platts, 1991) or within the dominant Euro-American Culture (Humphry & Ricciardelli, 2004). In general emerging evidence from these surveys gave conflicting results. Some studies suggested that non-western populations have fewer tendencies toward disordered eating (Lee, 1994; Ngai, Lee &, Lee, 2000) while others endorsed the view that eating disorders in non-western society were outpacing their western counterparts (Nasser, 1988). One explicit view emerging from these studies was the notion that ethnicity tends to be an independent risk factor for eating psychopathology as well as being a protective factor for some ethnic groups. Despite many reports on ethnicity and eating psychopathology, to our knowledge, there are few empirical comparative studies (e.g Edman & Yates, 2004; Caradas, Lambert & Charlton, 2001; le Grange, Telch & Tibbs, 1998) conducted in non-western settings specifically incorporating sub-cultural design (Sobal, 1998). From previous studies of these types, it was possible that non-western children living in western countries were not likely to be representative of their counterparts in the country of origin as migrating individuals tend to have psychosocial functioning that is different from individuals in the country of origin (Janssen et al., 2004; Fichter et al., 2004). Bearing in mind that eating disorders must be viewed within a socio-cultural paradigm, a study that explored different ethnic groups within one geographic location is necessary. This circumvents some insidious confounding factors that may arise as subjects are screened in two different locations with incompatible life-styles and different daily experiences that would impact on their attitude and behavior towards eating and weight. Sub-cultural comparisons, as used in the present study, within a society constitute 'powerful but under-appreciated strategies for examining cultural differences, and offer cultural variation within a common social, economics and political context that is constant for all sub-cultural group being studied' (cited in Sobal, 1998, p. 309).

The present sub-cultural comparison of Indian, Omani and Euro-American children suggested that despite having similar anthropomorphic functioning, the three ethnic groups appeared to have differences in their scores on eating attitude and behavior as scored on the EAT-26. The presently defined Euro-American cultural group had the lowest score while Indian teenagers had highest. The Omani teenagers lagged behind the Indians, but this was not statistically significant. Both Indians and Omanis differed significantly from their Euro-American counterparts. The present data suggest that non-western children had more tendencies for eating disorders than their Euro-American counterparts. Approximately 7% of the sample showed a tendency toward disordered eating pathology and the majority of these were non-western teenagers. The present finding further provided empirical support to the earlier observation that in non-western society eating disorder appeared to be as common as those reported in western industrialized countries. Although the present finding is consistent with some of the available literature, it is intriguing that eating disorder is higher among non-western populations, bearing in mind that the assessment measures were initially devised for western populations and eating disorder in developing countries was claimed to be due to westernization. Whether those who scored higher in EAT-26 are 'sub-threshold' for anorexia nervosa needs to be substantiated with further clinical interview. The present finding should be viewed with caution as the EAT 26 has been shown to give spurious results (Wilde & Emery, 2001). In the future studies, conventional clinical interview would be essential to collaborate the present finding as well as exploring socio-cultural correlates of eating disorder in non-western culture using cultural sensitive assessment measures.

2. Presence of Fear of Fat

Contradictory data have emerged on whether the core psychopathology involving relentless pursuit of thinness is also preoccupation among other cross-cultural populations. In western populations, manifestation of fat-phobia has been shown to fluctuate differently among various ethnic groups (Johnson et al., 2004; Williamson, 1998), suggesting that there is sub-clinical diversity even in the Western population. Studies from Asia suggest that the majority of anorexic patients tended to exhibit an absence of fear of obesity (Lee, 1994; Ngai, Lee &, Lee, 2000). To our knowledge, this potentially important aspect of eating disorders has not been looked at in the Arab part of the world. Many studies examining eating disorder from this region have focused solely on whether eating disorder is pathoplastic to westernization (e.g. Nasser, 1988; Abou-Saleh, Younis & Karim, 1998; Rasheed, 1998; Al-Subaie, 2000). The present study used a subscale from the Eating Disorder Inventory (Garner, Olmstead, & Polivy, 1985) the 'drive for thinness' index to measure the presence or absence of fat-phobia. The importance of fat phobia diagnostically has been eroded with studies suggesting conflicting results (Lee et al., 2001; Al-Adawi et al., 2001A: Simpson, 2002). Our data suggest that the Euro-American teenagers showed a significant tendency towards fat phobia. In contrast, such inclinations were relative lower among Indian and Omani teenagers, suggesting perception of body image in non-western adolescents is generally different from their western counterpart. In contrast, the majority of Euro-American students had strong desires or preoccupations with weight and body shape suggesting morbid fear of weight gain, an excessive concern with dieting or a strong desire for thinness, mindsets that were significantly different for students from Oman and Indian. In the literature, using the Goldfarb Fear of Fat Scale, which elicits fat phobia (Goldfarb, Dykens & Gerrard, 1984), Sjostedt, Schumaker & Nathawat (1998) have reported that Indian students scored significantly higher than their Australian counterparts on the EAT-26 but not on the fat-phobia scale. Similarly, Gupta et al. (2001) compared the severity of eating pathology among Indian children in India and their counterparts in Canada. They assessed the presence of eating disorder using a drive for thinness scale as well as other scales. They concluded that 'while Canadian and Indians scored similarly on some of the core features of eating-related disorder pathology, ...the nature of the underlying body image disturbance is different between the two groups. The Indian women tended to have a less distorted perception of their level of fatness than the Canadian women' (p. 197, quoted in Gupta et al., 2001). Also in a study that gauged anorexia without the central construct of fat phobia, it was shown that non-western students demonstrated more body image disturbance than their western counterparts did (Al-Adawi et al., 2002). The present data with other findings from elsewhere underscore the view that constructs of fat phobia may not be a universal preoccupation in some cross-cultural populations. This potentially important issue needed to be further empirically examined.

3. Presence of Somatization

As it was noted that subjects who did not endorse items of fear of fatness were also likely to complain of somatic distress, the question arises whether the lack of fat-phobia may be related to how certain populations around the world tend to verbalize their distress as noted in different context elsewhere (e.g. Kleinman, 1987; Nichter, 1981). In the present context, are Indians and Omanis styles of expressing distress contributing to the lack of fat-phobia and therefore is somatization in these ethnic group one of the idioms through which distress is communicated? It is worthwhile to note that lack of fat-phobia has been shown to be linked with complaints involving the stomach and digestive organs leading to poor appetite and diminished consumption of food. Therefore, it is possible that heightened somatic awareness tends to occur in response to psychological distress on a background of predisposing personality factors and culturally sanctioned behavior, but in adopting the sick role, a sense of wellbeing is achieved. In support of this contention, it has been shown that those who have been diagnosed as atypical or non fat-phobic tend have benign prognosis and less severe forms of psychopathology (Ramacciotti et al., 2002; Lee et al., 2001). Despite the potentially importance of addressing this issue, no previous study, to our knowledge, has examined the presence of somatization in an age group that is also vulnerable to eating disorder. This may be due to the long held assumption that eating disorder is a socio-cultural illness (Becker et al., 2004) and if somatic distress does occur in eating disorder it is as a pervasive body image disturbance rather than an integral part of the illness (Wiederman & Pryor, 2000). The absence of fat-phobia had been depicted as 'concealment' or 'denial' or 'atypical' manifestation of such disorder (Casper, 1998). Using a modified Bradford Somatic Inventory (Mumford et al., 1991), as expected, the study suggested the presence of somatopsychic expression in both Indian and Omani students. The Indian and Omani teenagers were more likely than their Euro-American counterparts to endorse the items linked to somatization. The clear demarcation between western and non-western adolescents is seemingly consistent with the view reported earlier that both Indian and Omani nationals tend to communicate distress somatopsychically (Al Lawati et al., 2000; Nichter, 1981). On the whole, from the present study, the indices of somatization were elevated in a subgroup of subjects and this was invariably related to their score in composite indices of eating disorder. In the literature, using screening instruments thought to be sensitive to local idioms of emotional distress, Ohaeri & Odejide (1994) and Mumford et al. (1987) have found the incidence of somatization ranges from 20% to 80% in various cultures among the developing countries. Complementing surveys from developing countries, Goldberg and Blackwell (1970) in UK, Giel & Le Nobel (1971) in the Netherlands, and Katon et al. (1984) in USA found similar patterns. In the Arab part of the world, various authors have reported high incidences of patients complaining of depression and anxiety and a variety of somatic symptoms (e.g. Hamdi et al., 1981; El-Rufaie et al., 1997; Racy, 1980; Pu et al., 1986; Al-Subaie et al., 1998). The frequent association of somatization and ethnicity and other morbidities suggested that the somatization would be a predisposing factor as well as idiom of distress and not simply a reaction to disability. The fact that somatic metaphor are part of how certain cultural groups communicate their distress gives rise to new ideas in the ongoing debate regarding core features of eating disorders. More studies are needed to explore how explanatory constructs involving somatopsychic idioms are related to lack of fat-phobia in other cross-cultural populations.

LIMITATIONS

Some limitations of this study should be highlighted. First, data collection with self-report questionnaires is likely to be inferior to the 'gold standard' interview (Dunn et al., 1999; McNamee, 2003; Prince, 2003). Some writers have suggested that as slimness is often considered to be a mass obsession, against the background of personal distress and lack of empowerment, there is the tendency for questionnaires to elicit spurious 'anorexic caseness' leading to diagnosis of "anorexia by proxy' or "pseudo-anorexics" (cited in Bruch, 1985, p.11). Notwithstanding such view, the cases identified as sub-threshold for anorexia nervosa were relatively small. Nevertheless, in order to circumvent such constrains on cross-cultural samples, qualitative interviews are likely to be more fruitful. However, carrying out protracted clinical interview would have been logistically impossible in the circumstances of the present study.

Secondly, although all the items of the screening instrument were carefully translated into Omani Arabic, their usefulness could still be obfuscated by certain subtle linguistic and conceptual misunderstandings that might not have been apparent during translation and piloting as causal attributions tend to differ from culture to culture. Similarly, although the Indian group studied in English medium schools, their native language is not English. Within the confines of the present study, it would be impractical to translate the assessment into various languages for what are apparently diverse groups of Euro-American and Indian students.

Finally, this study hinges on the assumption of ethnic homogeneity in terms of identity and functioning. However, the concept of ethnicity could be eroded with globalization and acculturation (Sobal, 1998) and therefore, ethnic groups that have been lumped in the present study should viewed with caution. Also, although there is obvious advantage of studying health related behavior in different ethnic groups dwelling in the same place in order to achieve ecological validity; it is possible such ethnic groups might not be typical of their respective countries. In the present study, the Indian and Euro-American children living in Oman might not be typical representatives of their respective countries.

Leaving aside the above-mentioned limitation and possible numerous others that are often inherent part of these types of studies, the present study, to our knowledge, is the first one of its kind to examine inter-ethnic differences in various variables related to eating disorders such as fear of fatness and somatization. The present study suggests that the performance of non-western adolescents (Omani, Indian) on assessment measures eliciting body image disturbance as indexed with attitude toward eating and weight, preoccupation with fatness and somatization were significantly different from their Euro-American counterparts. This complements the view that distress and stress are experienced in socio-cultural context (Siok et al., 2004).

Acknowledgment

We thank the staffs and pupils of the schools involved for their help and time in co-operating so fully with this study. We are grateful to Charles Asante for technical support.

References

Abdollahi P & Mann T (2001). Eating disorder symptoms and body image concerns in Iran: Comparisons between Iranian women in Iran and in America. *International Journal of Eating Disorders*, 30, 259-268.

Abou-Saleh MT, Younis Y & Karim L. (1998). Anorexia nervosa in an Arab culture. *International Journal of Eating Disorders*, 23, 207-212.

Agras WS, Brandt HA, Bulik CM, Dolan-Sewell R, Fairburn CG, Halmi KA, Herzog DB, Jimerson DC, Kaplan AS, Kaye WH, le Grange D, Lock J, Mitchell JE, Rudorfer MV, Street LL, Striegel-Moore R, Vitousek KM, Walsh BT & Wilfley DE. (2004). Report of the National Institutes of Health workshop on overcoming barriers to treatment research in anorexia nervosa. *International Journal of Eating Disorders*, 35, 509-521.

Al-Adawi S, Dorvlo AS, Burke DT, Moosa S & Al-Bahlani S. (2002A). A survey of anorexia nervosa using the Arabic version of the EAT-26 and "gold standard" interviews among Omani adolescents. *Eating and Weight Disorders*, 7, 304-311.

Al-Adawi S, Dorvlo ASS, Burke D, Al-Bahlani S, Martin RG & Al-Ismaily S. (2002B). Presence and severity of anorexia and bulimia among male and female Omani and non-Omani adolescents. *Journal of the American Academy of Child and Adolescent Psychiatry*, 41, 1124-1131.

Al-Adawi, S., Ghassany, H., Al- Naamani, A., Al-Sinawi, H., Martin, G., Chand, S.P., Al-Salmi, A., Zaidan, Z.A.J. & Al- Hussaini. A. (1999). Sub-clinical eating disorders: preliminary study of students in Muscat. *Oman Medical Journal*, 15, 29-29.

Al-Lawati J, Al Lawati N, Al Siddiqui M, Antony SX, Al Naamani A, Martin RG, Kolbe R, Theodorsson T, Osman Y, Al Hussaini AA & Al Adawi S. (2000). Psychological morbidity in primary healthcare in Oman: A preliminary study. *Journal for Scientific Research: Medical Sciences*, 2, 105–10.

Al-Riyami A, Afifi M & Mabry RM (2004). Women's autonomy, education and employment in Oman and their influence on contraceptive use. *Reproductive Health Matters*, 12, 144-154.

Al-Subaie A, Al Shammari S, Bamgboye E, Al Sabhan K, Al Shehri S & Bannah AR .(1996). Validity of the Arabic version of the Eating Attitude Test. *International Journal of Eating Disorders*, 20, 321 324.

Al-Subaie AS (2000). Some correlates of dieting behavior in Saudi schoolgirls. *International Journal of Eating Disorders*, 28, 242-246.

Al-Subaie AS, Bamgboye E, al-Shammari S, al-Sabhan KN, al-Shehri SN & Bannah AR. (1996). Validity of the Arabic version of the eating disorders inventory (EDI). *British Journal of Psychiatry*, 168, 636-640.

Al-Subaie AS, Mohammed K & Al Malik T. (1998). The Arabic self reporting questionnaire (SRQ) as a psychiatric screening instrument in medical patients. *Annals of Saudi Medicine*, 18, 308-310.

Altabe M (1998). Ethnicity and body image: Quantitative and qualitative analysis. *International Journal of Eating Disorders*, 23, 153-159.

American Psychiatric Association (1994). *Diagnostic and Statistical Manual of Mental Disorders* (4th edn.) American Psychiatric Association, Washington, DC.

Bagley CA, Character CD & Shelton L (2003).Eating disorders among urban and rural African American and European American women. *Women & Therapy*, 26, 57-79.

Barnett HL, Keel PK & Conoscenti LM (2001). Body type preferences in Asian and Caucasian college students. *Sex Roles*, 45, 867-878.

Becker AE, Burwell RA, Gilman SE, Herzog DB & Hamburg P (2002). Eating behaviours and attitudes following prolonged exposure to television among ethnic Fijian adolescent girls. *British Journal of Psychiatry*, 180: 509-514.

Becker AE, Keel P, Anderson-Fye EP &Thomas JJ. (2004). Genes and/or jeans?: Genetic and socio-cultural contributions to risk for eating disorders. *Journal of Addictive Diseases*, 23, 81-103.

Braun DL, Sunday SR &Halmi KA (1994).Psychiatric comorbidity in patients with eating Disorders. *Psychological Medicine*, 24, 859-867.

Brewis AA & McGarvey ST. (2000). Body image, body size, and Samoan ecological and individual modernization. *Ecology of Food and Nutrition*, 39, 105-120.

Cachelin FM, Veisel C, Barzegarnazari E. & Striegel-Moore RH. (2000). Disordered eating, acculturation, and treatment-seeking in a community sample of Hispanic, Asian, Black, and White women. *Psychology of Women Quarterly*, 24, 244-253.

Caradas AA, Lambert EV & Charlton KE (2001). An ethnic comparison of eating attitudes and associated body image concerns in adolescent South African schoolgirls. *Journal of Human Nutrition and Dietetics*, 14, 111-120.

Casper RC. (1998). Behavioral activation and lack of concern, core symptoms of anorexia nervosa? *International Journal of Eating Disorders*, 24, 381-393.

Chan B & Parker G. (2004). Some recommendations to assess depression in Chinese people in Australasia. *Australian and New Zealand Journal of Psychiatry*, 38, 141-147.

Contento IR, Basch C & Zybert P (2003). Body image, weight, and food choices of Latina women and their young children. Source: *Journal of Nutrition Education and Behavior*, 35, 236-248.

Davis C & Katzman MA (1999).Perfection as acculturation: Psychological correlates of eating problems in Chinese male and female students living in the United States. *International Journal of Eating Disorders*, 25, 65-70.

Drewnowski A, Pierce B & Halmi KA.(1988). Fat aversion in eating disorders. *Appetite*, 10, 119-131.

Duncan MC & Robinson TT (2004). Obesity and body ideals in the media: Health and fitness practices of young African-American women. *Quest*, 56, 77-104.

Dunn G, Pickles A, Tansella M & Vazquez-Barquero JL. (1999). Two-phase epidemiological surveys in psychiatric research. *British Journal of Psychiatry*, 74, 95-100.

Edman JL & Yates A (2004). Eating attitudes among college students in Malaysia: An ethnic and gender comparison. *European Eating Disorders Review*, 12, 190-196.

El Rufaie OE, Absood GH & Abou Saleh MT. (1997). The primary care anxiety and depression (PCAD) scale: a culture oriented screening scale. *Acta Psychiatrica Scandinavica*, 95, 119 24.

Fichter MM, Xepapadakos F, Quadflieg N, Georgopoulou E & Fthenakis WE.(2004). A comparative study of psychopathology in Greek adolescents in Germany and in Greece in 1980 and 1998--18 years apart. *European Archives of Psychiatry and Clinical Neuroscience*, 254, 27-35.

Friedman JM. (2004). Modern science versus the stigma of obesity. *Nature Medicine*, 10, 563-569.

Furnham A & Husain K (1999).The role of conflict with parents in disordered eating among British Asian females. *Social Psychiatry and Psychiatric Epidemiology*, 34, 498-505.

Garcia-Garcia E, Vazquez-Velazquez V, Lopez-Alvarenga JC & Arcila-Martinez D (2003). Internal validity and diagnostic utility of the Eating Disorder Inventory, in Mexican women. *Salud Publica De Mexico*, 45, 206-210.

Garner D, Olmsted M & Polivy J. (1983). Development and Validation of Multidimensional Eating disorder inventory for Anorexia nervosa and Bulimia. *International Journal of Eating Disorders*, 2, 15-34.

Garner DM & Garfinkel PE. (1979). The eating attitude Test: an index of the symptoms of anorexia nervosa. *Psychological Medicine*, 9, 273-279.

Garner DM, Olmstead MP & Polivy J (1985). Development and validation of multidimensional eating disorder inventory for anorexia nervosa and bulimia. *International Journal of Eating Disorder*, 2, 15-34.

Geier AB, Schwartz MB & Brownell KD. (2003). "Before and after" diet advertisements escalate weight stigma. *Eating and Weight Disorders,* 8, 282-288.

Germov J & Williams L. (1996). The epidemic of dieting women: the need for a sociological approach to food and nutrition. *Appetite*, 27, 97-108.

Giel R & Le Nobel CPJ. (1971). Neurotic instability in a Dutch village. *Acta Psychiatrica Scandinavica*, 47, 462-472.

Godart NT, Flament MF, Perdereau F & Jeammet P. (2003). Social disability in Anorexia nervosa and bulimia nervosa. *Encephale-Revue De Psychiatrie Clinique Biologique Et Therapeutique*, 29, 149-156.

Goldberg DP & Blackwell B. (1970). Psychiatric illness in general practices: a detailed study using new methods of identification. *British Medical Journal*, 2, 439-443.

Goldfarb LA, Dykens EM & Gerrard M. (1985).The Goldfarb fear of fat scale. *Journal of Personality Assessment*, 49, 329-332.

Gordon RA (2004). The global epidemiology of eating disorders: An update. *International Journal of Eating Disorders*, 35, 410-410.

Grant JE & Phillips KA. (2004). Is anorexia nervosa a subtype of body dysmorphic disorder? Probably not, but read on. *Harvard Review of Psychiatry*, 12, 123-126.

Gupta MA, Chaturvedi SK, Chandarana PC & Johnson AM. (2001). Weight-related body image concerns among 18-24-year-old women in Canada and India: an empirical comparative study. *Journal of Psychosomatic Research*, 50, 193-198.

Hamdi TI, Al-Hasani L, Mahmood A & Al-Husaini A. (1981). Hysteria: a large series in Iraq. *British Journal of Psychiatry*, 138, 177-178.

Havenaar JM, Poelijoe NW, Kasyanenko AP, Vanden-Bout J, Koeter MW & Filipenko VV. (1996). Screening for psychiatric disorders in an area affected by the Chernobyl disaster: The reliability and validity of three psychiatric screening questionnaires in Belarus. *Psychological Medicine*, 26, 837-844.

Hebebrand J, Casper R, Treasure J & Schweiger U (2004).The need to revise the diagnostic criteria for anorexia nervosa. *Journal of Neural Transmission*, 111, 827-840.

Helman CG. (1990). *Culture, Health and Illness*. (2rd edition). London: Wright.

Hoek HW & van Hoeken D (2003). Review of the prevalence and incidence of eating disorders. *International Journal of Eating Disorders*, 34, 383-396.

Humphry TA & Ricciardelli LA (2004).The development of eating pathology in Chinese-Australian women: Acculturation versus culture clash. *International Journal of Eating Disorders*, 35, 579-588.

James KA, Phelps L & Bross AL (2001). Body dissatisfaction, drive for thinness, and self-esteem in African American college females. *Psychology in the Schools*, 38, 491-496.

Janssen MM, Verhulst FC, Bengi-Arslan L, Erol N, Salter CJ & Crijnen AA (2004). Comparison of self-reported emotional and behavioral problems in Turkish immigrant, Dutch and Turkish adolescents. Social *Psychiatry and Psychiatric Epidemiology*, 39,133-140.

Johnson C, Crosby R, Engel S, Mitchell J, Powers P, Wittrock D & Wonderlich S. (2004). Gender, ethnicity, self-esteem and disordered eating among college athletes. *Eating Behaviour*, 5, 147-56.

Katon W, Ries RK & Kleinman A. (1984). The prevalence of somatization in primary care. *Comprehensive Psychiatry*, 1984, 25, 208 215.

Keel PK, Dorer DJ, Eddy KT, Franko D, Charatan DL & Herzog DB. (2003).Predictors of mortality in eating disorders. *Archives of General Psychiatry*, 60, 179-183.

Kiriike N, Nagata T, Sirata K, & Yamamoto N. (1998). Are young women in Japan at high risk for eating disorders? Decreased BMI in young females from 1960 to 1995. *Psychiatry and Clinical Neurosciences*, 52, 279–291.

Kleinman A. (1987). Anthropology and psychiatry: the role of culture in cross-cultural research on illness. *British Journal of Psychiatry*, 151: 447-454.

Ko C & Cohen H. (1998). Intraethnic comparison of eating attitudes in native Koreans and Korean Americans using a Korean translation of the eating attitudes test. *Journal of Nervous and Mental Disease*, 186, 631-636.

Kuboki T, Nomura S, Ide M, Suematsu H, Araki S. (1996).Epidemiological data on anorexia nervosa in Japan. Psychiatry Research, 62, 11-6.

Lasegue EC (1997). On hysterical anorexia. *Obesity Research*, 5, 492-497.

le Grange D, Telch CF & Tibbs J (1998).Eating attitudes and behaviors in 1,435 South African Caucasian and non-Caucasian college students. *American Journal of Psychiatry*, 155, 250-254.

Lee S, Chan YY & Hsu LK. (2003). The intermediate-term outcome of Chinese patients with anorexia nervosa in Hong Kong. *American Journal of Psychiatry*, 160, 967-972.

Lee S, Ho TP & Hsu LK. (1993). Fat phobic and non fat phobic anorexia nervosa: a comparative study of 70 Chinese patients in Hong Kong. *Psychological Medicine*, 23, 999 -1017.

Lee S, Lee AM, Ngai E, Lee DTS & Wing YK (2001). Rationales for food refusal in Chinese patients with anorexia nervosa. *International Journal of Eating Disorders*, 29, 224-229.

Lee S. (1994). The Diagnostic Interview Schedule and anorexia nervosa in Hong Kong. *Archives of General Psychiatry*, 51, 251-252.

Lee S. (1995). Self-starvation in context: towards a culturally sensitive understanding of anorexia nervosa. *Social Science and Medicine*, 41, 25-36.

Lee S. (1997). How lay is lay? Chinese students' perceptions of anorexia nervosa in Hong Kong. *Social Science and Medicine*, 44, 491-502.

Leff J. (1977). The cross cultural study of emotions. *Culture Medicine and Psychiatry*, 1, 317 350.

Lippincott JA & Hwang HS (1999). On cultural similarities in attitudes toward eating of women students in Pennsylvania and South Korea. *Psychological Reports*, 85, 701-702.

Longuenesse E. (1985). Indian workers in Oman. *Tiers Monde*, 26, 567-582.

McNamee R (2003).Efficiency of two-phase designs for prevalence estimation. *International Journal of Epidemiology*, 32, 1072-1078.

Mumford DB & Whitehouse AM. (1994). Sociocultural correlates of eating disorders among Asian school girls in Bradford. *British Journal of Psychiatry*, 34, 677-688.

Mumford DB, Bavington JT, Bhatnagar KS, Hussain Y, Mirza S & Naraghi MM. (1991). The Bradford Somatic Inventory: A multi-ethnic inventory of somatic symptoms reported by anxious and depressed patients in Britain and the Indo-Pakistan subcontinent. *British Journal of Psychiatry*, 158, 379-386.

Mumford DB, Minhas FA, Akhtar I, Akhter S & Mubbashar MH. (2000). Stress and psychiatric disorder in urban Rawalpindi - Community survey. *British Journal of Psychiatry*, 177, 557-562.

Mumford DB, Saeed K, Ahmad I, Latif S & Mubbashar MH. (1997). Stress and psychiatric disorder in rural Punjab a community survey. *British Journal of Psychiatry*, 170, 473 478.

Mumford DB, Whitehouse AM & Platts M (1991). Sociocultural correlates of eating disorders among Asian schoolgirls in Bradford. *British Journal of Psychiatry*, 158, 222-228.

Mumford DB. (1996). The 'Dhat syndrome': A culturally determined symptom of depression? *Acta Psychiatrica Scandinavica*, 94, 163-167.

Nakao M, Nomura S, Yamanaka G, Kumano H & Kuboki T. (1998). Assessment of patients by DSM-III-R and DSM-IV in a Japanese psychosomatic clinic. *Psychotherapy and Psychosomatics*, 67, 43-49.

Nakao M, Yamanaka G & Kuboki T. (2001). Major depression and somatic symptoms in a mind/body medicine clinic. *Psychopathology*, 34, 230-235.

Nasser M. (1986). The validity of the Eating Attitude Test in a non Western population. Acta *Psychiatrica Scandanica*, 73, 109 110.

Nasser M. (1988). Comparative study of the prevalence of abnormal eating attitudes among Arab female students of both London and Cairo Universities. *Psychological Medicine*, 16, 621-625.

Nasser M. (1994). Screening for abnormal eating attitudes in a population of Egyptian secondary school girls. *Social Psychiatry and Psychiatric Epidemiology*, 29, 25-30.

Ngai ESW, Lee S & Lee AM. (2000). The variability of phenomenology in anorexia nervosa. *Acta Psychiatrica Scandinavica*, 102, 314-317.

Nichter M. (1981). Idioms of distress: alternatives in the expression of psychosocial distress: a case study from South India. *Culture Medicine and Psychiatry*, 5, 379-408.

Nijenhuis ER, van Dyck R, Spinhoven P, van der Hart O, Chatrou M, Vanderlinden J & Moene F. (1999). Somatoform dissociation discriminates among diagnostic categories over and above general psychopathology. *Australian and New Zealand Journal of Psychiatry*, 33, 511-520.

Nishizono-Maher A, Miyake Y & Nakane A. (2004). The prevalence of eating pathology and its relationship to knowledge of eating disorders among high school girls in Japan. *European Eating Disorders Review*, 12, 122-128.

Ohaeri JU & Odejide OA. (1994). Somatization symptoms among patients using primary health care facilities in a rural community in Nigeria. *American Journal of Psychiatry*, 151, 728-731.

O'Keefe P & Lovell DM. (1999).Eating disorder inventory scores in Russia and Britain: A preliminary comparison. *European Eating Disorders Review*, 7, 129-135.

Omran AR & Roudi F. (1993). Oil jobs have big impact on heavily populated Middle East. *Population Today*, 21, 1-2.

Paquette MC & Raine K (2004). Sociocultural context of women's body image. *Social Scienceand Medicine*, 59, 1047-1058.

Peterson JE. (2004). Oman's diverse society southern Oman. *Middle East Journal*, 58, 254-269.

Pike KM. (1998) Long-term course of anorexia nervosa: response, relapse, remission, and recovery. *Clinical Psychology Review*, 18, 447-475.

Pina AA & Silverman WK. (2004). Clinical phenomenology, somatic symptoms, and distress in Hispanic/Latino and European American youths with anxiety disorders. *Journal of Clinical Child and Adolescent Psychology*, 33, 227-236.

Prince M. (2003). Commentary: Two-phase surveys. A death is announced; no flowers please. *International Journal of Epidemiology*, 32, 1078-1080.

Pu T, Mohamed E, Imam K & El-Roey AM. (1986). One hundred cases of hysteria in Eastern Libya a sociodemographic study. *British Journal of Psychiatry*, 148, 606- 609.

Racy J. (1980). Somatization in Saudi women: a therapeutic challenge. *British Journal of Psychiatry*, 137, 212-216.

Ramacciotti CE, Dell'Osso L, Paoli RA, Ciapparelli A, Coli E, Kaplan AS & Garfinkel PE.(2002). Characteristics of eating disorder patients without a drive for thinness. *International Journal of Eating Disorders*, 32, 206-212.

Rasheed P. (1998). Perception of body weight and self-reported eating and exercise behaviour among obese and non-obese women in Saudi Arabia. *Public Health*, 112, 409-414.

Rieger E, Touyz SW, Swain T & Beumont PJ. (2001). Cross-Cultural Research on Anorexia Nervosa: Assumptions Regarding the Role of Body Weight. *International Journal of Eating Disorders*, 29, 205-215.

Rubin LR, Fitts ML & Becker AE. (2003). "Whatever feels good in my soul": Body ethics and aesthetics among African American and Latina women. *Culture Medicine and Psychiatry*, 27, 49-75.

Russell SS. (2004).Population and development of the Arab Gulf States: The case of Bahrain, Oman and Kuwait. *Population and Development Review*, 30, 360-362.

Russell, GFM. (1970). Anorexia nervosa; its identity as an illness and its treatment. In JH Price (Ed.), *Modern Trends in Psychological Medicine* (Vol. 2, pp. 131-164). London: Butterworths.

Serrano E, Castro J, Ametller L, Martinez E. & Toro J. (2004).Validity of a measure of readiness to recover in Spanish adolescent patients with anorexia nervosa. *Psychology and Psychotherapy-Theory Research and Practice*, 77, (Part 1) 91-99.

Shimura M, Horie H, Kumano H, Sakano Y & Suematsu H. (2003). Reliability and validity of a Japanese version of the Eating Disorder Inventory. *Psychological Reports*, 92, 131-140.

Shroff H. & Thompson JK. (2004). Body image and eating disturbance in India: Media and interpersonal influences. *International Journal of Eating Disorders*, 35, 198-203.

Simpson KJ. (2002). Anorexia nervosa and culture. *Journal of Psychiatric and Mental Health Nursing*, 9, 65-71.

Siok TW, Perfetti CA, Jin Z & Tan LH. (2004).Biological abnormality of impaired reading is constrained by culture. *Nature*, 431, 71 - 76

Sjostedt JP, Schumaker JF & Nathawat SS. (1998). Eating disorders among Indian and Australian university students. *Journal of Social Psychology*, 138, 351-357.

Sobal J (1998). Cultural Comparison Research Designs in Food, Eating, and Nutrition. *Food Quality and Preference*, 9, 385-392.

Stacher G (2003).Gut function in anorexia nervosa and bulimia nervosa. *Scandinavian Journal of Gastroenterology*, 38, 573-587.

Strober M, Freeman R &, Morrell W (1999). Atypical anorexia nervosa: Separation from typical cases in course and outcome in a long-term prospective study. *International Journal of Eating Disorders*, 25, 135-142.

Sulaiman AJM, Al-Riyami A, Farid S & Ebrahim GJ (2001). Oman Family Health Survey 1995. *Journal of Tropical Pediatrics*, 47 (suppl), 1-33.

Szabo CP. (1999). Eating attitudes among black South Africans. *American Journal of Psychiatry*, 156, 981-982.

Turner H & Bryant-Waugh R (2004).Eating disorder not otherwise specified (EDNOS): Profiles of clients presenting at a Community Eating Disorder Service. *European Eating Disorders Review*, 12, 18-26.

Waller G, Babbs M, Wright F, Potterton C, Meyer C & Leung N.(2003). Somatoform dissociation in eating-disordered patients. *Behaviour Research and Therapy*, 41, 619-627.

Wang SS, Brownell KD & Wadden TA. (2004). The influence of the stigma of obesity on overweight individuals. *International Journal of Obesity and Related Metabolic Disorders,* XXXX

Watson TL & Andersen AE. (2003). A critical examination of the amenorrhea and weight criteria for diagnosing anorexia nervosa. *Acta Psychiatrica Scandinavica*, 108, 175-182.

Wiederman MW & Pryor TL. (2000). Body dissatisfaction, bulimia, and depression among women: The mediating role of drive for thinness. *International Journal of Eating Disorders*, 27: 90-95.

Wildes JE, Emery RE & Simons AD. (2001).The Roles of Ethnicity and Culture in the Development of Eating Disturbance and Body Dissatisfaction: A Meta-Analytic Review. *Clinical Psychology Review*, 21, 521-551.

Williamson L. (1998).Eating disorders and the cultural forces behind the drive for thinness: are African American women really protected? *Social Work in Health Care*, 28, 61-73.

Yates A, Edman J & Aruguete M. (2004). Ethnic differences in BMI and body/self-dissatisfaction among whites, Asian subgroups, Pacific islanders, and African-Americans. *Journal of Adolescent Health*, 34, 300-307.

Zahid MA, Motaal MAA & Razik MA (2001). Psychiatric morbidity among medical out-patients in Kuwait: Evaluation of a somatic inventory to identify the psychiatric from the non-psychiatric patients. *Medical Principles and Practice*, 10, 23-28.

Zaidan ZA, Burke DT, Dorvlo AS, Al-Naamani A, Al-Suleimani A, Al-Hussaini A, Al-Sharbati MM & Al-Adawi S. (2002). Deliberate self-poisoning in Oman. *Tropical Medicine and International Health*, 7, 549-556.

In: New Developments in Eating Disorders Research
Editor: Pamela I. Swain, pp. 93-122
ISBN 1-59454-542-1

Chapter 4

BODY SELF-IMAGE AND RISK FOR EATING DISORDERS IN A SAMPLE OF TEEN STUDENTS LIVING IN THE DISTRICT OF VARESE

Alberto Pellai and Luca Bassoli
Institute of Hygiene and Preventive Medicina at Università degli Studi di Milano

ABSTRACT

Adolescence is certainly the age of experimenting with a wide variety of rituals aimed at reaching full control on body changes, as well as on the social context teen-agers live within and start gaining their autonomy. Due to its cultural importance, dieting is one of these rituals frequently tried by adolescents as a fascinating way to deal with the body changes typical of puberty (Mallick M.J. et al, 1987).

INTRODUCTION

Body Perception in Puberty

Adolescence is certainly the age of experimenting with a wide variety of rituals aimed at reaching full control on body changes, as well as on the social context teen-agers live within and start gaining their autonomy. Due to its cultural importance, dieting is one of these rituals frequently tried by adolescents as a fascinating way to deal with the body changes typical of puberty (Mallick M.J. et al, 1987).

Through the control of his body figure, the adolescent is capable of representing and managing a number of changes and growing pubertal experiences typical of this age of evolution: redefinition of the relationships settled in infancy and strengthened in pre-adolescence, integration between sexuality and reproduction and furthermore, modifications of body figure and shape, stress towards aims of great social value, need to gain full autonomy in action and thought. Relationship with food becomes thus often ambivalent, oscillating between desire and reject, and it is charged with emotional values strictly connected with the adolescent's most intimate world and with his way of interrelating with the outer world. This can therefore explain why in puberty the physiological need of feeding as a consequence of hunger/satiety biological system turns into the expression of the evolving Self and of His uneasiness (Cuzzolaro M., 1997).

Body concern is actually started much prior to puberty, as evidenced by the anxiety and worry about body shape and dimensions detected in a research by the Harvard University among children of an age comprised between 8 and 10 years already. Approximately half of the female and one third of the male children interviewed reported to be dissatisfied with their body; most female children reporting dissatisfaction expressed the desire to be thinner, while nearly half of the dissatisfied male children to have a more muscular body (Collins M.E., 1991).

Confirmation to the above data comes from other surveys. Hill and Silver pointed out that, starting from 9 years of age, being overweight is a condition associated with higher social insecurity, scholastic failure, poor health state, lower physical strength and bad eating habits (Hill A.J. et al, 1992). As ascertained by a Swedish study, of a 7- and 8-year old sample girls, more than 20% reported to be concerned about their body shape and to have consequently tried to lose weight (Halvarsson K. et al, 2000).

Weight Control among Adolescents, a Behavior at Risk

Particular attention was focused by American Centers for Disease Control (CDC) on excessive accuracy in weight measurement among adolescents, individualized as a health risk factor, by enhancing a section of the Youth Risk Behavior Survey, carried out every year since the late 80's. The data surveyed indicated that the number of American teen-agers trying to loose weight has been constantly increasing, since in the last ten years the percentage of young girls under dietary restraint has grown from 43.5% up to 59.5%, the percentage of boys from 15.5% up to 26% (CDC 1991, 2000).

The problem seems to be specifically related with the current cultural attitude, which attaches to thinness a valuable aesthetic canon capable of ensuring a successful life. (Attie I. et al, 1995). The ideal bodily self-image of the adolescent derives in fact from his identification with someone else's body, as to say with those persons physically arising his admiration, from the mass media influencing messages and from the cultural environment as regards standards of beauty and physical shape (Levine M.P. et al, 1994). For example, photos shown in fashion magazines have a deep impact on girls' body size and weight perception; of 548 female teen-agers of an age comprised between 10 and 17 years interviewed by questionnaire, 69% reported to be influenced in their ideal self-bodily image, and 47% reported to wish to loose weight. (Field A.E. et al, 1999).

A number of young girls subject their bodies to heavy thinning efforts in a particular time of growth, when their body specifically requires enriching and strengthening, and not at all impoverishing and debilitating, with a deeply negative impact on their pubertal functional levels (organic, psychological and social), in every respect a behavior at risk.

Excessive weight concern and indiscriminate dietary restraint might, on one side, develop into a clear psychiatric pathology, but might also, independently of the latter, have a potential negative impact on the adolescent's mental and physical health and easily compromise his learning ability. A poor nutritional status, although not totally incomplete, may have, all the same and at any stage of puberty, negative effects on cognitive faculties and bad influence on scholastic performances and social acceptance. A reduced calorific intake of some nutritional principles leads in fact to memory diminution, reduced concentration power and irritability increase. A scarcely balanced diet in students finally translates into inactivity, indifference and reduced capacity of interrelating with the environment (Tufts University, 1998; CDC, 1996).

A deliberate and prolonged dietary restraint might develop in iron lack, the latter provoking in its turn weariness, shorter attention times, lessened capacities in physical and mental activities, weaker resistance to infections as well as a delay in growth and sexual maturity. American surveys report that 2-4% of teen-aged girls evidence lacks in iron (CDC, 1996).

Weight concern might as well affect the adoption of other at-risk behaviors. It is in fact noticed that cigarette smoking onset prevalence is higher among those adolescents on a diet or excessively worried about their weight, rather than among those satisfied with their body shape and weight. Female students of high schools, white girls and smoke-addicts, reported to use cigarette smoke to keep their weight and appetite under control (Tomeo C.A. et al, 1999).

The Problem Extent

Eating disturbances are highly complex chronic diseases, classified as psychiatric pathologies, which show in a wide range of aspects and various levels of seriousness. Their symptoms vary from a simple but indicative weight concern to a series of different eating pathologies correlated with a distorted perception of the body image; the most common forms are anorexia, bulimia, binge eating disorder (BED), along with other eating disturbs not otherwise specified but anyway so defined when symptoms do not allow for a more specific diagnosis.

BED is a form of eating disorder characterized by repeated episodes of uncontrolled "gobbling" not followed by common compensatory practices (self-induced vomit, laxative or diuretic remedies taking and/or over-training), but rather by a sense of depression, guilt and repulsion. Subjects suffering from BED have the tendency to be overweight, since to the elevated calorific intake they do not associate adequate energetic consumption. This eating disorder usually arises in puberty, specifically as the consequence of a significant loss of weight due to a slimming diet. For many authors, BED is the most common eating disorder, having a frequency rate of 0.7-4% among the general population and a relevant percentage among male subjects, too (Fairburn C., 1995).

Generally speaking, eating disorders affect all socio-economical categories as well as ethnic and cultural groups of all kinds (Dounchis J.Z. et al, 2000). The problem is mostly widespread among females (90% of all cases), although its diffusion is increasing among males (Carlat D.J. et al, 1997; Nelson W.L. et al, 1999). At present, approximately 1-4% of American young women suffer from disturbed eating attitudes (Yager J. et al, 1993) while anorexia nervosa is the 3rd chronic pathology among adolescent girls. Specifically, anorexia and bulimia are diffused among teen-aged girls with a frequency rate of respectively 0-0.8% and 0-1.9% (Hoek H.W., 1993 e Hoek H.W. et al, 1995), but the actual extent of the problem seems to be underestimated, as eating disorders not specifically diagnosed as the above two acknowledged pathologies are becoming more and more frequent (Zuckermann D. et al, 1986; Rodriguez A. et al, 2001).

Anorexia typical onset age is comprised between 14 and 18 years, while of bulimia a short time later, between late puberty and early adulthood.

Origins and Consequences

The origin of disturbed eating attitudes is so far not completely clear. Their development is the effect of a complex interaction of various factors, such as personality, genetic, biochemical and environmental features (family, society and culture).

For a better understanding of their evolution, has been taken as a reference a "multifactor" model in which predisposition factors such as overweight, inclination to depression, familiarity (further to the analysis of some hypothetical genetic proneness factors which might partially explain the familiarity surveyed, it has been noticed that eating disturbs tend to arise again within the same family) are associated with precipitating events such as physical or existential traumas, separations or conflicts.

In the latest few years, researchers have focused their attention mostly on the sociological origins of the problem. Besides to inner psychological factors and scarce self-consideration of physical growth, they have pointed out psycho-social factors involved in affecting the development of the adolescent's bodily perception: the environmental reactions and the way the adolescent reads them as compared with his changes in body shape (Levine M.P. et al, 1994). Mass media are actually among the most powerful instruments employed to deeply influence the adolescent's bodily self-perceptions, both directly and indirectly; a certain level of dependency on TV has been in fact identified among the population suffering from disordered eating habits. A survey carried out on a sample of teen-aged Italian girls, whose findings were consistent with American data, reported a longer time spent watching TV among girls with eating disturbs as well as a higher propensity on buying TV-advertised products when shopping, thus evidencing a meaningful difference if compared with the check-up sample girls without any eating disorder (Verri A.P. et al, 1997).

In the personal history of subjects suffering from eating disorders, it is rather common to notice anxiety or depression, substance abuse, episodes of sexual abuse in childhood and competitive sports activity. It needs mentioning a particularly low level of self-esteem, too, among individuals with anomalous eating habits (Nelson W.L. et al, 1999).

Owing essentially to the subject's early age, the consequences of eating disorders might be extremely serious; they might in fact be associated with an increase of osteoporosis and heart disease risks. Moreover, the mortality rate for psychiatric diseases among subjects suffering from eating disturbs is one of most elevated. It is assessed that one girl out of ten suffering from anorexia is likely to die from clinical complications associated with eating disturbs (National Institute of Mental Health, 1994).

Recent longitudinal research studies have shown the connection between eating disturbs and other high health-risk behaviors, such as cigarette smoking, alcohol and drug abuse, unsafe sexual intercourses and attempts to commit suicide (Neumark Sztainer D. et al, 1997).

It is therefore understood from the above data that eating disturbances are part of a complex behavior alteration as far as health is concerned in more general terms, and that they must be dealt with taking into consideration the plurality of the aspects involved. .

Owing to the socio-sanitary relevance of disturbed eating attitudes, with the aim to gain a more comprehensive perspective on their spreading at a national level as well as on those risk factors for the predisposition to and the development into pathology, a research on the topic was carried out within the district of Varese, province of Lombardy, Northern Italy. The research herewith illustrated allocated the widest sample of participants ever recruited for a survey of the kind in Italy.

Rationale

The current study was intended for accurately surveying the needs of the high school students population within the district of Varese as regards eating disturbs. In spite of clear clinical and epidemiological evidence, and though the experience of those professionals working at close contact with adolescents indicate a constant increase in the prevalence of cases of disturbed eating attitudes, no surveys can be found in Italy capable of illustrating the problem and defining its true extent.

In the year 2000, a community diagnosis concerning risk behaviors among students had been produced within the district of Varese, which pointed out eating disturbs as a crucial point. A two-year health education program has already been put into practice, based on an empowerment strategy which, through peer education, helped students to acquire the proper resources to effect conscious behavioral choices.

To plan specific preventive interventions, an exact and systematic evaluation of the prevalence rate of all those deranged eating attitudes, not yet acknowledged as pathologies but capable of developing if not cared for and treated, were mostly needed.

This study's goal was the preparation of community diagnosis as regards the number of eating disorders among the population of high school students within the district of Varese, and the school promotion of guidelines for bringing to effect dedicated interventions of primary and secondary prevention.

The tool for the current study is a questionnaire specifically "tailored" for the purpose and pre-tested among a sub-sample of high-school students in a pilot survey. The questions, investigating on personal details and most common risk behaviors, regarded in particular the perception of one's self-image, weight concern, bodily self-esteem and eating habits.

Specifically, the questionnaire contained three reliable and valid instruments taken from international literature: the EAT, (Eating Attitude Test, Garner et al. 1982), the Collins schematic silhouettes (Collins ME, 1991) and the MSCS- Multidimensional Self-Concept Scale (Bracken BA, 1992).

Participants were recruited by clustering a sample of High Schools within Varese district, from which a further sample-section was selected.

Questionnaires were handed out in the school year 2001/2002, within each single class by specifically trained staff who followed a standard procedure. To ensure total anonymity and freedom in answering, respondents were asked to fill in their questionnaires outside their class in absolute privacy, to put it into an envelope, close, seal and finally re-deliver it the following day to the same researchers.

The data collected, entered into and elaborated by EpiInfo 6, a word processing database and statistics program edited by C.D.C., are illustrated in the current study, in keeping with the first of its goals, as to say providing a community diagnosis to be employed for planning future interventions.

Statistical analysis was performed using the Chi Square Test and defining pvalues ≤ 0.05 as statistically significant.

RESULTS

Sample Population

Questionnaires were given out to 100 classes of students attending 20 High Schools within the District of Varese in the school year 2001-2002; 1743 questionnaires validly filled in were gathered up, which equaled and exceeded the expected sample number (1500).

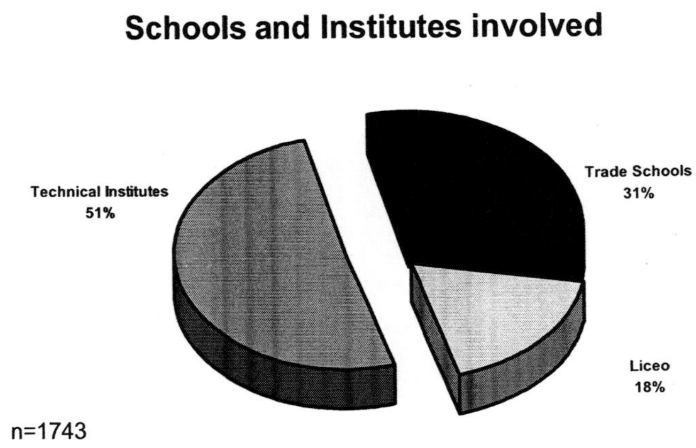

The total number of students participating to the current survey was 2035 (students who enlisted the sample schools and were present in class the giving-out day), with a return percentage up to 86.8% (corresponding to 1767 questionnaires given back). Fully blank questionnaires (24, corresponding to 1.4% of the return percentage) were left out from the analysis.

The percentage of students participating to the research varied according to the different kind of Schools and Institutes. In the school with the lowest number of participants, 61.3% of validly filled-in questionnaires were returned to the research staff, in all other schools more than 75% and in some cases more than 90% of questionnaires were handed back.

In recruiting the participant schools, a wide range of different courses and studies was selected; the final sample consisted essentially of students attending Technical Institutes (51.0%), followed by a lower number attending Trade Schools (31.3%) and Liceo (17.7%).

Among respondents, the percentage of girls (53.5%) is higher than boys (46%), homogeneously distributed among the five-year classes (nearly 20% in each class). The highest differences are noticed between I-year and V-year classes, attended respectively by 23.4% and 16% of respondents. 7.5% of the interviewed students attended private schools.

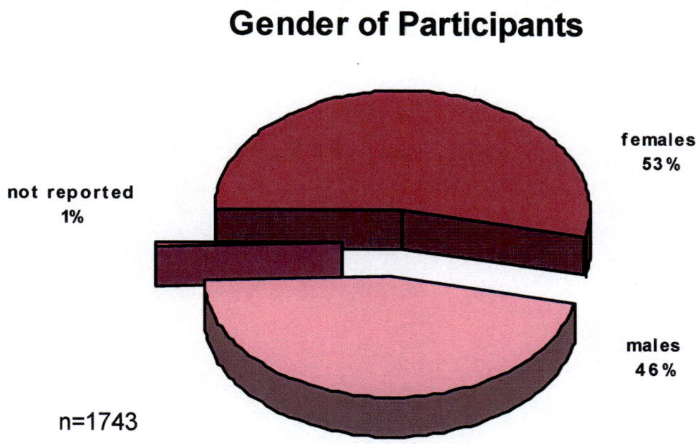

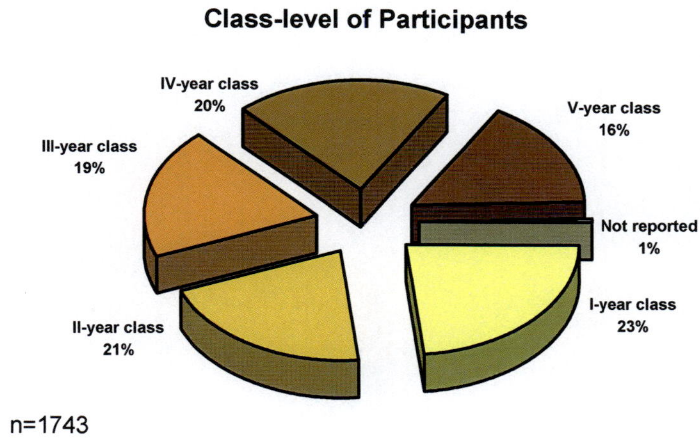

In compliance with the data provided by the Ministry of Education, University and Research as regards State Schools within the District of Varese in the school year 2001/2002 the total number of students was 31951, divided as follows: 35.8% attending Liceo, 21.6% Trade Schools and 42.6% Technical Institutes. Students were distributed among the five-level courses with the following percentages: 24.7% in I-year, 22.3% in II-year, 20.1% in III-year, 16.9% in IV-year and 15.9% in V-year. ISTAT data referring to school year 1997/1998 reported, among the 34.069 total students of Varese District ,a higher number of girls (51.4%), and a percentage of private school students up to 12.8%.

Auxological Data

The auxological measurements below were self-reported by students on their questionnaires. It must be considered, however, that a number of participants gave incomplete or missing answers, and that the percentage of dissatisfying questionnaires with missing details on weight and height was comprised between 6% and 7%.

Reported average height was 169 cm, average weight 60 Kg and average Body Mass Index (BMI) 20.9.

Average height in cm

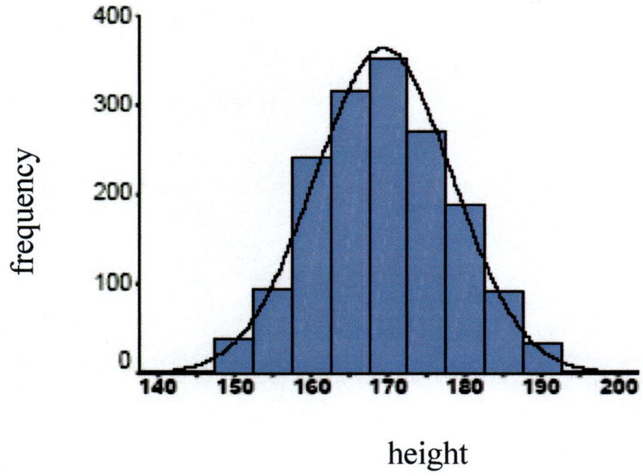

Average weight in kg

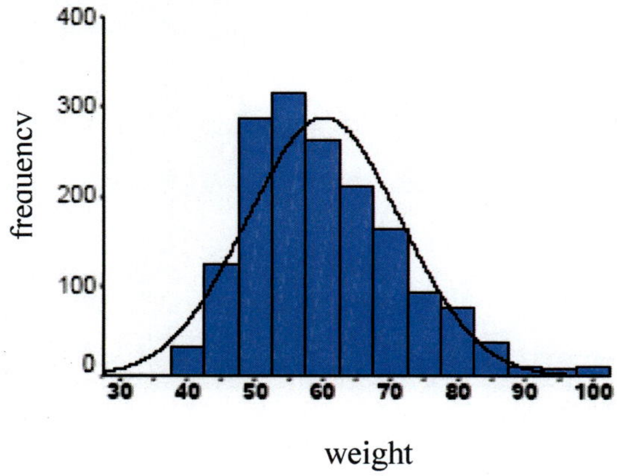

BMI

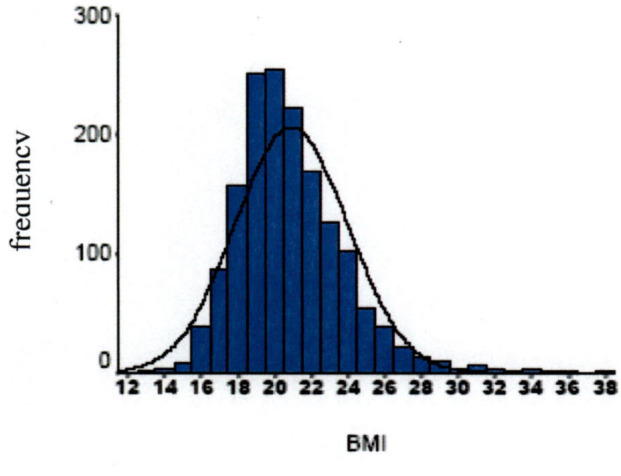

As expected, average height, weight and BMI resulted higher in boys.

Boys	Girls
Average height: 175.2	Average height: 164,3
Average weight: 65.8	Average weight: 55,2
Average B.M.I.: 21.4	Average B.M.I.: 20,5

Height, weight and B.M.I. globally increased with the class level, their value being then stabilized among students attending III-IV-V year courses.

Auxological data for class-level

Class		N		Mean	Median	S.A.D.	Min.	Max.
		Valid	Missing					
1	Reported height cm	372	35	167,4	168,0	8,515	140,0	199,0
	Reported weight kg	376	31	58,03	55,00	11,298	30,00	95,00
	BMI	360	47	20,69	20,02	3,304	13,33	37,78
2	Reported height cm	331	29	168,7	169,0	9,132	150,0	199,0
	Reported weight kg	339	21	58,36	57,00	0,2884	35,00	95,00
	BMI	327	33	20,49	20,24	2,793	14,03	35,56
3	Reported height cm	315	16	170,3	170,0	9,282	140,0	194,0
	Reported weight kg	312	19	61,04	59,00	11,554	35,00	100,0
	BMI	307	24	20,94	20,45	3,181	14,88	47,09
4	Reported height cm	335	20	170,6	170,0	8,757	150,0	192,0
	Reported weight kg	334	21	62,32	60,00	11,412	40,00	100,0
	BMI	330	25	21,33	20,81	2,929	14,71	38,09
5	Reported height cm	266	15	170,3	170,0	8,461	150,0	193,0
	Reported weight kg	266	15	61,79	60,00	11,468	41,00	100,0
	BMI	260	21	21,25	20,62	3,006	15,09	34,89

s.a.d. = Standard/average deviation

Auxological Data Classification

Since a specific question concerning the participant age was missing from the questionnaire, a strict comparison with other surveys, generally based on categorizing per participants' age is not possible, precise auxological references cannot be given either. Statistics on the basis of on the reported data must also take into account the tendency, mainly noticed among overweight or obese respondents, to overestimate their height and underestimate their height, which might result in a trend towards normality of their B.M.I.

On the basis of B.M.I categories, it is possible to categorize respondents according to the OMS classification (1997), specifically made for adult people and indicated in the table beside. If the same adult body size ranges are applied to adolescents, it follows that a young boy 1.75 m tall should weigh between 57 and 77 kg to have a body size in the average B.M.I category, while a young girl 1.64 m tall between 50 and 67 kg.

Weight classification		
B.M.I.)	**Class**	**Comorbility risk**
< 18,5	Underweight	Increased
18,5 – 24,9	Average	Average
25 – 29,9	Overweight	Increased
30 – 34,9	I degree obesity	Moderate
35 – 39,9	II degree obesity	Severe
≥40	III degree obesity	Highly severe

Students for B.M.I. size ranges (% with IC95%)

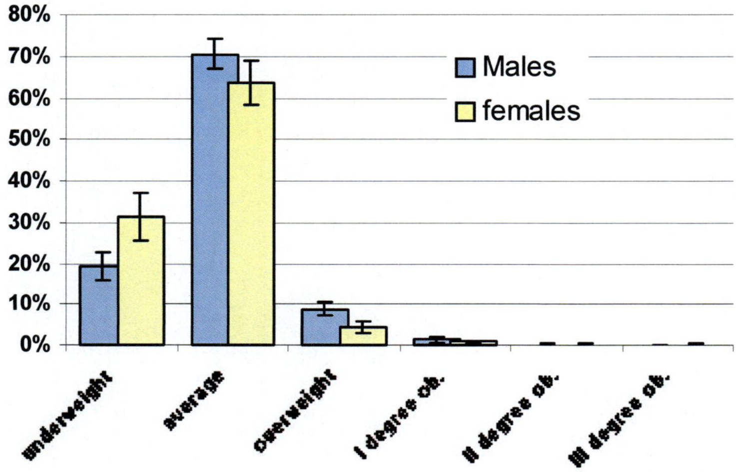

It must be considered, however, in reading the results that the application of adult body B.M.I. categories to adolescents does not produce immediate interpretation, but permits on the other hand to overcame some obstacles of practical nature (the latter essentially consisting in the lack of consistent findings and in the undetected participants' age), and to operate cross-references and comparisons within the various study sections. By applying B.M.I. categories to the sample students, it was noticed that they ranked asymmetrically, as shown in the bar graph beside. A higher number of both boys and girls had a body size in the underweight B.M.I. category than in overweight. Specifically 31.1 % of respondent girls ($IC_{95\%}$ 25.4%-36.9%) and 19.4% of respondent boys ($IC_{95\%}$ 16.0%-22.7%) ranked in underweight B.M.I. class, while only 5.4% of girls and 10.2% of boys ranked in overweight/obese B.M.I. categories. Students' B.M.I. increased with their age from I to V High School level classes with a corresponding progressive diminution in the number of students ranking in underweight category. The percentage of overweight-excessively fat students did not change significantly. If frequencies for gender are examined, although starting percentages were quite similar in I-year classes, the bar graphs below show a progressive reduction much more evident in underweight boys than girls, as the class level is higher. The percentage of underweight boys is reduced from 30.3% to 10.2%, that of girls from 35.4% to 25.7%. Since they are referred to different students attending different classes, data are indicative only and should be confirmed by surveying the evolution of a same cohort of students from I- to the V-year classes.

B.M.I. for class-levels - girls -

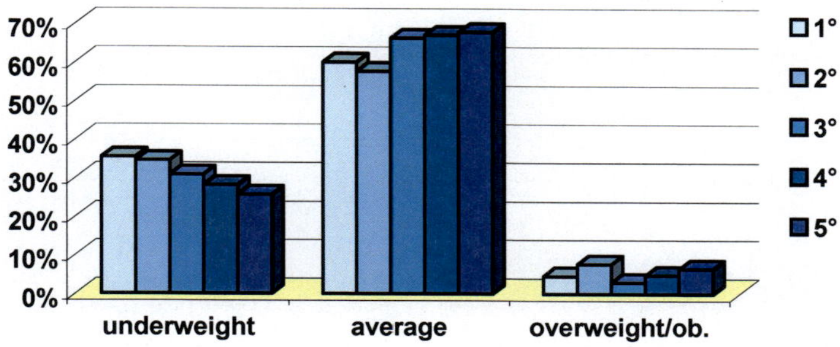

B.M.I. for class-levels - boys -

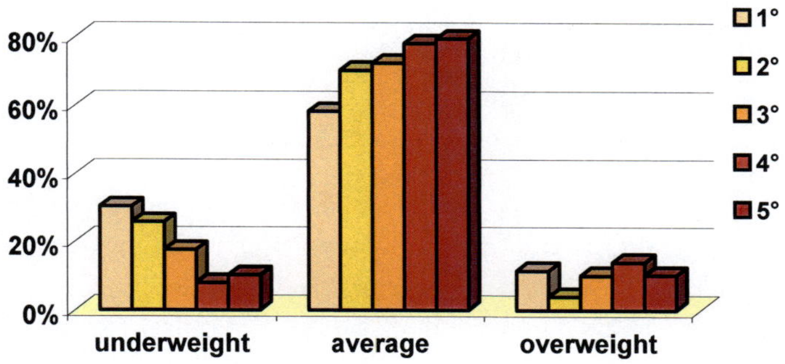

Family and Interfamilial Relationships

The reported standard family was generally composed of both parents (89%) with at least one brother or sister (82%).

Among other reported situations, 7.1% lived with one separated/divorced parent only, and 3.6% with one parent only for other not specified reasons.

The difference detected for gender was not significant either by living with both parents (90.3% of boys and 88.1% of girls), or by having any brother or sister (81% for boys and 83% for girls). Finally, 7.6% of female respondents reported separated or divorced parents vs. 6.4% of male respondents, with no statistically significant difference.

It was commonly reported (60.6%, $IC_{95\%}$ 57.5%-63.7%) that at least one family member had once been on a slimming diet, with a more elevated prevalence of girls than boys (64.1% vs. 56.6%), the difference being at the limit of significance. This percentage was significantly higher among respondents with brothers or sisters, 54% of sole sons/daughters vs. 63% of brothers/sisters.

	Interrelationships with the mother			
	frequency		percentuage	
	females	males	females	males
Good	787	689	84,4	86,0%
Indifferent	51	55	5,5%	6,9%
Conflictin	87	50	9,3%	6,2%
Not report.	7	7	0,8	0,9%

	Interrelationships with the father			
	frequency		percentuage	
	females	males	females	males
Good	691	648	74,1%	80,9%
Indifferent	132	85	14,2%	10,6%
Conflictin	82	47	8,8%	5,9%
Not report.	27	21	2,9%	2,6%

	Interrelationships with brothers/sisters			
	frequency		percentuage	
	females	males	females	males
Good	583	502	62,6%	62,7%
Indifferent	81	81	8,7%	10,1%
Conflictin	111	75	11,9%	9,4%
Not report.	157	143	16,8%	17,9%

On the contrary, no significant difference was noticed among respondents living with one divorced/separated or with both parents. Interrelationships with family members were rated as globally satisfying. 85% of the interviewed students rated relationship with their mother as good, 6% as indifferent and 8% as conflicting, while 1% did not give any answer. As regards relationship with the father, it was rated by 77% as good, 13% as indifferent and 7% as conflicting; 3% did not give any answer. A worse situation was reported as regards relationships with brothers or sisters: 17% gave no answers on the matter, 63% rated them as good, 9% as indifferent 11% as conflicting.

Girls reported slightly more conflicting relationships with all family members than boys, the discrepancy being closer to statistical significance only with the father, although.

Being sole son/daughter appeared to have no significant influence in evaluating relationships with parents. If analyzed by class, none of the above data evidenced a well-defined trend.

Extra-Familial Interrelationships, Reading, TV-Watching and Sporting Activities

The assessment of extra-familial relationships by male and female respondents did not evidence any significant difference. Of the sample students, 42.2% rated their extra-familial relationships as extremely satisfying, 54.6% as rather satisfying and 2.9% as dissatisfying, while 0.3% did not give any answer. The percentage of "rather satisfied" students tended to increase in the higher classes to "extremely satisfied" students' detriment, respectively 48% and 50% attending I-year and 63% e 34% attending V-year classes. The assessment was not significantly influenced by respondents weight category, since the most relevant difference detected was among "extremely satisfied" students, 43.1% of them underweight, 42.5% average and 36.8% overweight/excessively fat. No significant differences in rating extra-familial interrelationships were noticed among respondents living with both parents or with one separated/divorced parent only. It is anyway worth mentioning that, among the latter, the percentage of "dissatisfied" respondents resulted 5.7%, vs. 2.6% of the former.

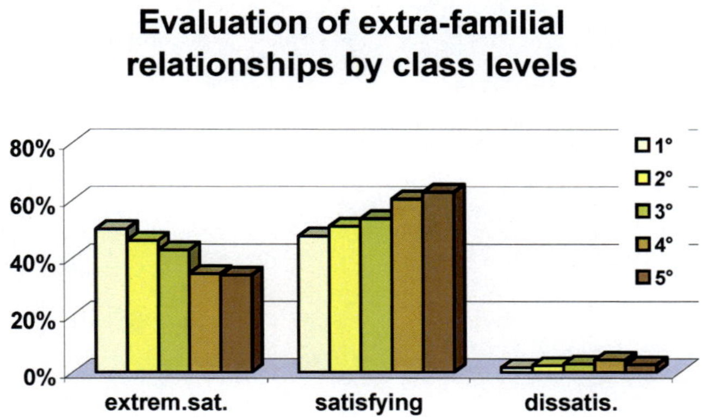

Interfamilial relationships did not seem to affect extra-familial ones.

Of the sample students, 28.9% ($IC_{95\%}$ 23.4%-34.4%) reported to participate in competitive sporting activities; 29.8% ($IC_{95\%}$ 26.9%-32.8%) in sporting activities at amateur level and 40.8% ($IC_{95\%}$ 34.1%-47.5%) in no sporting activity at all. A significant difference was detected when examining frequencies by gender, with 43.1% ($IC_{95\%}$ 38.4%-47.8%) of competitive and 29% ($IC_{95\%}$ 25,5%-32,5%) of amateur male athletes, vs. 16.7% ($IC_{95\%}$ 13.6%-19.8%) of competitive and 30.6% ($IC_{95\%}$ 26.1%-35.1%) of amateur female athletes. 27.6% of boys ($IC_{95\%}$ 22.5%-32.6%) and 52,1% of girls ($IC_{95\%}$ 46.3%-58%) did not participate in any sporting activity. Among I-year class students, a higher percentage of respondents reported to participate in sports at a competitive level (37%) than at amateur level (26%) or in no sports (37%). The higher the class attended, the lower the number of competitive athletes (from 37.4% among I-year down to 17.8% among V-year course students), with an increase in the percentage of non-sporting students (from 36.6% to 48.8%) as well as of amateur athletes (from 26% to 33.5%), the latter in a less regular way, although.

No significant differences were found by average B.M.I and sporting activity level, B.M.I. being slightly lighter among non-sporting (20.6) than among sporting respondents (21.1). Better evaluations of their extra-familial interrelationships were reported by respondents participating in sports, described as fully satisfying by 48.3% of competitive athletes and by 42% of amateur-level athletes, vs. 38.2% of non-sporting respondents.

Extra-school sporting activities: girls participation

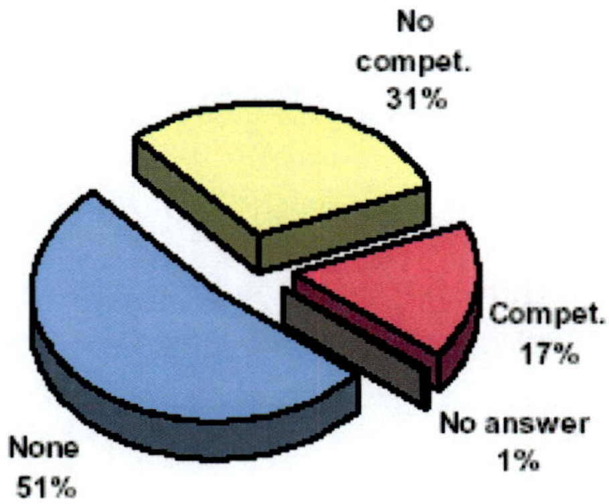

Extra-school sporting activities: boys participations

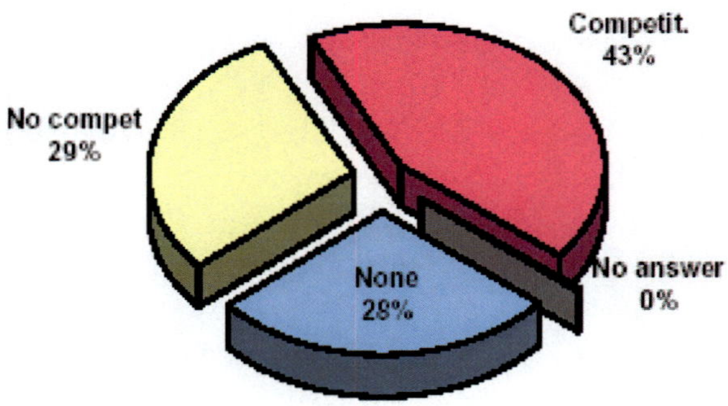

Sports in the five-level classes

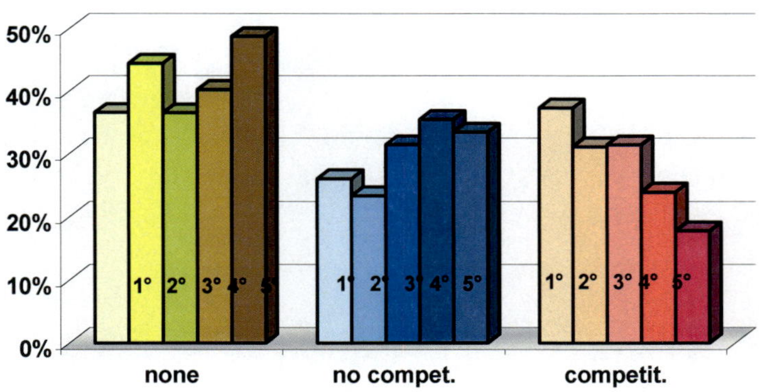

Time spent in watching TV appeared quite variable, averaging two hours and fifteen minutes a day, without any significant difference between boys (2 h and 14 m) and girls (2 h and 17 m). I-year class students reported a longer TV-watching time (2 h and 25 m), which appeared progressively reduced in higher classes (2 h and 1 m among V-year class students).

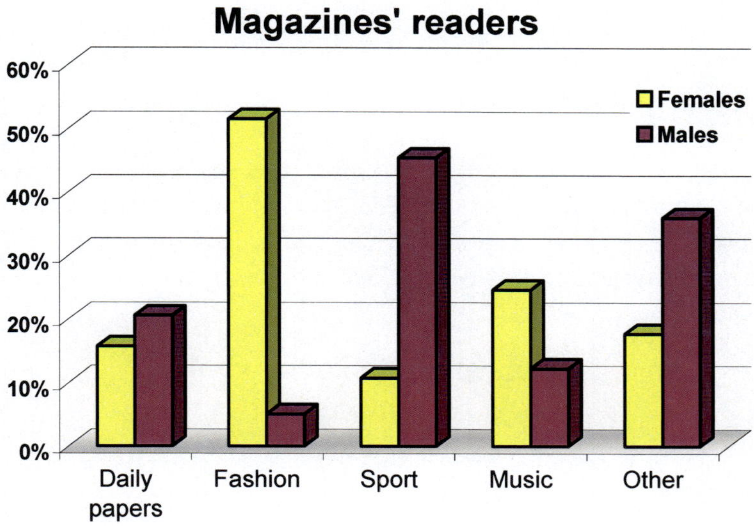

Overweight or obese respondents spent a slightly longer time in watching TV (2 h and 26 m) if compared with average (2 h and 13 m) and underweight (2 h and 19 m), the difference being not statistically significant. Sports practicing did not influence TV-watching time either, slightly longer among non-sporting respondents (2 h and 19 m) than amateur (2 h and 10 m) or competitive athletes (2 h and 16 m). No significant differences were detected either by evaluating interfamilial/extra-familial relationships, being sole son/daughter or living with separated/divorced parents. As far as magazine reading was concerned, only 18% of the sample students reported to spend time in reading daily newspapers, with a slightly higher prevalence in boys rather than in girls (21% of boys vs. 16%). Nearly half of the female respondents reported to be readers of "fashion-health-beauty" magazines, vs. 5% of male respondents only. A reversed situation was detected as regards sports and motoring magazines, circulating among 45% of male and 5% of female respondents. 19% of the sample students were readers of music magazines, circulation being higher among girls (25%) than boys (12%). Finally, 36% of boys and 18% of girls read magazines on other subjects.

By analyzing data for class-levels, it was noticed from I- to V-year courses an evident increase in respondents reading daily papers (from 14% to 22%) and "fashion-health-beauty" magazines (from 26% to 39%) and a reduction in respondents reading "sports and motoring" (from 29% to 17%) and music magazines (from 24% to 12%). Magazines on other subjects had a similar circulation in the various class-levels.

When examining frequencies for weight, average B.M.I. appeared lower in female readers of fashion magazines (BMI 20.1 kg. $IC_{95\%}$ 19.8-20.4) if compared with non-readers (20.9 Kg. $IC_{95\%}$ 20.5-21.2), the difference being statistically significant. Ideal B.M.I. resulted lighter among female readers of fashion magazines (18.7 kg $IC_{95\%}$ 18.5-18.9) if compared with other kinds of magazines (19.3 kg $IC_{95\%}$ 19.1-19.6). Similar results were noticed among the small number of boys reading the same type of publications.

As expected, sports magazines are mostly read by those respondents practicing sporting activities, no significant differences were surveyed between readers' and non-readers' B.M.I., however. The same can be said of music magazines and newspaperspapers readers' and non-readers' B.M.I.

Tobacco and Marijuana Smoking

56.2% ($IC_{95\%}$ 52.2%-60.3%) of the interviewed students reported to have experienced smoking a whole cigarette at least once in their lives. As expected, the number of those who experimented cigarette smoking was lower among I-year class students (45.7%) than among other level students (II-year: 58.1%; III-year: 58.6%; IV-year: 58.0%; V-year classes: 64.1%)

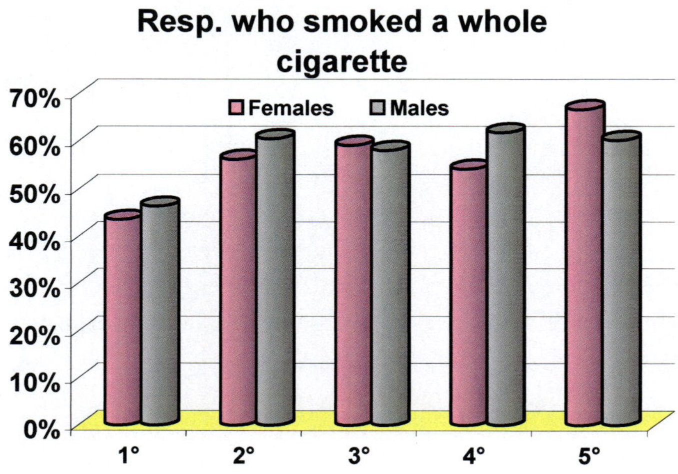

Two clear discontinuities were surveyed in the trend of smoking students' number: the percentage was increased by nearly 13% between I- and II-year course students, unchanged between II- and IV-year course students' and increased again by a further 6% between IV- and V-year course students. By data analysis for sex, it was noticed that, while among I- and II-class students the difference was the same for both boys and girls, among IV- and V-year class it concerned girls essentially, who, in their last year level experimented cigarette smoking in higher percentage than boys. Obviously, the above data do not allow for proper statistic comparison, possible only through a longitudinal research study.

No gender differences were detected among non-smoking students, percentages resulting 42% of males and 43% of females.

Among those who smoked a cigarette at least once, the first experience's average age resulted 14 years, boys smoking at an earlier age (13.7 years) than girls (14.3 years). Globally, 2.8% of students reported to have experienced a cigarette at 10 years or younger, 11.2% at 11-12 years of age, 27.2% at 13-14 years of age, 13.1% at 15-16 years of age and 2% at 17 years or older. It must be considered that the above assessments were made on a sample of students of different ages, thus determining a frequency overestimation among lower classes students. Moreover, examining the reported data by class-levels, it was noticed that participants tended to place their first smoking experience within an age range close to theirs at the time of the interview. Questions aimed at counting smoke-addicts revealed 36.3% of sample students ($IC_{95\%}$ 32.4%-40.3%) had smoked cigarettes at least once over the month before the survey, frequency being slightly higher among boys (38.7%) than girls (34.2%). Of those who experienced smoking a whole cigarette, 2 out of 3 participants reported to have smoked during the previous month (64% $IC_{95\%}$ 60.7%-67.3%), boys being more numerous (66.9%) than girls (61.3%).

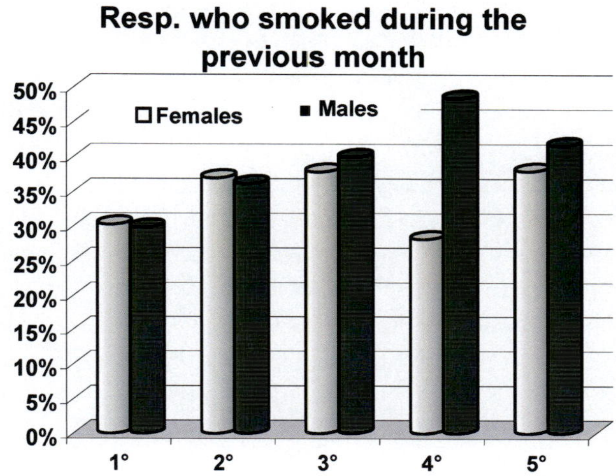

I-year class smoking students resulted 30.2; V-year were 39.5%, without any statistically significant difference.

Average smoking, calculated on the percentage of 30-day smokers, was 20 days, with a small difference between boys (19.6) and girls (20.3). By examining frequencies by class-levels, a more elevated means of smoking days was pointed out among students of the higher classes, being 16.1 days in I-class courses vs. 24.7 days in V-class courses.

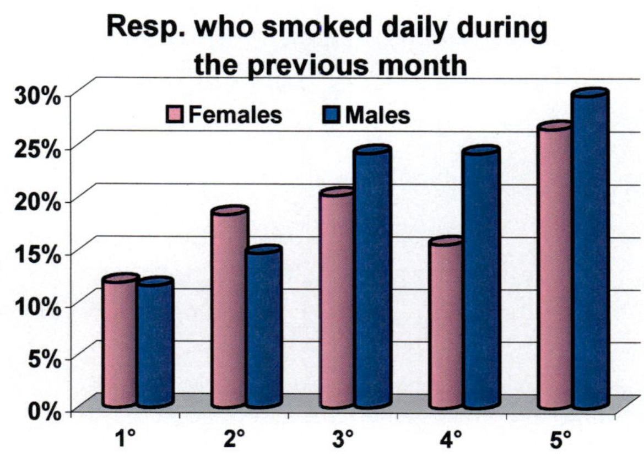

Of those who smoked during the previous month, most participants (50.4%) reported daily cigarette-smoking, with no difference between males and females (males: 49.1%; females: 51.7%).

The number of regular smokers is the lowest among I-year course students (36.7%); it is progressively increased as the level is higher and it is nearly doubled among V-year course respondents (70.3%). Of the whole sample, 11.7% ($IC_{95\%}$ 8.3%-15.1%) every-day smokers attend I-year courses, 27.9% ($IC_{95\%}$ 20.2%-35.5%) V-year courses.

The reported average number of cigarettes a day during the previous month resulted up to 6.1, slightly lower among girls (5.8 cigarettes a day) than boys (nearly 6.4 cigarettes a day) without a significant difference.

No significant discrepancy was detected either in the number of cigarettes a day by class-level, being the lowest among I-year class students (5.6 cigarettes a day) and the highest among V-year class students (6.7 cigarettes a day).

It was finally noticed that the average number of cigarettes a day increased with the number of smoking days a month, from 2.1 cigarettes a day on 1 to 6 smoking days within the previous month, up to 8.4 cigarettes a day on 30 smoking days.

By a cross-analysis of frequencies for smoking habit by weight category, the percentage of those who had experience of smoking a cigarette is higher among average weight subjects (59.1%), and lower in underweight (51.9%) or overweight/obese subjects (48.9%). Average smoking onset age is similar in the three weight categories, slightly lower among overweight/obese students (13.6 years) than underweight (13.9 years) and average weight (14 years). Of those students who reported smoking during the previous month, 38.5% were average weight, 33.15 overweight/obese and 31.6% underweight. Similar findings were noticed in examining frequencies for average number of smoking days over the previous month (20.8 average weight, 18.8 underweight, 15.7 overweight/obese) by the average number of smoked cigarettes (respectively 6.5, 6 and 5.4).

As regards the way weight affects smoking habits, different frequencies were noticed by gender. The percentage of average weight male smokers resulted higher (63,3% $IC_{95\%}$ 58%-68,6%) than overweight/obese (43,9% $IC_{95\%}$ 34%-53,8%) or underweight (40,6% $IC_{95\%}$ 31,9%-49,4%), the difference being statistically significant. No significant differences were on the contrary detected among female smokers by the same variable (underweight 56.9%, average 54.9%, overweight/obese 58%). Similarly, 44.1% ($IC_{95\%}$ 37.9%-50.4%) of average weight male respondents vs. only 24.5% ($IC_{95\%}$ 18,6%-30,4%) of underweight and 28% ($IC_{95\%}$ 17,9%-38,2%) of overweight obese smoked over the previous month, the percentages among female respondents being respectively 35.5% of underweight, 32.9% of average and 42% of overweight/obese.

Cannabis use was another at-risk behavior investigated by the questionnaire of the current study. 29.4% of the sample students ($IC_{95\%}$ 24.8%-34.1%), most of them males (males 36.6%; $IC_{95\%}$ 31.7%-41.4%; females 23.4% $IC_{95\%}$ 18.5%-28.3%). reported at least one instance of cannabis smoking in their lifetime. The percentage of cannabis-using students was noticed to grow with the class-level, from 19.2% among I-year up to 35.9% among V-year course students.

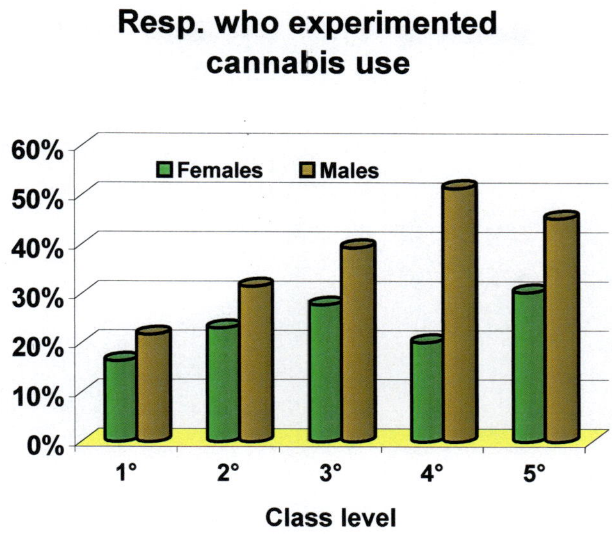

It was evidenced from the data collected that a high percentage of occasional marijuana users (25,2%; $IC_{95\%}$ 20.8%-29.6%) limited the marijuana smoking instances to once or twice, practically to one or two experimentation episodes. Progressively lower percentages of students reported to have used cannabis from 3 to 9 times (21.5%; $IC_{95\%}$ 17.1%-25.9%), from 10 to 19 times (14.0%; $IC_{95\%}$ 11.3%-16.7%) and from 20 to 29 times (10.7%; $IC_{95\%}$ 7.7%-13.7%). By analyzing frequencies on the contrary point of view, a relevant number of participants (24.5% $IC_{95\%}$ 19.5%-29.4%) reported to have smoked cannabis more than 40 times in their lifetime.

Besides reporting a lower frequency of cannabis use, girls appeared less prone to repeat the first-time experience: among respondents who experimented the substance, it is definitely higher the number of regular smokers with 40 instances of use or more (30.0% of males vs. 17.0% of females) and lower that of occasional smokers, with 1 or 2 instances (22.1% of males vs. 29.6% of females).

Effectively, to hypothesize an "optimistic" assessment of marijuana use frequency, answers were re-calculated considering the mean between the highest and the lowest given cannabis uses (i.e. 3 to 9 instances of cannabis use = 6 instances) and the lowest given use in the last choice (40 uses or more = 40 uses), with a total average instances of cannabis smoking of 17.3 times in lifetime, which by gender resulted in 19.2 instances among males and 14.8 among females.

When examining frequencies for class-levels, the average use frequency in lifetime resulted the lowest among I-year course students (14.3) and the highest among IV-year (19.0), with a diminution among V-year course students.

By limiting the analysis to the previous 30 days, an "optimistic" assessment made through the above-illustrated method evidenced a frequency crest among II-year (6.3 instances of cannabis use) and the lowest level of use among V-year class students (3.3 instances), with a higher prevalence of male users (6.5 uses during the prior 30 days) than female (3.4 uses).

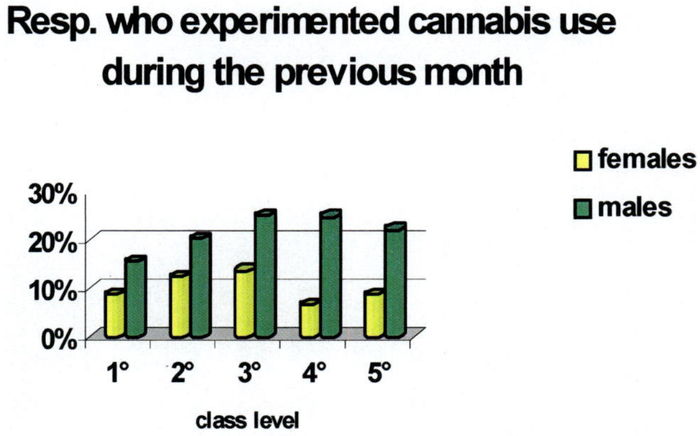

15.3% ($IC_{95\%}$ 12.1%-18.4%) of the interviewed students reported to have used cannabis during the prior 30 days (recent users) with a lower percentage of girls (10.0% $IC_{95\%}$ 7.2%-12.8%) than boys (21% $IC_{95\%}$ 17.4%-25.3%), the discrepancy by gender being statistically significant.

III-year course students reported the higher frequency (19.3%), I-year (12.3%) and V-year students (13.9%) the lowest.

Through a comparison between the two questions investigating on cannabis use, it was noticed that among those who had experimented the substance in their lifetime, the percentage of recent users progressively decreased as the class-level attended increased, frequency rates being 61.5% among I-year and 38.6% among V-year class students.

Reported using instances during the prior 30 days resulted mostly 1 or 2 (35.6% $IC_{95\%}$ 29.8%-41.4%), less frequently 3 to 9 (28.8% $IC_{95\%}$ 23.6%-34.0%), 10 to19 (12.3% $IC_{95\%}$ 8.8%-15.8%), 20 to 39 (3.8% $IC_{95\%}$ 1.9%-5.6%) or "40 or higher" (10.6% $IC_{95\%}$ 7.0%-14.3%). Coherently with the above assessments of average cannabis use instances, boys resulted more prone to use cannabis than girls (answer "40 instances of use or higher" reported by 12.4% of boys vs. 6.7% of girls; answer "20 to 39 instances" reported by 5.4% of boys vs. 1% of girls).

Relationship between body weight and cannabis use, distinctly analyzed by gender, were consistent with the findings of the section concerning tobacco smoking.

The percentages of girls experimenting cannabis for weight categories are quite similar (underweight 24.8%, average 22.8%, overweight/obese 22%); the same can be said of female recent smokers (underweight 10.7%, average 9.6%, overweight/obese 10%).

It is significantly higher, on the other hand, the frequency of average weight male respondents who reported experimenting or using cannabis during the previous 30 days (respectively 42.9% $IC_{95\%}$ 37%-48.9% and 24.6% $IC_{95\%}$ 19.3%-30%) than underweight (19.4% $IC_{95\%}$ 15.1%-23.6% and 12.3% $IC_{95\%}$ 9%-15.5%) or overweight/obese (25.6% $IC_{95\%}$ 17.2%-34% and 15.9% $IC_{95\%}$ 7.9%-23.8%).

Using frequency during the previous month did not show any significant difference by weight categories either. The average frequency of male respondents resulted 11.4 instances of cannabis use (specifically 12.9 instances in underweight, 11.4 in average weight and 9 in overweight/obese), of female respondents 8.2 instances (respectively 7.5, 8.2 and 11.8).

Sexuality

29.2% of the interviewed students ($IC_{95\%}$ 24.0%-34.6%) reported to have already had complete sexual intercourse, with practically no difference between boys (29.2% $IC_{95\%}$ 23.0%-35.4%) and girls (29.1% $IC_{95\%}$ 23.4%-34.9%).

The percentage of sexually involved respondents increased with class-level attended, starting from 14.7% ($IC_{95\%}$ 11.0%-18.5%) in I-year up to 48.8% ($IC_{95\%}$ 37.9%-59.6%) in V-year courses.

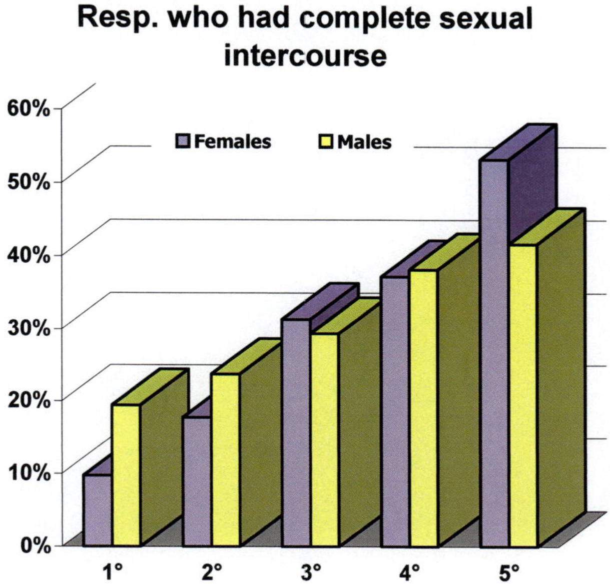

As shown by the graph beside, a higher number of I-year course boys than girls (19.4% vs. 9.7%) reported to have had sexual intercourse, while the opposite tendency was detected among V-year class students (41.7% vs 53.2%).

Among those V-year class sexually involved males, the first intercourse reported age resulted 13 years or younger in 8.9%, 14 years in 4.4%, 15 years in 15.6%, 16 years in 33.3% and 17 years or older in 37.8% of cases, with a resulting average age of 15.9 years. Of V-year class sexually involved females, 7.7% reported 14 years, 16.5% 15 years, 25.3% 16 years and 48.4% 17 years or older, with a first intercourse average age of 16.2 years.

By comparing information given by those who had had sexual intercourse and those who had not, no significant discrepancies were noticed for B.M.I. or intra- and extra-familial relationship assessments.

Among those students sexually involved, instead, it was noticed a significantly higher percentage of cigarette smokers, up to 84.1% ($IC_{95\%}$ 80.1%-87,8%) vs. 44.5% ($IC_{95\%}$ 41.1%-47.9%) of those not involved.

Likewise, 59.5% ($IC_{95\%}$ 54.3%-64.7%) of sexually involved respondents reported to have experimented cannabis use, significantly much more elevated than those not yet involved (17.1%, $IC_{95\%}$ 13.7%-20.5%).

Moreover, among cigarette-smokers or cannabis-users, the number of smoking days or cannabis-use instances during the previous month appeared higher in those respondents who had had sexual intercourse. The latter reported cigarette smoking on an average number of 15 days a month and cannabis use in two instances over the same period, while those not sexually involved reported an average number of 4 smoking days out of 30, and only one use of cannabis over three months. The last question on sexuality investigated the prevalence of sexual victimization on students. 4% ($IC_{95\%}$ 2.8%-5.2%), of respondents gave affirmative answer to the question "*Have you ever experienced any abuse or assault of sexual nature*?" girls being more numerous than boys (respectively 4.5%, $IC_{95\%}$ 3.0%-6.0% vs. 3.5%, $IC_{95\%}$ 2.0%-4.9%). No defined trend was noticed for class-levels.

Body Self-perception

Students were asked their current body weight and their ideal weight. Further to the comparison between the two data, it appeared evident that the population of students desired an average reduction of their body weight of 2.7 kg ($IC_{95\%}$ 2.1-3.2). As expected, girls expressed a higher level of body dissatisfaction than boys. Excess body weight among boys resulted lower than 1 kg ($IC_{95\%}$ 0.5-1.4), and more than 4 kg ($IC_{95\%}$ 3.9-4.6) among girls, the difference being statistically significant.

The graph shows that the perception of the excess weight is more evident among average B.M.I. subjects. Girls ranking in average weight B.M.I. category (BMI 18.5-25) expressed the desire to lose an average excess weight of nearly 5 kg, boys of 0.5 kg only.

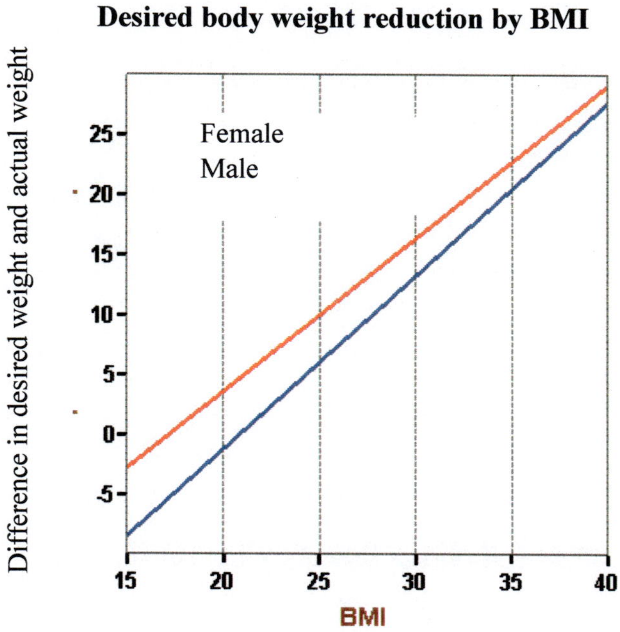

By locating on the regression lines the hypothetical ideal weight, the resulting B.M.I. would correspond to 20.8 for males and 17.2 for females, values ranking in underweight category. As a consequence, if B.M.I. were calculated on the basis of the desired weight, once boys and girls could get thinner to reach their ideal weight, 21% of males and 52% of females would be underweight, with respective average B.M.I. up to 21.2 and 19. These hypothetical B.M.I. values are quite close to the lowest normality standards (18.5), but are consistent with the reported data, desired average weight resulting 65 kg for boys (average height 1.75) and 51 kg for girls (average height 1.64).

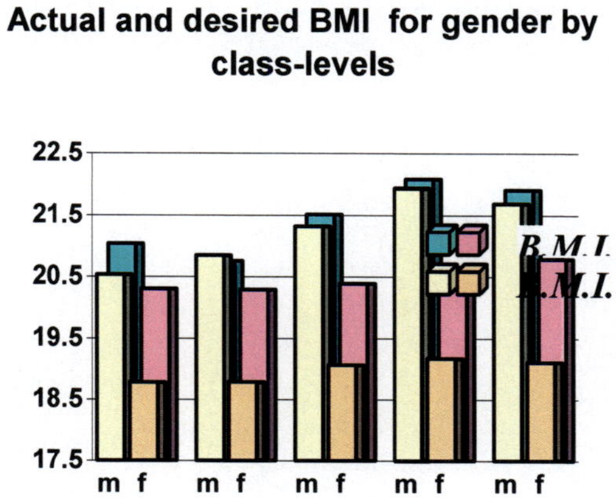

If examined by class-levels, reported data showed that the problem of overweight self-perception is common among I-year course students already with an evident gender connotation, and remains unchanged in girls up to their V-year course.

A further assessment of the participants' body self-perception was given by Collins schematic silhouettes, aimed at measuring the body dissatisfaction level through a morphologic comparison between current body size and desired body shape.

The answers obtained were consistent with the previous findings: on a 9-point scale, the average value of current body perception was 3.66, of ideal body shape 3.22, with an average discrepancy of 0.45. Difference resulted however 1 point in girls and nearly zeroed in boys. Given that Collins standard body shape for both males and females is represented by the fourth silhouette, the test evidenced that girls, although perceiving themselves thinner than average, still desired to lose weight and have a smaller body.

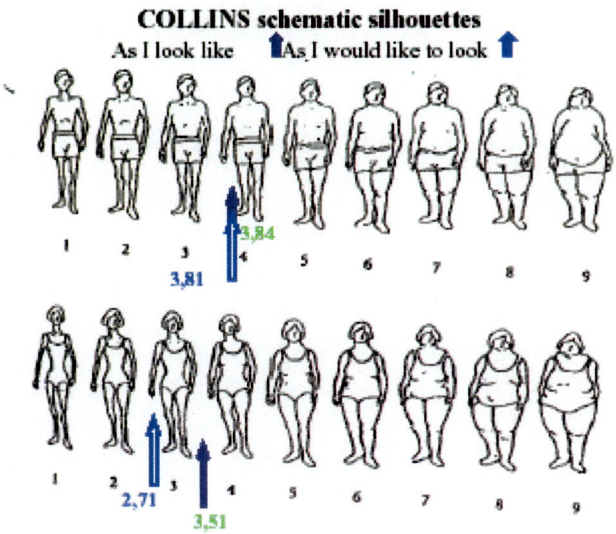

Actually, by associating Collins silhouettes with B.M.I. weight categories, it was noted that the third silhouette represented a sort of "borderline", since most underweight and a wide number of average weight respondents of both sex identified their body shape with it.

In conclusion, most girls indicated as their ideal body shape a silhouette between the second and the third (mean 2.7), thus desiring an ideal body shape ranking in underweight B.M.I. category.

EAT 26 Results

The Eating Attitude Test is a 26-item self-report questionnaire used to screen adolescents at risk for eating disorders such as anorexia and bulimia. If properly scored, answers can be employed to determine a score for classifying at-risk respondents. A cut-off score of 20 on the overall EAT scale was used in the present study to identify participants with eating disturbances as at-risk subjects for eating pathologies.

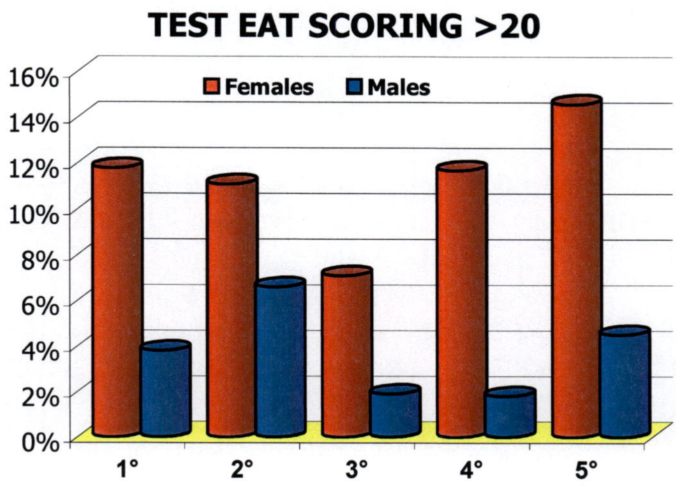

Of the sample students, 7.8% ($IC_{95\%}$ 6.0%-9.6%) scored at 20-point "at-risk" cutoff or above, with a significantly higher percentage of girls (11.3%, $IC_{95\%}$ 9.0%-13.5%) than boys (3,6% $IC_{95\%}$ 1.8%-5.5%).

No statistically significant discrepancies or univocal trends were noticed by class-level.

If examined for B.M.I., the percentage of adolescents scoring at 20 or above in the EAT did not put in evidence any significant difference either; the number of underweight and overweight respondents (respectively 9.1% and 8.8%) who scored "high" resulted slightly more elevated than average (7.2%), although.

Actually, average B.M.I. of students scoring at or above the 20-point cutoff in the EAT (21.3 $IC_{95\%}$ 20.7-21.9) resulted slightly heavier than those scoring under (20.9 $IC_{95\%}$ 20.6-21.2), with no significant discrepancy at all.

On the contrary, by analyzing for gender the number of desired kilograms (kg) to be lost by the EAT score, it resulted evident that girls who scored at 20 or above desired to lose a mean of 6.2 kg ($IC_{95\%}$ 4.9-7.5) vs. 4.0 kg ($IC_{95\%}$ 3,6-4,4) of girls scoring under, a statistically significant difference. Among boys, the discrepancy was even more impressive, respectively of 4.8 kg ($IC_{95\%}$ 3.7-5.9) vs. 0.9 kg ($IC_{95\%}$ 0.4-1.3).

Moreover, among EAT high-scoring students, it appeared significantly more elevated the percentage of those who have experimented cigarette-smoking (73.5% vs. 54.8%) and who have reported one family member on a slimming diet (71.3% vs. 59.7%). Both differences were consistent with findings by girls only.

Differences by other variables were not significant, such as tobacco smoking during the previous 30 days (49.3% of those scoring at 20 or above vs. 35.2% of those scoring under), cannabis using (36% vs. 28.9%), complete sexual involvement (38.2% vs. 28.%) and one or more reported sexual abuse (11% vs. 3.4%).

Self-esteem and Body Self-concept

Respondents were asked "*Are you happy with who you are?*" for a global assessment of their self-esteem.

44.6% of them ($IC_{95\%}$ 39.6%-49.6%) answered affirmatively, 49.2% ($IC_{95\%}$ 44.7%-53.7%) answered *"partially"*, while 5.8% ($IC_{95\%}$ 4.4%-7.2%) answered negatively.

Boys reported higher levels of self-esteem, since 58.2% of them ($IC_{95\%}$ 53,6%-62,8%) resulted fully satisfied with themselves, 38.3% ($IC_{95\%}$ 34.2%-42.5%) partially satisfied and 2,8% only ($IC_{95\%}$ 1.4%-4.4%) dissatisfied. percentages among girls were respectively 33% ($IC_{95\%}$ 29.8%-36.3%), 58.6% ($IC_{95\%}$ 54.9%-62.2%) and 8.3% ($IC_{95\%}$ 6.2%-10.3%). The reported self-esteem levels resulted slightly different for classes, but without any univocal trend.

The level of body self-satisfaction among respondents, obtained by Bracken Multidimensional Self-Concept Scale, averaged 94.4. A significant gender discrepancy was noted, since the average MSCS score resulted 97.7 ($IC_{95\%}$ 96.1-99.2) in boys vs. 88.7 ($IC_{95\%}$ 87.6-89.7) in girls.

Table 1. MSCS scoring table

Score	Self-esteem level
lower than 66	extremely negative
between 66 and 75	very negative
between 76 and 85	slightly negative
between 86 and 115	average
between 116 and 125	slightly positive
between 126 and 135	very positive
higher than 135	extremely positive

For a better understanding of the test results, reported bodily self-esteem values were classified according to a scoring table compiled by Bracken on the basis of data collected from a sample of American adolescents. (See table 1).

The bar graph below shows that 65% of the sample students reported an average level of body self-concept, 28% a lower than average and 5% a higher than average level; 2% did not give any answer on the matter.

Findings evidenced a neat gender difference in the students' bodily self-perception. 74% of male respondents reported in fact an average level of body self-esteem, 9% higher and 15% lower than average, vs. 58% only of average female respondents Moreover, the number of females reporting higher levels of body self-esteem resulted nearly zeroed, while it was increased up to 38% the percentage of those reporting lower.

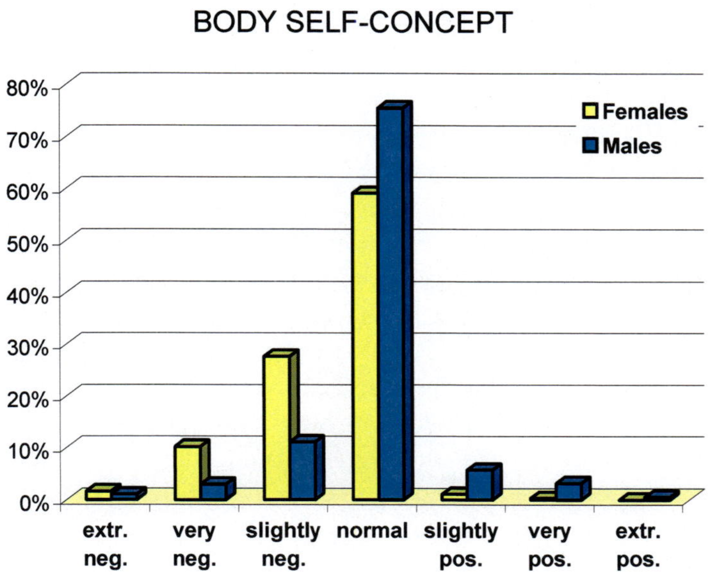

Among the latter, 70% scored slightly negative, 26% very negative and 4% extremely negative.

Among participants who scored in the EAT high range, the level of bodily self-concept resulted significantly lower (85.5 $IC_{95\%}$ 82.7-88.4) than among others (93.4 $IC_{95\%}$ 91.8-95.1), the lowest resulting among girls with a 7-point discrepancy vs. a limited 2.1-point difference among boys.

For different weight categories, average weight respondents showed a higher level of bodily self-esteem (94.3) than underweight (91.0) or overweight (85.6).

DISCUSSION

Findings from the current survey are consistent with the consideration that body image, as well as its full control, plays a fundamental role in puberty, since it becomes the expression of a deeper self-dissatisfaction along with the willingness to dominate both physical changes and emotional difficulties typical of that age. The need for identification with stereotypes along with the social urge to feel accepted by peers stimulate in both male and female adolescents a range of different behaviors aimed at controlling body changes, with the final purpose of gaining self-autonomy and personal appreciation.

Data regarding distorted self-image are worrisome, as serious warning signs of inner anxiety and intra-psychic tension capable of generating in adolescents useless and harmful self-constricted dietary restraints. Moreover, as evidenced in the section dedicated to cigarette-smoking and cannabis-use, a dissatisfying body self-perception appears most often associated with substance abuse, perhaps in the vane attempt to soothe pain and psychological distress deriving from it.

If considered within school context, the problem reveals a much wider extent than it might seem, thus becoming of crucial importance. Apparently normal girls in the opinion of teachers, parents and friends feel daily weight-related uneasiness and often in a concealed way, due to the secretive nature of eating disturbances, behave consequently. An extremely elevated percentage of girls are constantly keeping their weight under control, thus dispersing mental and physical power that could be otherwise employed. A further important consideration on the basis of the above analysis, a number of weight-concerned subjects are well aware of being average weight.

Besides to clear pathologies, in a lot of other common weight-controlling strategies such as sports practicing, the limit between health advantages and at-risk behavior isn't so neat. Sporting certainly needs a more detailed analysis than the current as regards both training frequency and intensity. It is well known, in fact, that subjects suffering from anorexia have an overtraining tendency, exercising much more than required to improve health or enhance performances. Subjects with clear eating pathologies generally take time away time to school activities and interrelationships and go on at any rate, in spite of their illness.

It is worth pointing out that 8% of the interviewed girls reported self-induced vomit after eating as a weight-controlling strategy, perhaps at school where it is easier not to be noted, with a mean of at least one girl for each class level. The datum points out that serious disordered eating symptoms that might easily develop into eating pathologies are more common and widespread than so far noticed.

Slimming tablets or remedies resulted frequently taken by adolescents to keep their weight under control; their consumption is noted to increase with the adolescents' age as the training frequency with the same purpose decreases. This weight-controlling strategy is probably deeply influenced by commercial ads, their number increased in the last few years along with the types of slimming products available on the market.

It can be finally observed that adolescents often follow more than one strategy to control or lose their weight, with higher probabilities that a disturbed attitude might in a close future develop into a true eating pathology.

The problem extent, as step by step defined by the current study findings, is certainly wide, although not directly evident, and needs proper attention both at school and within the family. Every education effort in preventing, recognizing and treating the problem of disturbed eating attitudes must be encouraged.

Specifically, school health educators and school health service personnel might be of great help in providing the students with the possibility of dealing with the matter at class, in encouraging adolescents to recognize their uneasiness and openly communicate it, to teach them a critical way of "reading" the mass media messages, to address them with basic nutrition information, to explain the risks of a restricted caloric intake as well as the benefits of a well-balanced diet meeting energy needs for growth and development.

School is certainly the privileged environment to recognize the problem for early diagnosis and easy resolution, but it is above all the most suited place to provide adolescents with sound foundations for their adult being and self-esteem building-up, so that they might become aware of their potentialities as well as of the pressure constantly exerted on them by the prevailing culture, demanding the sacrifice of physical and psychic well-being in the cause of a stereotyped "look".

REFERENCES

Attie I., Brooks-Gunn J., The development of eating regulation across the life span, in Cicchetti D., Cohen D.J., *Developmental psychopathology* (vol.2), New York, Wiley, 1995, 332-368.

Bracken BA MSCS- Multidimensional Self-Concpet Scale Austin, *PRO-ED,* 1992.

Carlat D.J., Carmargo C.A., Herzog D.B., Eating disorders in males: a report on 135 patients, *American Journal of Psychiatry,* 1997, 154 (8): 1127-1132.

CDC, Centers for Disease Control and Prevention, Body weight perceptions and selected weight-management goals and practices of high school students, United States 1990. *MMWR* 1/11/1991, 40 (43); 741, 747-50.

CDC, Centers for Disease Control and Prevention, Department of Health and Human Services, Guidelines for School Health Programs to Promote Lifelong Healthy Eating. MMWR 4/6/96, 45 (RR-9). Tradotto "Educazione alla salute" a cura di Pellai A. e Marzorati P., *Franco Angeli* 2001.

CDC, Centers for Disease Control and Prevention, Youth Risk Behaviour Surveillance, United States 1999. *MMWR* 9/6/2000, 49 (SS 05); 1-96.

Collins M.E., Body figure perceptions and preferences among preadolescent children, *International Journal of Eating Disorders,* 1991, 10(2): 199-208.

Cuzzolaro M., Disturbi del comportamento alimentare in adolescenza, in Pissacroia M. (ed.), Trattato di psicopatologia dell'adolescenza, *Piccin* 1997, 287-311.

Dounchis J.Z., Hayden H., Wifley D.E., Obesity, Eating Disorders, and Body Image in Ethnically Diverse Children and Adolescents, in Thomson J.H., Smolak L. (eds), *Body Image, Eating Disorders, and Obesity in Children and Adolescents: Theory, Assessment, Treatment, and Prevention,* Washington DC: American Psychological Association, 2000.

Fairburn C., Overcoming binge eating. A new scientifically based program, London, New York: Guilford Press, 1995

Field A.E., Cheung L., Wolf A.M., Herzog D.B., Gortmaker S.L., Colditz G.A., Exposure to the mass media and wieght concerns among girls, *Pediatrics*, 1999, 103(3): E36.

Garner, D.M., Olmsted, M.P., Bohr, Y. and Garfinkel, P.E. (1982). The eating attitudes test: Psychometric features and clinical correlates. *Psychological Medicine, 12*, 871-878.

Halvarsson K., Lunner K., Sjoden P.O., Assessment of eating behaviours and attitudes to eating, dieting and body image in pre-adolescent Swedish girls: one-year follow-up, *Acta Paediatrica,* 2000; 89: 996-1000.

Hill A.J., Oliver S., Rogers P.J., Eating in the adult world: the rise of dieting in childhood and adolescence, *British Journal of Clinical Psychology,* 1992; 31: 95-105.

Hoek H.W., Bartelds A.I.M., Bosveld J.J.F., Van der Graaf Y., Limpens V.E.L., Mainwald M., Spaaij C.J.K., Impact of urbanisation on detection rates of eating disorders, *American Journal of Psychiatry,* 1995; 152: 1272-78.

Hoek H.W., Review of epidemiological studies of eating disorders, *International Review of Psychiatry,* 1993; 5: 61-74.

Levine M.P., Smolak L., Hayden H., The relation of sociocultural factors to eating attitudes and behaviours, *Journal of Early Adolescence,* 1994; 14: 472-91.

Mallick M.J., Whipple T.W., Huerte E., Behavioral and Psychological traits of weight-conscious teenagers: a comparison of eating-disordered patients and high-and low-risk groups, *Adolescence,* 1987, 85(12): 157-68.

National Institute of Mental Health, *Eating Disorders,* 1994.

Nelson W.L., Hughes H.M., Katz B., Searight H.R., Anorexic eating attitudes and behaviors of male and female college students, *Adolescence,* 1999, 34(135): 621-33.

Neumark Sztainer D., Story M., Toporoff E., Himes J.H., Resnick M.D., Blum R.W., Covariation of eating behaviours with other health-related behaviours among adolescents, *Journal of Adolescence Health,* 1997, 20(6): 450-8.

Pellai A., Sancini S. Eating attitudes and Behaviours in a sample of teenage Italian Students in Pamela I. S (edited by) Focus on Eating Disorders Research., New York, *Nova Biomedical Books,* 2003: 57-68

Rodriguez A., Novalbos J.P., Martinez J.M., Ruiz M.A., Fernandez J.R., Jimenez D., Eating disorders and altered eating behaviours in adolescents of normal weight in a Spanish city, *Journal of Adolescence Health,* 2001, 28. 338-45.

Tomeo C.A., Field A.E., Berkey C.S., Colditz G.A., Fraiser A.L., Weight concerns, weight control behaviours, and smoking initiation, *Pediatrics,* 1999; 104 (4): 918-24.

Tufts University School of Nutrition Science and Policy. Statement on the link between nutrition and cognitive development in children. Boston: Center on Hunger, Poverty and Nutrition Policy, 1998.

Verri A.P., Verticale M.S., Vallero E., Bellone S., Nespoli L., La televisione e i disturbi del comportamento alimentare, *Minerva Pediatrica,* 1997, 49: 235-43.

Yager J., Andersen A., Devin M., Mitchell J., Powers P., Tates A., American Psychiatric Association practice guidelines for eating disorders, Am J Psychiatry, 1993, 150: 207-28.

Zuckermann D., Colby A., Ware N., Lazerson J., The prevalence of bulimia among college students, *American Journal of Public Health,* 1986, 76: 1135-7.

In: New Developments in Eating Disorders Research
Editor: Pamela I. Swain, pp. 123-133

ISBN 1-59454-542-1

Chapter 5

BULIMIC BEHAVIOR IN ADOLESCENT ATHLETES

Maria Lúcia Bosi*[*]*, and Fátima Palha de Oliveira
Federal University of Rio de Janeiro - Brasil

ABSTRACT

Introduction

Eating disorders are today an increasing problem among teenagers and young adults specially females. In the case of bulimia the estimated prevalence is between 3 and 5% and the average age it starts is around 20 years. It is known that its etiology is complex and depends on biological, psychological, and social factors as well as more specific characteristics as, for example, the practice of sports that in some cases leads to these disorders. The close relation between corporal image and performance makes the female athletes a group particularly vulnerable to problems of bulimic behavior due to the emphasis in weight control that they are frequently submitted. However the studies available are still insufficient to characterize the amplitude and distribution of the problem.

Objective

The aim of the present work is to evaluate bulimic components of behavior among adolescent female endurance runners.

Methods

From a total of 40 athletes affiliated with the Track and Field Federation of Rio de Janeiro, 17 female endurance runners (16 ± 1.8 years old) and 32 post-menarche, non-

[*] Rua Octávio de Rezende, 1060/600; Meireles – Fortaleza; Ceará – Brazil; email: malubosi@nesc.ufrj.br

athletic adolescents (15.0 ± 1.4 years) were examined. The athletes were training for at least 2 years (15 ± 7 hours/week).
The body composition was esteemed by the anthropometric method and percent body fat (%F) and Body Mass Index (BMI) were calculated. Bulimic behavioral components (frequency and severity) were evaluated using the Portuguese version of BITE (Bulimic Investigatory Test, Edinburgh), a self-rating scale.
A control group of 32 non-athlete volunteers in the same age group were also evaluated. Calculation of parameters, descriptive data statistics and comparison (Anova one way) of the variables were performed with the softwere Statistica for windows (5.1, 1998), with a significant level of $p \leq 0{,}05$.

Results and Discussion

Scores above the normal limit of 10 were recorded for 35.3% of the athletes (6 individuals), including 29.4% (4 individuals) that reported unusual behavioral components, suggestive of a tendency toward bulimia. One individual scored above 20, indicating a possible clinical case of bulimia. On the scale of severity of the symptoms, a score of 5 (considered moderately severe) was recorded in one case.

Conclusions

The athletes in this group are in risk to develop eating disorder, considering their preoccupation with weight control and the use of inadequate means of keeping within the desired range – including restrictive practices such as fasting along with intense physical activity.

Key words: Bulimia, Eating Disorders, Athletes.

INTRODUCTION

Eating disorders are defined as deviations in eating behavior that correspond essentially to anorexia nervosa and bulimia nervosa. Depending on the classification used, non-specific eating disorders may also be included, such as compulsive or binge eating[1].

A number of authors[2-5] have pointed out that anorexia and bulimia appear to be on the rise in recent years, affecting in particular young (adolescent) women, a population that is at the highest risk for these disorders. Both bulimic and anorexic behaviors are resistant to treatment, and anorexia nervosa can be lethal in 5% to 20% of the cases in which it occurs[3]. Individuals with these disorders have in common an excessive preoccupation with weight and diet, as well as self-dissatisfaction and a distorted self-image.

In addition, the disorder referred to as compulsive periodic eating – a syndrome included in Appendix B of the DSM-IV[6] – must be considered a serious problem in the population as a whole[7,8] since it is closely correlated with obesity, a condition that is widely recognized as a public health problem among adults in Brazil[9-13].

Bulimia nervosa, the primary focus in this study, is estimated to affect between 3% and 5% of adolescents and young adults in the female population[14].

This syndrome is characterized by repeated bouts of overeating and an excessive preoccupation with the control of body weight, leading the patient to adopt extreme measures so as to mitigate the 'fattening" effects of ingested food.

Individuals with bulimia consume large quantities of food, especially when subjected to stressful situations, and subsequently develop compensatory behaviors in order to avoid gaining weight and to alleviate the sense of guilt and shame evoked by uncontrolled eating[15].

Because of the "secret" character of this ritual, bulimia is difficult to diagnose, especially in its initial phase, and is therefore difficult to prevent as well as to treat at an early stage.

Although the prevalence of bulimia among female athletes in Brazil has not been adequately documented, reports from other countries indicate a higher frequency than among non-athletes, especially in certain sports[18] that emphasize leanness for performance and appearance the athletes. Thus, gymnasts, long-distance runners, dancers, and figure skaters are more prone to developing eating disorders and related problems than those who compete in nonweight-restricting sports such as volleyball or football[18]. The prevalence of eating disorders is higher among female athletes than nonathletes[19,20] and the estimates of eating disorders among athletes range between 15% to 62%[21]. Sundegot-Borge[21] observed a hight prevalence of eating disorders and the inadequate weight control was significantly higher among bodybuilders (34%) and those who practice sports tha require low body mass (27%). For technical (13%) or team sports (11%), the prevalence was lower, and the control present a prevalence of 7%.

The close relationship between corporal image and physical performance makes female athletes especially vulnerable to the development of bulimic behaviors and other eating disorders, in view of the emphasis given to weight control as part of the training regime. Rosen and Hough (apud Ruud, 1996) point to the influence exerted by coach' comments about athletes' weight and form as an important factor in promoting adoption of abnormal eating behaviors. In addition, the prescription of restrictive diets at an early age, especially in the absence of professional supervision, can lead to serious damage to an athlete's health and consequently to her athletic performance. The reduce plasma volume impaired thermoregulation and nutrient exchange, decreased glycogen availability and decrease buffer capacity in the blood are a possible explanation for reduced performance, especially after rapid weith reduction[22].

Inadequate nutrition can cause in female athletes, whose energy requirements are different from those of non-athletic women, problems such as amenorrhea, loss of bone density, anemia, and behavioral anomalies such as bulimia and/or anorexia. Inadequate eating habits can give rise to mineral depletion and osteoporosis, making bones more fragile. Osteoporosis is one component of the so-called *women athletes' triad* (amenorrhea, eating disorder, and osteoporosis) that results from dietary intake that is unequal to the athlete's daily energy demand. The literature indicates that 90% of those who suffer from osteoporosis are women[23], a statistic that coincides with the distribution of bulimia and other eating disorders.

Eating disorders constitute not only a significant clinical picture among individuals, but also an increasingly troublesome question of public health[1]. Statistics for Latin America show that in the last 10 years there has been a nearly exponential increase in eating disorders, leading to coefficients of prevalence and incidence greater than those in the United States.

In Brazil, it has been estimated that about 19% of female students exhibit symptoms of bulimia[26] – that is, behavior that can be taken to indicate that a full-blown clinical manifestation of bulimia nervosa is imminent. In addition, in one of the few population studies available, a survey in Pelotas (in the state of Rio Grande do Sul) showed a prevalence of 13.8% in the practice of anomalous eating behaviors, indicating subclinical development of the classical syndromes, while 30.2% exhibited behavior characteristic of individuals at risk and 11.3% clearly showed abnormal eating behavior that could be classified among the non-specific eating disorders[3].

Nevertheless, there are clearly recognizable precursor stages of these disorders, and they are much more prevalent than the fully developed clinical disorders[1]. From the point of view of prevention, it is essential to be able to recognize these early signs. This implies cooperative interaction between the investigative teams and family members.

Among the identified subclinical syndromes are the use of restrictive diets, the practice of self-induced vomiting, and the use of laxatives, diuretics and/or anorexogenic drugs, associated with strenuous physical activity. Any of these signs can serve as a warning to take action against further development of the clinical disorders.

These considerations define a context in which research on this topic can be expected to provide feedback that will be useful to the services, the teaching and the training of future investigators on this topic. The objective of the present study is to help define the dimensions of the problem in one of its specific manifestations – bulimia and its behavioral precursors – within a population that is at risk: female adolescent athletes in training for a specific event. We present it as a first step in an already expanding effort to include other sports and population groups, in the expectation of contributing to the definition and comprehension of a complex theme that involves bio-psychic, epidemiologic, anthropologic, sociologic economic and historical aspects[27-32] – and therefore one that requires an interdisciplinary approach capable of integrating these different facets.

Material and Method

A transverse study design was employed, using subjects from a population that is considered to be at greatest risk for the development of eating disorders: adolescent females, especially athletes[33, 34].

The sample consisted of 17 adolescents (15.9 ± 1.8 years) chosen at random from a population of 40 adolescent athletes who were registered at the time in the *Track and Field Federation of Rio de Janeiro*. The athletes were training for at least 2 years (15 ± 7 hours/week). Criteria for including these individuals in the study were as follows:

- All 17 athletes had been engaged in a systematic training program under supervision of a professional trainer, in different athletic clubs in Rio de Janeiro, for at least two years, on an average of 15 hours per week.
- All were training for endurance events of 800 m or more.

- All of the individuals chosen had been classified above fifth place in a recent juvenile competition in the state of Rio de Janeiro.

Also evaluated was a control group of volunteers consisting of 32 post-menarche, non-athletic adolescents aged 15.0 ± 1.4 years.

In order to evaluate the presence and intensity of bulimic behaviors, the Bulimic Investigatory Test of Edinburgh (BITE)[26, 35] was used. This is a self-administered questionnaire consisting of 33 questions, with two subscales – one related to the symptoms and one to the severity of the symptoms. The scale for symptoms is subdivided into High (20 points or more), Medium (10 to 19 points) and Low (below 10 points). The scale for severity of symptoms is subdivided into Light (score below 5), Moderate (5 to 9) and Severe (greater than 10), and is used in those cases where the score in the first scale (symptoms) is greater than 10. In the present study, the Portuguese version was used[26]. Results were tabulated according to frequency (absolute and relative values).

To obtain a profile of the athletes' body composition he follow anthropometrical measurements were taken:

Skinfolds thikness (mm:) The mean of three skinfold measurements were registraded for the following points: triceps, medium axilla, subscapula, suprailiac, abdomen, biceps, thigh, and leg, using a Cescorf compass with a precision of 0.1 mm.

Body weight (kg, precision of 50 g) and height (m, precision of 1 mm) — in lightbclothing and without shoes — were measured using calibrates scales.

From the measures fond, the parameters were calculated:

The percentage of body fat (%F)[36] was obtained from body density estimated according to the equation developed by Withers et al. (1987)[37] specifically for female athletes. The percentage of body fat in the control group was calculated as described by Jackson et al.(1980)[38].

The Body Mass Index was calculated as the ratio of weight (kg) to h eight (m^2) (BMI= weight / Heigth^2)[39].

The anthropometric readings are reported as average and standard deviation for the group. Calculation of parameters, descriptive data statistics and comparison (t Student) of the variables were performed with the softwere "Statistica for windows" (6.0, 2001). The statistical significance level adopted in these analyses was 5% ($p \leq 0.05$).

This study was carried out with the written consent of the participants, who were also informed about the planned use of the data obtained.

Results and Discussion

The characteristics of the subjects' body composition are shown in Table 1.

Table 1. Anthropometric Characteristics

Group	Age (years)	Weight (Kg)	Height (cm)	Body fat (%)	BMI (Kg/m^2)
Athletes (17)	15.9 ± 1.8	49.3 ± 5.2	161.9 ± 5.6	22.0 4.2	18.8 ± 1.9
Controls (32)	15.0 ± 1.4	58.0 ± 11.0	162.5 ± 6.5	26.5 ± 8.1	22.0 ± 4.0
T Student (p)		0.004*		0.044*	0.004*

BMI= Body Mass Index; * signifficant difference $p \leq 0{,}05$.

Athletes had weight, body fat and body mass index significantly lower than the control group, but there are no significant difference for age and height.

This result is to be expected for endurance runners, whose training is directed toward increasing their aerobic resistance. One of the adaptive responses to this training is a greater reliance on lipids as a source of energy. This adaptation has a pronounced impact on body composition of female athletes who run long distances, and they tend to have less body fat than athletes in other sports[23].

Studies have found that , even with body mass within normal populations standarts,it is significant the numbers of yong women unhappy with their weight and that do inappropriate practices to reduces body mass[24]. The young athletes had a aditional pressure concern body size and shape by the social influence for thinness, anxiety about athletic performance and negative self-appraisal of athletic achievement[25].

Our investigation confirm this possibility when observed that in spite of the normal ranges[23] encountered for body mass, body fat and body mass index among the athletes, the results of the BITE questionnaire indicated the presence of pre-bulimic behaviors and even, in one case, a possibility of bulimia.

RESULTS OF THE BITE

Analysis of the athletes' answers to the BITE (Table 2) indicated that 35.3% (n=6) had scores above 10, the limit of the normal range. Of this percentage, 29.4% responded with an anomalous pattern (scores of 10 – 19), indicating behavior suggestive of a risk of bulimia. A value above 19 identified one individual (5.9% of the total) as a strong possibility of having fully developed bulimia. In the control group, a smaller proportion (21.8%) had scores in the 10 to 19 range, i.e. above the normal limit. The result is in accord of Sundegot-Borgen[21] thatobserved a higth prevalence of eating disorders in athletes (18%) than in no-athletes (5%).

On the scale for severity one athlete had score greater than 10 (severe) and the others (n=5) achieved scores below 5 (light).

Table 2. Result of the BITE

	ATHLETES	CONTROL
Synptom Scale		
HIGH (> 20 points)	**5,9** %	0%
MÉDIUM (10 – 19 points)	29,4 %	21,8%
LOW (or within normal range) (below 10 points)	64,7 %	78,2%
Severity Scale Applied when changes in the synptom scale were found		
SEVERE (greater than 10)	**16,6** %	0%
MODERATE (5 to 9 points): clinically signifficant	0%	9,4 %
LIGHT (score below 5 points): clinically **non** signifficant	83,3 %	87,5%

Table 3 presents some of BITE questions were one can see the concern with weigth control and practice of dietary restrictions, particulary fasting, which are conflicting with physical activities.

The result of revealed the abnormal eating behaviors in athlete and control groups, that reflect a possible subclinical eating disorder syndromes[40]. The subclinical cases have a higth prevalence among athletes[41] and the early identification and intervention in these groups may prevent development of the eating disorder[42].

Table 3. Among The Findings, a Number of Replies Suggested Bulimic Behavior

Behavioral characteristic	Prevalence in athletes	Prevalence in controls
1 – Fear (horror) of getting fat; eating large quantities of food very rapidly	58.8%	46.8%
2 – Fasting for an entire day	52.9%	18.7%
3 – Accustomed to eating when not observed	52.9%	31.2%
4 – Worried about lack of control over eating	47.1%	53.1%
5 – Feeling of guilt when eating	41.2%	53.1%
6 – Obsessive thoughts about food	29.4%	31.2%

Questions from BITE, portraing dietary practice and emitional attiitude

Less frequently, other types of behavior were also mentioned by the athletes, including a tendency to eat more when anxious (17.6%); fluctuations in weight (23.5%); and feelings of shame about food and one's own eating habits (17.6%).

Oliveira *et al.* [43] show in athletes of differents sports modalities the presence of worriment about body weigh, combined with a mild distortion of body image and also the practice of dietary restriction. The authors alerted to such parcial eating disorder syndromes associed to systematic and exhaustible physical exercise is a risk factors of eating disorders.

From the data of these study, it is apparent that the athletic individuals in this group are in risk to develop bulimia, especially considering their preoccupation with weight control and the use of inadequate means of keeping within the desired range – including restrictive practices such as fasting along with intense physical activity (table 2).

In addition to the risk of these young athletes' developing eating disorders, it is disturbing to find these signs of abnormal eating behavior in a group that is undergoing rapid physical development and is under training. A systematic training program generates a daily energy demand that requires adequate attention to nutrition. A long-term low energyy intake may impede the athlete from reaching her full potential and, moreover, lead to a negative consequences, such as inadequate carbohydrate, protein, vitamin and mineral intake, increased risk of injury and increased risk of illness [44].

At the other extreme, the loss of control over food intake is an element that stands out, along with feelings associated with these practices – guilt, shame, fear, anxiety – a whole gamut of emotions that are characteristic of bulimia and represent a psychic suffering that should not be neglected, not only because of the emotional vulnerability of this age group but also because of the pressure associated with performing well in a highly competitive milieu. It is relevant to consider the possibly synergistic effects of these emotional factors in contributing to the development of eating disorders as well as to the difficulty in managing them.

Conclusion

As we have tried to show, eating disorders, including bulimia, represent a disturbing problem that appears to be increasing, especially among adolescent females and young women. With regard to female athletes, nutritional planning should focus on bulimia as a possible complication of the close relationship between diet and training for sports, considering the daily demands with regard to weight and form, as well as the stress of competition.

In fact, it is no surprise that in the self-administered test included in the present report there appear multiple behavioral signs pointing toward individuals at risk of developing bulimia, or even with clinically apparent bulimia, still in a comparatively mild form.

Professionals who deal with this segment of the population – MD's, physical education teachers, psychologists and nutritionists, among other specialists – need to be well informed and trained to identify and manage bulimia. Detecting signs of this disorder and intervening at an early stage are essential in order to preserve not only an athlete's performance but also her health, recognizing that a healthy diet and mental stability are fundamental to physical activity.

In the future, further studies should be aimed at evaluating the dimensions of the problem in this and other groups at risk, as well as broadening the field of inquiry to include a qualitative description of the genesis of these behaviors -- still an engima in many aspects.

Acknowledgment

We thank Professor Marta Sorenson for revision of the article and the staff of the LABOFISE. This study was parcially funded by FAPERJ AND FUJB.

A preliminary version of this study were publicated as short comunication in Brasilian Journal of Psychiatry, 2004, 26(1):32-34.

REFERENCES

[1] American Psychiatric Association. *Diagnostic and Statistical Manual of Mental Disorders*, 4th Ed. Washington: American Psychiatric Association; 1994.

[2] Russell, G. Bulimia Nervosa: an ominous variant of anorexia nervosa. *Psychol. Medicine*, 1979, 9:429-48.

[3] Nunes, MAA. Prevalência de Comportamentos Alimentares Anormais e Práticas Inadequadas de Controle de Peso em Mulheres de 12 a 21 anos em Porto Alegre. PortoAlegre, 1997. Dissertação (mestrado). Universidade Federal de Pelotas.

[4] Nunes, MAA . Influência da Percepção do peso e do índice de massa corporal nos comportamentos alimentares anormais. *Revista Brasileira de Psiquiatria,* 2001 23:21-7.

[5] ANDRADE, AC. Para além dos sintomas: a trilogia do desamparo no vivido de mulheres com transtornos do comportamento alimentar. Dissertação de Mestrado/Universidade Federal do Ceará. Mestrado em saúde Pública/Departamento de saúde Comunitária. 2000.

[6] Manual diagnóstico e estatístico de transtornos mentais DSM-IV. Tradução de Dayse Batista. Porto Alegre: Artes Médicas; 1995.

[7] Appolinário, JC. transtorno do comer compulsivo. In: Abuchaim, ALG, Appolinário, JC; Nunes, MAA; Coutinho, W; *et al.*, editores. Transtornos Alimentares e Obesidade. Porto Alegre: Artes Médicas; 1998; 40-46

[8] Appolinário, JC. Transtorno da compulsão alimentar periódica e transtorno obssessivo-compulsivo: partes de um mesmo espectro? *Revista Brasileira de Psiquiatria*, 2001 23:38-40.

[9] Hollis, JM. Une affaire de famille. Montreal: Éditions Sciences et Culture; 1992.

[10] Hoek, H. The Distribution of eating disorders. In: Brownell, KD; Fairburn, CG, editores. Eating Disorders and Obesity. A Comprehensive Handbook. New York: The *Guilford Press;*1995.

[11] Gigante, DP. Prevalência de obesidade em adultos e seus fatores de risco. *Revista de Saúde Pública*, 1997 31:236-46.

[12] Sichieri, R. Epidemiologia da obesidade. Rio de Janeiro: *Editora UERJ;* 1998.

[13] Jimenéz, R. La percepción de la función familiar y el desarrollo psicosexual en el adolescente obeso. *Revista de Investigación Clinica*, 1992 44:525-30.

[14] Morandé, G; Carrera, M. Anorexias nerviosas y bulimias. Una epidemia actual en adolescentes? Algunos aspectos en discussion. *Revista de Psiquiatria do Chile*, 1988, (1):19-28.

[15] Castilla, D; Bastin, C. La boulimie: mieux se connaître pour en guérir. Paris: Éd. Robert Laffont; 1998.

[16] Maine, M. Anorexie, boulimie, pourquoi? Paris, Barretle-bas: Le souffle d'or, 1997.

[17] Paleo, MC. Anorexia y bulimia nerviosa – comunicacion humana y sistemas humanos. Centro Médico de Mar del Plata, 7, p. 16-19, 1994. Mimeo.

[18] Ruud, JS. Nutrition and the female athlete. New York: *CRC Press;* 1996.

[19] Sundgot-Borgen, J. Eating disorders in female athletes. *Sports Med*icine 1994 17:176-88.

[20] Yeager, KK; Agostini, R; Nattiv, A; Drinkwater, B. The female athlete triad – disordered eating, amenorrhea and osteoporosis. *Medicine andScience in Sports and Exercise,* 1993 25:775-7.

[21] Sundgot-Borgen, J. Prevalence of eating disorders in elite female athletes. *International Journal of Sport and Nutrition,* 1993 3:29-34.

[22] Fogelholm, M. Effects of the body weight reduction on sports performance. *Sports Medicine,* 1994 4:249-67.

[23] Mcardle, WD; Katch, FI; Katch, VL. Essencials of exercise physiology. second edition. Philadelphia: *Lippincott Williams and Wilkins;* 2000.

[24] King, MA. Eating disorders in a general practice population: prevalence, characteristics and follow-up at 12 to 18 months. *Physichol Mededicine,* 1989 14:211-18.

[25] Williamson, DA; Netemeyer, RG; Jackman, LP; Anderson, DA; Funsch, CL; Rabalais, JY. Structural equation modeling of risk factors for the development of eating disorder symptoms in female athletes. *International Journal of Eating Disorders,* 1995 17:387-93.

[26] Cordás, TA; Hochgraf, PB. O BITE: Instrumento para avaliação da bulimia nervosa. Versão para o português. *Jornal Brasileiro de Psiquiatria*, 1993 42:141-4.

[27] Bourdieu, P. La domination masculine. Paris: Seuil; 1998.

[28] Leloup, JY. O corpo e seus símbolos: uma antropologia essencial. 3ª edição Petrópolis: Vozes, 1998.

[29] Guillemot, A; Laxenaire, M. Anorexie mentale et boulimie – le poids de la culture. 2e édicion. Paris: *Masson;* 1997.

[30] Breilh, J. El Genero entrefuegos: inequidad y esperanza. Quito: *CEAS;* 1996.

[31] Pasini, W. Nourriture & amour. Paris: *Payot;* 1994.

[32] Balasc, C. Désir de rien. Paris: *Aubier;* 1990.

[33] Kaplan, HI; Sadock, BJ; Grebb, JA. Compêndio de psiquiatria. 7ª edição. Porto Alegre: *Artes Médicas;* 1997.

[34] Nunes, MAA; Ramos, DC. Anorexia nervosa: classificação diagnóstica e quadro clínico. In: Nunes, MAA; Coutinho, W; *et al.* Transtornos alimentares e obesidade. Porto Alegre: *Artes Médicas;* 1998; 21-30.

[35] Henderson, M; Freeman, CPL. A self-rating scale for bulimia. The BITE. *British Journal of Psychiatry,* 1987 50:18-24.

[36] Siri, WE. Gross composition of the body In: Lawrence, J; Tobias, CA. Advanced in biological and medical physics. New York: *Academic Press;* 1956.

[37] Withers, RT; Whittingham, NO; Norton, KL; Laforgia, J; Ellis, MW; Crockett, A. Relative body fat and anthropometric prediction of body density of female athletes. *European Journal of Applied Physiology*, 1987 56:169-80.

[38] Jackson, AS; Pollock, ML; Ward, A . Generalized equation for predicting body density of women. *Medicine and Science in Sports and Exercise,* 1980 12:175- 82.

[39] Quetelet, A. Antropométrie ou mesure dês différentes facultes de l'homme. Bruxelles: C.Muquardt; 1870.

[40] Nunes, MAA. Prevalência de comportamentos alimentares anormais e práticas inadequadas de controle de peso em mulheres de 12 a 21 anos em Porto Alegre. Porto Alegre [Dissertação de mestrado]. Porto Alegre (RS): Universidade Federal de Pelotas; 1997b.

[41] Grange, D L; Tibbs J, Noakes, T. Implication of a diagnosis of anorexia nervosa in a ballet school. *International Journal of eating disorders,* 1994 4:369-76.

[42] Bassoe, HH. Anorexia/Blimia nervosa: the development of anorexia nervosa and of mental symptom. Tratament and the outcome of the disease Acta *Psychiatrica Scandinavica,* 1990 82:7-13.

[43] Oliveira, FP; Bosi, MLM; Vigário, PS; Vieira, RS. Eating behavior and body image in athletes. *Revista Brasileira de Medicina do Esporte (Brasilian Journal of Sport Medicine),* 2004 9:1-8.

[44] Grandjean, AC; Ruud, JS; Reimers, KJ. Nutrition. In: Women in sport. Drinkwater, BL, editor. Australia: *Blackwell Science;* 2000; 120-31.

In: New Developments in Eating Disorders Research
Editor: Pamela I. Swain, pp. 135-147
ISBN 1-59454-542-1

Chapter 6

ANOREXIA OF AGING

Claudia Savina, Lorenzo M. Donini [*] ***and Carlo Cannella***
Istituto di Scienza dell'Alimentazione – Università di Roma "La Sapienza" (Italy)
Casa di Cura Villa delle Querce – Nemi (Rome – Italy)

ABSTRACT

Independence and self–esteem are strongly related to physical and mental function which in turn are largely determined by nutritional status and physical activity. Food is an integral part of our well-being and quality of life. It extends beyond simply satisfying hunger and providing nourishment. Specific foods have a symbolic meaning and particular food habits are influenced by religious, cultural, social and emotional experience.

Elderly people showing interest towards food, nourishment and keeping a good appetite, in most cases still are vital human beings full of interests and quite independent. Behavioural characteristics before mentioned describe the picture of the elderly aging with "a good health", known in medical literature as *Healthy Aging*.

Aging is normally associated with body weight gain in individuals who fail to decrease food intake in proportion to the age-related decline in energy expenditure. However, decreases in body weight are common in elderly individuals (over 70 years of age) who do not eat enough to meet energy demands.

Age related reduction in energy intake is largely a physiologic effect of healthy aging and reveals itself with a loss of eating need and pleasure. This reduction intake may predispose to the harmful anorexic effect of psychological, social and physical problems that become increasingly frequent with aging. The physiological anorexia of aging increases the propensity for developing pathological anorexia and weight loss when an older person falls ill with either a medical or a psychological illness [1]. A 10% loss of body weight over 10 years is consistently associated with increased mortality and functional disability [2].

Weight loss is one of the pathognomonic signs of malnutrition (whether energetic or protein-energy) which may negatively influence the clinical outcome of rehabilitation

* Università di Roma "La Sapienza"; Istituto di Scienza dell'Alimentazione; Ple Aldo Moro, 5 – 00185 Roma (Italia); e-mail: lorenzomaria.donini@uniroma1.it; tel.: +39.06.4969.0216; fax: +39.06.4991.0699

programmes, confirming that a convenient nutritional status helps the achievement of such a condition and it is absolutely essential when recovering from acute illnesses [3].
A further demonstration of the importance of nutritional status has been pointed out by several studies showing that, after sixties of age, weight loss is associated to a decline in muscle mass and consequently in muscle strength. The picture just mentioned is well-known as *sarcopenia,* which plays a main role in the beginning of: frailty, functional and metabolic impairments, physical disabilities that expose the elderly to an increased risk of falls and protein-energy malnutrition. The obese elderly also affected by protein malnutrition configure the so called *fat frail* who obtains worse outcomes in rehabilitation programmes [4].

Epidemiology of Anorexia of Aging in the Elderly

From an epidemiological point of view, nutritional surveys showed a low to moderate prevalence of frank nutrient deficiencies in free living elderly groups. The SENECA-EURONUT study, enrolling cognitively intact and free living elderly from twelve European nations, found that dietary intakes were often below the recommended levels established for younger adults but this was not reflected in the indicators of nutritional status [5]. The National Health and Nutrition Examination Survey has clearly shown a linear decline in food intake from 20 to 80 years in both men and women even if this change could be caused by a greater incidence of pathological causes in elderly people [6]. In another research the authors found that food intake was lower in older persons than in younger: their data showed that the major decrease was due to a decrease in fat (55%) rather than in carbohydrate (40%) [7]. According to different record of cases and nutritional parameters, data are worst in institutionalised older persons whose rates of protein energy malnutrition range from 30 to 60% [8-10].

Definition of Anorexia of Aging

Age-related anorexia may be defined as an unintentional decline in food intake, and, as a result, of body weight, that begins near the end of life; it represents a sign of a failure to preserve steady state levels of body weight and energy stores. The regulation of food ingestion is an extremely complex process with multiple fail-safe mechanisms able to preserve that the feeding drive remains intact. Food intake can be considered to be under the regulation of a central feeding drive influenced by a peripheral satiation system and receiving further feedback signals from fat cells, absorbed nutrients and circulating hormones. Animal and human studies suggest that alterations at multiple levels of this system occur with aging, resulting in the physiologic anorexia of aging.

Absence of obvious pathology associated distinguishes, according to some authors, the *physiological anorexia of aging* (due to appetite, taste and olfactory acuity, dental status, physical activity, ...) from *pathological anorexia*, a phenomenon characterised by increased resting energy expenditure, elevated cytokines and muscle and fat wasting related to disease (acute and chronic diseases, disability, ...). It is however difficult to verify the real absence of underlying disease and this may influence the prevalence, in different settings, of anorexia of aging [2].

A third form of anorexia in elderly is related to *environment* (age, sex, income, cooking facilities, retirement/leisure time, education, distance to food store, availability of transportation, social activity, self-esteem, symbolism of food, mental awareness, …) and *iatrogenic conditions* (use of drugs, …).

1. Physiological Anorexia of Aging

Energy Balance in the Elderly

In the elderly we have a disregulation of energy balance and food intake control. After an overnight fast, older tend to be less hungry than younger persons and after a standard meal older persons report a greater degree of satiation than younger.

Older individuals are also less capable of returning to their previous weight after a perturbation of their food intake than younger are and even after refeeding, older persons return to a lower weight than previously. Young people significantly increase their energy intake following underfeeding while elderly do not and their energy needs remain somewhat depressed relative to their previous weight maintenance requirements.

Healthy older persons ingest less energy than younger men do over a single meal. However, when given a preload (e.g. yoghurt) elderly fail to adequately regulate their food intake, overeating 10-30%, whereas younger had a more precise regulation of their food intake.

These findings are consistent with the suggestion that a lack of the normal ability to regulate energy intake contributes to impaired energy regulation in old age. However, rather than a loss of the ability to regulate energy intake, this being an independent factor, weight loss may be caused in the elderly by the combination of a reduction in the ability to regulate food intake and other adverse events [11-13].

Altered Regulation of Food Intake Control

In the elderly, more rapidly acting or more potent inhibitory satiety signals may contribute to the altered regulation of satiation system. The passage of nutrients into the small intestine and their absorption contribute to stimulate the release of hormones. These include cholecystokinin (CCK), glucagon-like peptide-1, glucose-dependent insulinotropic peptide, insulin and amylin, all of them with proven or putative satiating effects. CCK is probably the most important satiating hormone and is thought to be responsible of 20% of the signals responsible for meal termination. It causes simultaneous contraction of the gallbladder and relaxation of the sphincter of Oddi, thus releasing bile into the duodenum, and stimulates pancreatic enzyme secretion. CCK acts together, in a synergic way, with other hormones or neurotransmitters as serotonin, corticotrophin releasing factors, histamine, glucagon and somatostatin. CCK also activates vagal afferent fibres that terminate in the brainstem. The effects of CCK are mediated by an increase in the contractile activity of the pylorus, which slows gastric emptying and increases the sensitivity to gastric relaxation. Animal studies have shown greater levels and an increased satiating effect of CCK in older compared with younger animals. Many authors found that elderly patients with idiopathic senile anorexia had increased plasma concentrations of CCK compared with age-matched controls.

The regulation of the satiation system is under the control of the adaptive relaxation of the stomach fundus: dilatation allows it to act as a reservoir for food before passing along the antrum. In fact gastrointestinal sensory signals induced by relaxation of food contribute to initial sensations of fullness during a meal. With aging, food tends to pass more rapidly from the fundus into the antrum and then to remain longer there, leading to earlier and greater degree of antral relaxation. The degree of antral relaxation is directly proportional to the development of satiation after ingestion of a meal. Most studies suggest that the rate of gastric emptying slows in older compared with younger persons. For this reason, the elderly frequently complain of increased fullness and early satiation during a meal.

The decrease of the adaptive relaxation of the fundus stomach in the elderly is associated with the reduction of the number of neurons in the myenteric plexus and with the reduction of nitric oxide (NO), a short-lived gas produced by the endothelial and neuronal cells and inducible nitric oxide synthase. NO is a transducer of the effects of a number of hormones in the control of feeding like leptin and NPY. NO delays gastric emptying by altering pyloric tone and it seems to play an important role for both receptive and adaptive relaxation of the fundus of the stomach to food. Even if the condition may not be the same in humans, in studies with older animals there is a decrease in messenger RNA for NO-synthase with aging [14-18].

Decline in food intake in the elderly may be due to the altered regulation of peripheral feedback signals as those coming from fat cells. Leptin is produced by fat cells and is responsible for appetite modulation: the effect of elevated leptin levels, especially in men, may cause anorexia. One mechanism whereby leptin inhibits food intake and stimulates energy expenditure involves altered transcription of hypothalamic neuropeptides. Leptin decreases the expression of orexigenic peptides (NPY, agouti-related peptide, melanin-concentrating hormone) and increases mRNA levels of anorexic peptides (propiomelanocortin, cocaine and amphetamine-related transcript). Studies in humans have demonstrated that, after adjustment for body fat, a significant inverse relationship between serum leptin and age exists. However leptin concentrations are not dramatically altered with aging and seem to be more related to body fat than aging per se leaving open the possibility that disrupted leptin signals, as opposed to increased leptin levels, occurs in age-related energy imbalance such as anorexia.

Peripheral feedback signals may come from the rate of peripheral nutrient utilisation and the plasma nutrient concentrations that influence circulating messages relating to overall fuel status. Elderly have difficulty in maintaining their internal state and this can be due to changes in regulatory systems as it happens for example for salt and water homeostasis.

Aging is associated with a decline in homeostatic capabilities so that the elderly is less sensitive to both internal and environmental changes. Circulating glucose is thought to be one of the signals of hunger in younger adults and detection of hypoglycemia may be impaired in older individuals. With aging, even if glucose impairment is not quantitatively important, glucose may still be an important mediator of changes in the regulation of food intake.

Also circulating hormones may influence food intake. Insulin as been suggested to act as a satiety agent by affecting the expression of neuropeptides such as NPY and insulin concentrations increase with aging as a result of increased insulin resistance. At the moment, there are no data supporting the role of insulin in the development of the anorexia of aging.

Nevertheless animal studies have reported that hyperglycemia and or hyperinsulinemia may be causes of the greater satiating effects of glucose in older subjects.

Sex hormones are well recognised to regulate appetite: testosterone increases food intake Thus the reduction of testosterone levels in older males may play a role in the reduction of food intake (increasing leptin levels) and in the loss of muscle mass (sarcopenia) [1, 2, 15, 19, 20].

The opioid feeding drive, mediated in particular by dinorphin (but also by beta-endorphins and enkefalines), plays an important role in driving fat intake in animals and humans, in determining the palatability of food and in initiating and terminating eating. A decrease in concentrations of endogenous opioid peptides and in their effectiveness, related to the decrease in opioid receptors, occurs with aging: elderly patients with idiopathic senile anorexia seem to have lower levels of cerebrospinal fluid and plasma β-endorphin.

Central feeding drive may be influenced also by neuropetide Y (NPY) that is the most potent orexigenic agent. The effects of NPY are predominantly on food rich in carbohydrate. NPY is less effective in increasing food intake in older than in younger animals and its concentrations decline with aging especially in Alzheimer's dementia patients.

In elderly patients with idiopathic senile anorexia some authors found an increased ratio of tryptophan, a serotonin precursor, to large neutral amino acids in the cerebrospinal fluid. Elevated brain serotonin level causes satiety.

The issue concerning the production of interleukin with anorexic action in geriatric age is disputable (IL6, TNFα). Researches, up to now, did not give any univocal result; some of them showed an increased production of IL6 also without any chronic or acute illness in course, while others did not reach similar conclusions.[16, 17, 21-24].

Alterations in the Hedonic Qualities of Food

The enjoyment of food depends not only on its taste but also on its smell as it approaches the mouth and on the release of volatile organic substances within the mouth. In addition food temperature and texture, as well as masticatory sounds, all produce the ultimate sensory experience.

Throat dryness in elderly is frequent and related to either a progressive atrophy of the salivary glands, or to the lack of nutrients (Zn), besides, drugs use (such as diuretics, anticholinergic drugs, drugs for treatment of Parkinson's disease, tricyclic antidepressants...). Poor dentition or ill fitting dentures are often mentioned as a factor affecting the nutrition of elderly people and even masticatory efficiency of removable denture is much less than that of complete natural dentition.

Subtotal or total edentulism is not only an oral disease but also a disease affecting the quality of life and the healthy status since it deeply limits the hedonistic component of feeding that is only apparently a commonplace feature. In particular, edentulism alters food selection, forcing the elderly to change the basket of the basic foods of his own nutrition. In fact, the elderly, even wearing dentures, above all if bad fitting, because of the reduced masticatory efficiency, tend to avoid specific foods such as those of hard, fibrous texture, as meat, fruits (es.: apples, pears, ...) and vegetables (es.: raw carrots, raw fennels, ...). For this reason, both the edentate elderly, who does not wear dentures and whose hula are physiologically sclerous, and the elderly who wear partial or total dentures, even though well fitting, decide to select soft texturing foods in order to reduce or eliminate oral pain. The texture therefore is the main organoleptic characteristic used as coping behaviour. By means of this behaviour the elderly: 1. does not reduce total energy intake since selected foods are generally rich in simple sugar, saturated fats and cholesterol and are even able to cause overweight or obesity in those ones with oral disease; 2. reduces the intake of animal protein, vitamins e minerals.

Also, a reduced masticatory efficiency is thought to lead to a preference for foods of softer consistency, high in sugar content. However few relationships with macronutrients intake have been observed.

According to most studies, a functionally inadequate dental status affects micronutrient intake: for edentulous subjects in the SENECA study intakes of carbohydrates and vitamin B6 especially, but also to a lesser extent for vitamins C and B1, dietary fibre, calcium and iron, were reduced .

Also the masticatory efficiency may be negatively affected by drugs like muscle relaxants or benzodiazepines, in case of illnesses seriously compromising motility (Parkinson's disease, cerebrovascular disease, major depression,...), the musculature efficiency, generally speaking (myasthenia, hypothyroid myopathia, ...) or that regarding the mouth in particular (oculo-pharingeal muscular distrophy, cerebrovascular accident, ...) [25-26].

Aging is characterized by a reduction in sensorial perceptions: visus sharpness decreases, olfactory and gustative thresholds increases, hearing and tactile discriminative capacity decreases. These changes negatively affect the hedonistic feature of all the step of feeding. Elderly food choice is done in order to: make shopping easier (stocking of great quantity of foods versus variety, precooked food), facilitate meal preparation (cooking a lot of foods which is stocked in the fridge and consumed after being warmed up exposing the elderly to reduced intake of vitamins), facilitate ingestion (soft, easy to chew foods which do not exacerbate oral pain during chewing and swallowing).

Taste and smell are key determinants of the palatability of food. With advancing age and mainly related to chemosensory losses, taste and smell changes occur: this can lead to poor appetite, inappropriate food choices and lower nutrient intake.

In the elderly we have a reduction of taste papillae and an increase in taste thresholds, sweet taste being less affected than other modalities (sour, salt, bitter) and salt showing the highest increase. Similarly older persons are less capable to identify different compounds. Taste dysfunction also results from certain diseases, medications, surgical intervention, malnutrition and environmental exposure, bad oral hygiene or when a dental prosthesis is used.

In contrast with the variability in taste changes, the ability to smell declines progressively with age in relation to diseases or medications while older persons rate flavour as the most important determinant of their food choice. With aging, threshold losses have been reported for multiple odorants and many disorders affecting smell perception like anosmia, hyposmia and dysosmia increase in severity with advancing age. Some authors found that older persons preferred food having a greater flavour concentration. Addition of simulated food flavours to meats, vegetables and other foods to amplify smells to compensate for chemosensory losses has been shown to be helpful in an elderly population resulting in an improved immunity and functional status, palatability and food acceptance.

Sight is basic for eating behaviour. By sight it is possible to evaluate: shape, dimension, appearance, and colour of foods. Colour plays a very important role in food choice since it allows to assess food appearance, it arouses expectations of taste, odour, texture, healthiness; it also provides signs about maintenance of food. In food choice or rejection sight is the first control point parallel working with experiences and memories. In fact, people are reticent when tasting differently coloured food (this fact suggest that food choice or rejection is made up by a complex evaluation based on both sensory perceptions and memories) [27-28].

2. Pathological Anorexia of Aging

Medical Conditions

Despite being apparently healthy most of the elders suffer from one or more chronic conditions, which may produce anorexia, malabsorption and increased metabolism, alone or combined.Anorexia often is an underrated symptom in the clinical management of patients suffering from acute and chronic diseases. Besides what already stated about depression and oral disorders, decline in food intake in the elderly may be due to medical conditions such as disability (even if little information exists on the association of disabilities and macronutrient intakes, limitations in daily life activities are considered a key cause of weight loss), gastrointestinal disorders and malabsorption deficiencies (swallowing disorders are both associated with aspiration and decreased food intake; dyspepsia is extremely common in older persons and is associated with anorexia; persons with intestinal bacterial overgrowth have been shown to lose weight associated with both anorexia and malabsorption; helicobacter pylori infection prevalence increases with age and may play a role in anorexia), acute and chronic infections (chronic obstructive pulmonary disease, for example, produces anorexia secondary to oxygen desaturation and increased metabolism due to increased activity of the respiratory muscles), hypermetabolism and hypercatabolism (causing increased energy and protein requirements and producing their anorectic and wasting effects by releasing cytokines).

In particular these cytokines have a powerful anorectic effect that is mediated by: leptin (release and action on leptin receptor), direct stimulus of Corticothropin Releasing Factor, the increase $PGE_{1\alpha}$ levels , or inhibition o anorectic peptides release (dynorphin, NPY, galanina, MCH).

Leptin is a peptide hormone belonging to the helical cytokines family (IL-6, IL-11, leukmia inhibitory factor, ciliary neurotrophic factor). Further the leptin receptor is homologous to the gp 130 signal-transducing molecule that it is also associated with the IL-6 receptor (transducers 1 e 3 signal activation) which activity decreases with aging. It seems that signal transducers transcription factors may have a basic role in AA pathogenesis. The same postreceptor pathway is activated by endotoxin, lipopolysaccharides e anorectic cytokines.

Among elderly patients Alzheimer's dementia is frequent and it is one of the dwindles of geriatric failure to thrive. It is however still unclear whether weight loss precedes or follows dementia and whether it is caused by low levels of energy intake or by a hypermetabolic state. In people affected by dementia some changes concerning the control of feeding intake (disregulation of the central opioid feeding drive, CCK increase, reduced levels of plasma and brain NPY and brain neuroepinephrine, changes in sensorial perception) add to problems concerning deterioration of mental status, (loss of memory of the latest meal, apraxia of eating, agnosia with difficulties in interpreting sense data related to vision, taste, smell or touch, distraction from eating during mealtime), changes in behavioural function (circadian shift in intake preponderance of calories consumed at breakfast) and the loss of the Activities of Daily Leaving (inability to buy food, to cook meals, to feed themselves and feeding time lengthening) thus creating a serious risk as far as nutrition is concerned.

Patients with Parkinson's disease often exhibit eating problems: most of them show a decrease sense of smell, a cognitive decline, a loss of motivation to eat related to depression, difficulties in starting to eat owing to increased need to external stimulation or in performing the acts of eating. Drugs given for the treatment of Parkinson's disease may cause anorexia and further contribute to decreasing food intake.

Many medical conditions, as those affecting the nervous system (Alzheimer's disease, epilepsy, multiple sclerosis, Parkinson's disease, ...), or those affecting the nutritional sphere (chronic renal failure, cancer, zinc – vitamin B12 – niacin deficiencies, ...), endocrine diseases (diabetes mellitus, hypothyroidism, ...), local inflammations (allergic rhinitis, bronchial asthma, sinusitis, ...) and viral infections (acute viral hepatitis, influenza-like infections, ...) may also affect the sense of taste and smell [29-36].

3. Anorexia of Aging Secondary to Iatrogenic or Environment Conditions

Loss of Motivation to Eat

One of the causes of anorexia of aging is the loss of motivation to eat that may be due to depression and social networks loss or deterioration.

Social factors, like poverty, inability to shop, to feed one's self, to prepare and cook meals, can contribute to decreased food intake in the elderly.

Less energy is acquired during meals taken alone than during meals eaten in company, difference in energy intake being about 30%. An extensive friendship network may be positively related to appetite and nutrient intake while widowhood may cause a decrease in meal enjoyment, poorer appetite and weight loss. Providing nutrition food via specific social programs may not overcome the eating problems associated with social isolation. Such data are generally used to suggest that social eating promotes overeating and obesity, but another interpretation is that eating alone, in the elderly especially, leads to undernourishment and weight loss.

Energy intake is greater when a variety of foods is provided than when only a single food is available. Dietary variety has been shown to decline as age increases, with sensory impairment, poverty, loneliness and widowhood. Variety of foods is positively correlated with nutritional quality and has been associated with health outcomes.

Hospitalisation or the institutionalisation in a nursing home, independently from physical acute illness, forecasts a reduction of feeding intake; all this bounds up to worsening of mood, to the perception of a likely future loss of the family environment besides the loss of all of those non-biological values nevertheless attributed to food intake. The foods we eat as well as when, where and how we eat them are decisions based on individual choices and lifetime habits. In a nursing home or in a hospital these choices are limited. Therefore, many elders refuse to eat because they do not like the food they are served or because the food is of different ethnicity. In a recent survey, only 23% of the residents in a nursing home were very satisfied with the food and 58% stated choice and control over food to be very important. Nursing home residents or hospital patients may also reject food to punish a staff member who has not been kind to them, as a way to manipulate the staff itself, to get more attention or to refuse a dietary prescription.

Depression has been shown to be one of the most important treatable causes of weight loss in both community and institutional settings. Depression is related to loneliness, low self-esteem, intolerance against the environment, retirement from job, loss of a relative or a pet, hospitalisation or retirement in a nursing home.

The mechanism behind anorexia in depression has not been fully elucidated. There are some evidence that depression increases corticotrophin releasing factor (CRF) levels, suggesting a role for CRF causing anorexia and weight loss in the elderly.

The prevalence of depression is high in the elderly. Geriatric Depression Scale (GDS) scores above the cut-off of 5 were found in about 12% of the men and 28% of the women enrolled in the SENECA study. There was a significant negative correlation between GDS score and cholesterol blood levels. Successful treatment of depression in nursing home residents results in reversal of weight loss. Weight loss and anorexia were found to be important symptoms related to increased mortality in depressed elderly.

Refusal to eat can be part of an indirect self-destructive behaviour (ISDB) a form of covert, indirect and perhaps unconscious suicidal behaviour. ISDB is defined as an act of omission or commission that causes self-harm that leads indirectly and over time to the patient's death. Persons can omit behaviours that would sustain life and health like prescribed treatments or food. ISDB has been shown to be associated with a direct suicidal potential, dissatisfaction with the treatment program and life in general, confused reasoning and judgement, poor prognosis for discharge, absence of religious commitment and significant losses in the patient's life. Some older people decrease their food intake few months before dying: for those patients who feel an excessive burden of life, refusing food is an acceptable method for terminating their lives.

Nervous or "tardy" anorexia can recur in older persons who were previously weight restrictors. Eating disorders have been considered illness of adolescence and young adulthood but few cases of later onset (over 50 years of age) presentation have been reported. Patients with belated anorexia have a persistently depressive mood but a lesser degree of disturbed body image and of preoccupation with weight, eating and shape [33-35, 37-46].

Prescription Medicines

Comprising 12% of the population, elderly persons consume 35% of prescription drugs in the United States. Epidemiological studies indicate that the mean number of medications used by community-dwelling elderly over the age of 65 ranges from 2.9 to 3.7 medications [47]. The side effects of these drugs are a major cause of weight loss in older persons both free-living or institutionalised. Drugs can affect nutritional intake by decreasing appetite (digoxin, amiodarone, spironolactone, cimetidine, amitriptyiline, most antibiotics, metronidazole, ...), causing malabsorption, nausea or vomiting (sorbitol, theophyllin elixir, laxatives, ...), increasing metabolism (excess thyroxine replacement, theophylline, ...), depleting body's mineral stores (aluminium or magnesium hydroxide antacids , ...). In addition drug induced depression, cognitive impairment and constipation may cause food refusal [14, 31, 32, 34, 35].

Over 250 drugs have been clinically reported to alter taste and/or smelllike drugs to lower cholesterol or lipids in blood (fibrates, statines, ...), antihistamines, drugs to fight infectious diseases (antibiotics, fluoroquinolones, ...), to treat cancer, for arthritis and pain (corticosteroids, ...), for asthma and breathing problems (β-adrenergic agonists, ...), for hypertension (ACE inhibitors, Ca-channel-blockers, ...) and heart disease (nitroglycerin patches, ...) besides muscle relaxants and drugs for treatment of Parkinson's disease or epilepsy, drugs to improve mood.

Compared to young individuals, the average detection thresholds for elderly individuals, with one or more medical conditions and taking an average of 3.4 medications, were 11.6 times higher for sodium salts, 4.3 times higher for acids, 7.0 times higher for bitter compounds, 2.7 times higher for sweeteners [27, 36].

Management of Anorexia of Aging

It is very important to keep into consideration and face anorexia of aging in due time. Consequences, as stated, can be extremely serious and deeply affect both patient's mobility, mortality and quality of life. Therefore, it will be of the utmost importance to insert a special evaluation of the nutritional risk in the Comprehensive Geriatric Assessment, that must be performed in all elderly patients at admission, and constantly evaluate the nutritional status and their feeding intake of the older patients using specific method (Eating Behaviour Scale [47], Blandford Scale [48], Mini Nutritional Assessment [49], ...), to identify and treat the underlying disease (acute and chronic infections, depression, ...) when possible, to institute environmental and behavioural modifications (changing in atmosphere during mealtime, providing favourite foods, increasing food flavours, seeking companionship during meals, increasing physical activity, ...), to both increase staffing levels and to organise staff better to produce higher quality feeding assistance during mealtimes [50], to use, in selected cases, appetite stimulants (megestrol acetate, cyproheptadine, growth hormone, ...), to plan early nutrition rehabilitation programs (liquid supplements, enteral feeding) and nutritional education programs for caregivers (using methods such as the Nutritional Calendar [51]; these programs should enable the caregiver to establish a minimal evaluation of the nutritional state, to know the nutritional value of basic food , to cope with eating behaviour disorders, ...) [20, 35, 52-54].

Conclusion

Food intake can contribute to improve older people well-being and quality of life. Therefore despite some dietary interventions are unlikely to reduce disability or extend life expectancy, they may be still worthwhile if they enhance an elderly individual's well-being or quality of life.

We need further studies to better understand factors contributing to poor nutrition in the elderly, such as changes in various neurotransmitters, to develop preventive (reduction of risk factors, improvement of nutritional assessment, ...) and treatment strategies (nucleotides, increased energy and nutrient density food, improving taste and smell, ...).

Dietary related interventions in older adults should aim to prevent decline and to extent possible restore or to maintain function and quality of life. Interventions need to be acceptable, so that to integrate other health promoting strategies and be continually monitored and assessed to evaluate their effectiveness.

In elderly people, also relation to their cultural and emotional value, traditional food, even if it is known for not being always nutritionally sound, should be preferred. However innovations in agriculture and food technologies will increasingly allow us to assure a richer content of nutrients and beneficial phytochemical and a reduced content of inhibitory and anti-nutritional factors. These changes also present their risks as nothing in human evolutionary experience have prepared those who are exposed to these novel foods to the particular chemical composition they are made up with.

REFERENCES

[1] Morley JE: Anorexia, body composition and ageing. *Curr Opin Clin Nutr Metab Care* 2001, 4, 9-13Horwitz BA, Blanton CA, McDonald RB: Physiologic determinants of the anorexia og aging. *Annu Rev Nutr* 2002, 22, 417-43

[3] Gazewood JD, Mehr DR: Diagnosis and management of weight loss in the elderly. *J Fam Pract* 1998, 47, 19-25

[4] Stevens J: Impact of age on association between weight and mortality. *Nutr Rev* 2000, 58, 129-137

[5] Euronut-SENECA De Groot CGPM, Van Staveren WA, Hautvast JGAJ eds: A concerted action on nutrition and health in Europe. *Eur J Clin Nutr* 1991, 45 suppl, 3, S1-196

[6] Anonimous. Daily dietary fat and total food energy intakes. 3rd NHANES, phase III 1988-1991. *MMWR Morb Mortal Wkly Rep* 1994, 43, 116-25Wurtmann JJ , Lieberman H, Tsay R: Calorie and nutrient intakes of elderly young subjects measured under identical conditions. *J Gerontol* 1988, 43, B174-180

[8] Sullivan DH: The role of nutrition in increased morbidity and mortality. *Clin Geriatr Med* 1995, 11, 661-674

[9] Elmstahl S, Steen B: Hospital nutrition in a geriatric long-term care medicine. *Age Ageing* 1987, 16, 73

[10] Ahari M, Kimigiar M: Food intake and body mass index in the privately institutionalised elderly. *Int J Vit res* 1997, 67, 41

[11] Elia M, Ritz P, Stubbs RJ: Total energy expenditure in the elderly. *Eur J Clin Nutr* 2000, 54, S3, 92-103

[12] Henry CJK: Mechanisms of changes in basal metabolism during ageing. *Eur J Clin Nutr* 2000, 54, S3, 77-91

[13] Elia M: Organ and tissue contribution to metabolic rate. In: Energy metabolism. Tissue determinants and cellular corollaries. JM Kinney & HN Tucker Eds, New York, *Raven Press,* 1992, pp 62-8

[14] Morley JE: Anorexia of aging. *Am J Clin Nutr* 1997, 66, 760-73

[15] MacIntosh CG, Horowitz M, Verhajen MAMT, Smout AJPM, Wishart J, Morris H, Goble E, Morley JE, Chapman IM: Effect of small intestinal nutrient infusions on appetite, gastrointestinal hormone release and gastric myoelectrical activity in young and older men. *Am J Gastr* 2001, 96, 4, 997-1006

[16] Martinez M, Arnalich F, Hernanz A: Alterations of anorectic cytokine levels from plasma and cerebrospinal fluid in idiopathic senile anorexia. *Mech Ageing Dev* 1993, 72, 145-53
[17] Martinez M, Hernanz A, Gomez-Cerezo J: Alterations in plasma and cerebrospinal fluid levels of neuropeptides in idiopathic senile anorexia. *Regul Pept* 1993, 49, 109-117
[18] MacIntosh CG, Morley JE, Wishart J, Morris H, Jansen JB, Horowitz M, Chapman IM: Effect of exogenous cholecystokinin (CCK)-8 on food intake and plasma CCK, leptin, and insulin concentrations in older and young adults: evidence for increased CCK activity as a cause of the anorexia of aging. *J Clin Endocrinol Metab* 2001 Dec;86(12):5830-7
[19] Roberts SB: Energy regulation and aging. *Nutr Rev* 2000, 58, 91-7
[20] Morley JE: Decreased food intake with aging. *J Gerontol A Biol Sci Med Sci* 2001 Oct;56 Spec No 2(2):81-8
[21] MacINtosh CG, Sheehan J, Davani N, Morley JE, Horowitz M, Chapman IM: Effects of aging on the opioid modulation of feeding in humans. *JAGS* 2001, 49, 1518-1524
[22] Arnalich F, Hernanz<A, Vazquez JJ, Amores A: Cell mediated immune responses and cytokine production in idiopathic senile anorexia. *Mech Aging Dev* 1994, 77, 67-74
[23] Beharka AA, Meydani M, Leka LS, Meydani A, Meydani SN: Interleukin-6 production does not increase with age. *J Gerontol* 2001, 56A, B81-8
[24] Yeh SS, Wu SY, Levine DM, Parker TS, Olson JS, Stevens MR, Schuster MW: The correlation of cytokine levels with body weight after megestrol acetate treatment in geriatric patients. *J Gerontol A Biol Sci Med Sci* 2001 Jan;56(1):M48-54
[25] De Groot CPGM, van Staveren WA, de Graaf C: Determinants of macronutrients intake in elderly people. *Eur J Clin Nutr* 2000, 54, S3, 70-6
[26] Haller J, Weggemans RM, Lammi-Keefe CJ, Ferry M: Changes in the vitamin status of elderly Europeans. *Eur J Clin Nutr* 1996, 50, S2, 32-46
[27] Schiffman SS, Graham BG: Taste and smell perception affect appetite and immunity in the elderly. *Eur J Clin Nutr* 2000, S3, 54-63
[28] Mulligan C, Moreau K, Brandolini M, Livingstone B, Beaufrère B, Boire Y: Alterations of sensory perceptions in healthy elderly subjects during fasting and refeeding. *Gerontology* 2002, 48, 39-43
[29] Reynish W, Andrieu S, Nourhashemi F, Vellas B: Nutritional factors and Alzheimer's disease. *J Gerontol A Biol Sci Med Sci* 2001 Nov;56(11):M675-80
[30] Young KW, Greenwood CE: Shift in diurnal feeding patterns in nursing home residents with Alzheimer's disease. *J Gerontol A Biol Sci Med Sci* 2001 Nov;56(11):M700-6
[31] Chrischilles EA, Foley DJ, Wallace RB, Lemke JH, Semla TP, Hanlon JT: Use of medications by persons 65 and over. *J Gerontol* 1992, 47, M137-144
[32] Carr-Lopez SM, Phillips SM: The role of medications in geriatric failure to thrive. *Drugs Aging* 1996, 9, 221-5
[33] Bernstein M, Tucker K, Ryan M: Higher dietary diversity is associated with better nutritional status in frail elders. *FASEB J* 1999, A695
[34] Kane RA, Caplan AL, Urv-Wong EK: Everyday matters in the lives of nursing home residents. *JAGS* 1997, 45, 1086-93
[35] Marcus EL, Berry EM: Refusal to eat in the elderly. *Nutr Rev* 1998, 56, 163-171

[36] Schiffman SS: Perception of taste and smell in elderly persons. *Crit Rev Food Science Nutr* 1993, 33, 17-26

[37] De Castro JM, De Castro ES: Spontaneous meal patterns of humans. *Am J Clin Nutr* 1989, 50, 237-47

[38] McIntosh WA, Shifflett PA, Picou JS: Social support, stressful events, strain ,dietary intake and the elderly. *Med Care* 1989, 27, 140-53

[39] Rosenbloom CA, Whittington FJ: The effects of bereavement on eating behaviours and nutrient intakes in elderly widowed persons. *J Gerontol* 1993, 48, S223-9

[40] Thompson MP, Morris LK: Unexplained weight loss in the ambulatory elderly. *JAGS* 1991, 39, 497-500

[41] Morley JE, Kraenzle D: Causes of weight loss in a community nursing home. *JAGS* 1994, 42, 583-5

[42] Yesavage JA, Brink TL, Rose TL: Development and validation of a geriatric depression rating scale. *J Psych Res* 1983, 17, 27

[43] Haller J, Weggemans RM, Ferry M, Guigoz Y: Mental health: MMSE and GDS of elderly Europeans in the SENECA study of 1993. *Eur J Clin Nutr* 1996, 50, S2, 112-6

[44] Morley JE, Kraenzle D: Weight loss. *JAGS* 1995, 43, 82-3

[45] Pulska T, Pahkala K, Laippala P; Kivela SL: Depressive symptoms predicting six-year mortality in depressed elderly finns. *Int J Geriatr Psych* 2000, 15, 940-6

[46] McIntoch JL, Hubbard RW: Indirect self-destructive behaviour among the elderly. *J Gerontol Soc Work* 1988, 13, 37-48

[47] Tully MW, Lambros Matrakas K, Muir J, Musallam K: The Eating Nehaviour Scale. *J Geront Nurs* 1997, july, 9-15

[48] Blandford G, Watkins LB, Mulvihill MN, Taylor B: Assessing abnormal feeding behaviour in late stage dementia. Research and Practice in Alzheimer Disease: Weight loss & Eating behaviour in Alzheimer's patients. B. Vellas, Rivière S, Fitten J Eds, Serdi, Paris, 1998, pag. 47-64

[49] Guigoz Y, Vellas B, Garry PJ: Mini Nutritional Assessment. *Facts and Research in Gerontology,* 1994, 4 (suppl 2), 113-43

[50] Simmons SF, Osterweil D, Schnelle JF: Improving food intake in nursing home residents with feeding assistance: a staffing analysis. *J Gerontol A Biol Sci Med Sci* 2001 Dec;56(12):M790-4

[51] Riviere S, Lauque S, Vellas B: Health promotion programme: nutrition and Alzheimer's disease. Research and Practice in Alzheimer's Disease, Serdi ed, Paris, pag. 93

[52] Rivière S, Gillette-Guyonnet S, Voisin T, Reynish E, Andrieu S, Lauque S, Salva A, Frisoni G, Nourhashemi F, Micas M, Vellas B: A nutritional education program could prevent weight loss and slow cognitive decline in Alzheimer's disease. *J Nutr Health Aging* 2001, 5, 295-9

[53] Thomas DR, Ashmen W, Morley JE, Evans WJ: Nutritional management in long-term care: development of a clinical guideline. Council for Nutritional Strategies in Long-Term Care. *J Gerontol A Biol Sci Med Sci* 2000 Dec;55(12):M725-34

[54] Wilson MM, Purushothaman R, Morley JE: Effect of liquid dietary supplements on energy intake in the elderly. *Am J Clin Nutr* 2002 May;75(5):944-7

In: New Developments in Eating Disorders Research
Editor: Pamela I. Swain, pp. 149-167
ISBN 1-59454-542-1

Chapter 7

PSYCHOPATHOLOGICAL DIMENSIONS IN EATING DISORDERS (E.D.)

Giancarlo Di Pietro [*1], ***Fulvio Sorge*** [1], ***Anna Chiacchio*** [2], ***Caterina Crispo*** [2], ***Felice Iasevoli*** [2], ***Vittorio Schiavone*** [2], ***Simona Palmieri*** [2], ***Raffaele Basso*** [2], ***Fabio Panariello*** [2], ***Luigi Valoroso*** [2] ***and Giovanni Muscettola*** [3]

University "Federico II" of Naples; Department of Neuroscience and Behaviour Science Psychiatry Division

[1]Researcher in Psychiatry; [2] Students from the Residency Program in Psychiatry (Specialty degree); [3] Professor in Psychiatry

ABSTRACT

The exploration, the comprehension and the definition of the underlying psychopathological dimensions and/or concomitant to Eating Disorders are everything but exhaustive. On the one hand, the ED present themselves as dysfunctional, transnosographic and multiform behaviour, on the other hand, they tend to mask various underlying pathologies, including structural, pathological descriptions. While the coexistence of the depressive, anxious and personality spectrum pathology is recognised, it is not yet clear if the eating pathology, in its various forms, should be understood as an expression of illness, therefore also structured in an organic dimension, or if, on the other hand, it is a defensive attempt to 'self-cure' another affection of psychic nature and origin. Both theories are probably valid, and in the clinical practise we can outline syndromes of the first kind, the second kind, or even mixed.

The main purpose of a psychiatric interview is that of expanding the observation viewpoint of the problem, to look for new connections with other hidden dimensions and to "reframe" the symptom in a more complex and integrated dimension with the other parts of the personality.

But what are the themes that are frequently more noticeable in people affected by ED?

* Viale Colli Aminei, 461, is. 29; 80131 Napoli (Italy); Tel.: 081 7462652; Fax: 0817462378; E-mail: dipietro@unina.it

For this purpose, using some cases as starting points for reflection, we will present psychopathological focus areas that seem to be particularly significant in the observation clinic of the ED: feelings and emotions, the depressive spectrum, the rapport with the body, and that with the family.

INTRODUCTION

The exploration, the comprehension and the definition of the underlying psychopathological dimensions and/or concomitant to Eating Disorders are everything but exhaustive. On the one hand, the ED present themselves as dysfunctional, transnosographic and multiform behaviour, on the other hand, they tend to mask various underlying pathologies, including structural, pathological descriptions. While the coexistence of the depressive, anxious and personality spectrum pathology is recognised, it is not yet clear if the eating pathology, in its various forms, should be understood as an expression of illness, therefore also structured in an organic dimension, or if, on the other hand, it is a defensive attempt to 'self-cure' another affection of psychic nature and origin. Both theories are probably valid, and in the clinical practise we can outline syndromes of the first kind, the second kind, or even mixed.

Even if the structured, repetitive, symptomatic manifestation flattens the person in stereotyped behaviour and thoughts, each clinical case presents unrepeatable characteristics, and each pathological manifestation presents profound diversities from one case to another. In the food pathology, the tendency towards the flattening and to the stereotyped repetition of pathological behaviour seem particularly evident: the female sex, the teenage years, a negative relationship with food and nourishment, a conflicting relationship with their body, are the substratum., the fertile soil for the development of pathological behaviour, and once that this behaviour has become habit, they also become a strong support to the necessity of existence, a firm safety anchor towards the other difficulties and risks that life demands.

We want to underline the defensive significance of the ED that, before becoming symptoms, are attempts at adapting, compared to the relationship difficulties between the Ego, and the World (Others).

The refusal to incorporate the food necessary to survival often expresses the omnipotent childish desire to dominate it, proving to yourself and to the world that you don't need it, on the contrary, stuffing yourself excessively with food, and then vomiting it, means destroying it.

In both cases, food assumes the significance of EVERYTHING, it is the 'pars pro toto', laden with inalienable and extraordinary symbolic meanings, the "Totem", built to be adored and annihilated. When this happens, all the emotions concentrate on it, the "Totem" dominates the person, this person's feelings recognise only one, inflexible point of reference: the "Totem" itself.

The behaviour hardens into a series of rituals for which you no longer understand the sense, the purpose, even less the choice: looking at yourself in the mirror. checking your weight, rationing the quantity of food, visualising the material expelled, organising the day on the necessity of carrying out all the rituals.

And it is exactly this "NECESSITY" which becomes the prevailing psychological dimension, while choice and free will become a distant memory, the shadow of a person now lost.

From this point of view, how can we not think about the deceptive choice freely made by the drug addicts at the time when they are "forced to choose" to use drugs?

In the clinical work with ED we frequently meet people who have lost their real identities, and, in many cases, their very capacity to think.

Their relationship with food, and everything connected with it, completely invades their minds and conversations, even those with their psychiatrists. Behaviour and feelings which began as attempts to resolve some other problems, have become a mask, a prosthesis for their lost identity.

Often, behind the mask there seems to be nothing, a psychotic dimension with an extreme distance between conscience, and authenticity of the person, other times, the awareness, even partial, of the underlying dynamics opens conflicts which end in an attitude, even more defensive, of passive resignation, scepticism or unjustified fear: it is difficult to accept and to decide to change the path of your own life, even when you find out that you are living it partially and inauthentically.

The way back is never easy, finding and repairing the broken threads requires time and patience, and often suffering and determination. But above all, it requires a certain sense of direction of their conscience which frequently is lacking in those who have found "AWAY from themselves" the cause of their own suffering, as in patients with ED, and drug addicts: a kind of introversion, a capacity to acknowledge that, in the folds of their own minds, it is possible and necessary to look for the pieces of the puzzle of their own personality, buried and forgotten under the heavy blanket of the symptom's habit.

A meeting with a specialist in this field can open new possibilities of comprehension of the ailments, even though this does not always correspondent to a cure and a change.

The main purpose of a psychiatric interview is that of expanding the observation viewpoint of the problem, to look for new connections with other hidden dimensions and to "reframe" the symptom in a more complex and integrated dimension with the other parts of the personality.

But what are the themes that are frequently more noticeable in people affected by ED?

For this purpose, using some cases as starting points for reflection, we will present psychopathological focus areas that seem to be particularly significant in the observation clinic of the ED: feelings and emotions, the depressive spectrum, the rapport with the body, and that with the family.

The reports reproduced are part of the formation programme of the students from the Residency Program in Psychiatry (Specialty degree), and refer to the first testing of patients who flocked to the outpatients' department of Food Behaviour Ailments of the Psychiatric Clinic of the 'Federico II' University of Naples in 2004.

The meeting took place in a room specifically adapted for outpatient visit, and was carried out by a student under the direct supervision of a senior psychiatrist; in addition, the completion of a clinical file was required (CIDA – Di Pietro & coll. 2000) and in a different space and phase, and the administering of specific tests for ED: Eating Disorder Inventory (EDI 2, Garner et al., 1983) Eating Attitude Test (EAT, Garner et al., 1979), Symptom Checklist (EDI-SC, Garner et al., 1983), (SCL 90, De Rogatis et al., 1976), Body Uneasiness

Test (BUT, Cuzzolaro, 1999), Beck Depression Inventory (BDI, Beck et al., 1961), and Short Form 36 (SF 36, Apolone et al., 1997, 1998).

At the end of this diagnostic procedure, to which the patient gave his previous informed consent, the students were asked for a case description, which was then examined and discussed collectively.

CASE 1 – TERESA

Teresa, a 17-year-old brilliant high school student and the older of two sisters, both raised in a middle class family, (first) came to our psychiatric unit with signs of unhealthy eating behaviour.

Teresa is 1.73 m tall. Her present weight is unknown, for she strongly refuses to take her weight. However, we do know that during the past year, she reached a maximum of 63 kg and a minimum of 59 kg.

Her menarche was attained at the age of 9 and has always been regular.

Because her parents separated in the summer of 2003, Teresa, together with her mother and younger sister, moved in with her mother's relatives. It was around this time that the misuse of food, which gradually worsened over time, began to surface. Actually, her pathology emerged as she began asking for nutritional counselling to lose a few extra kilos. Although she was prescribed a diet, she never followed it, for she considered the plan too lenient and rich in calories. Accordingly, on her own initiative, she made it stricter and began to eat less and less so as to reach the ideal weight of 55 kg. Up to today, without ever weighing herself, she keeps feeling fat and relentlessly continues her negative eating habits. Among other things, she isolated herself from her family and friends, because she feels deeply resentful of anyone trying to urge her to eat adequately. Finally, Teresa has never used laxatives and diuretics but spends a lot of time doing physical exercises and other hyperkinetic activities, such as going up and down stairways, in the hope of burning additional calories.

The patient underwent her medical consultation first in the presence of her mother and then alone. In the first case, she was overwhelmed with anger, cried and bitterly complained of feeling sad and depressed. By contrast, in the second case, she seemed quite withdrawn and rational. When we asked her how she felt, she replied that she was fine and downplayed her condition by withholding information from us about her pathological behaviours, which were later reported by her mother. From this first interview, it was clear that Teresa was in oppositive attitude, as demonstrated by her refusal to take any of the diagnostic tests as well as by her reluctance to accept any advice on how to be helped and eventually treated, and that she resented the presence of her mother. Teresa was very reserved and quite withdrawn during the interview. Surprisingly, despite the patient's conflicting relationship with her mother and relatives, it emerged that she still missed her grandmother, who had been dead for three years , and that she was very close to her father, who had returned home to help her.

From our observations, this patient meets the criteria for the anorexic type of Eating Disorder Non Otherwise Specified (EDNOS). Specifically, Teresa's clinical case clearly reflects those personality traits common among people with anorexia, both before the onset of the disorder and after its occurrence. In fact, she is a well raised middle class teenager and a brilliant high school student who appreciates company. Overall, she is a role model daughter up until her problems arise. In the same way, her family environment mirrors that which characterizes the lives of anorexic patients: mother-father separation, absence of a father figure, and an increasing mother-child conflicting relationship. Other typical aspects refer to her state of oppositive attitude as well as her refusal to receive any help. Such aspects are generally so compelling that the warning signs of eating disorders are often overshadowed by them.

Indeed, according to Hilde Bruch (1982, 1983), a deep unresolved psychological problem of the emotional Self may be the underlying condition for an ongoing oversensitive preoccupation with food and weight-gain. The author underlines the presence of a mother-daughter conflict stemming from the mother's incapability of realizing her daughter as an entity completely apart from her own, thus imposing her needs and emotions on the little girl rather than trying to help her daughter overcome her emotional turmoil. This situation leads to a disownment of Ego limits, and to a failure of a body-image creation. The author also defines anorexia as the patient's attempt to take care of herself. In doing so, the patient seeks to attain a sense of individuality and self-reliance through body discipline. Therefore, the adolescent will first revolt against her mother and then will use food as her substitute: fasting or eating and then vomiting could represent the patient's unconscious desire to reject or free herself from her mother. Bruch's description reminds us of Winnicot's concept of the False Self (Winnicott, 1971). According to his theory, the eating disorder represents a battle between the False Self and the True Self in an effort to assert the latter. Actually, in the separation-individuation process, theorized by the psychoanalytic authors, the most onerous task for adolescents is to separate themselves emotionally from their parents, particularly from their mother. Such separation, though, yields only an illusory autonomy. In fact, the adolescent could still alternate between the desire for autonomy and the desire for dependence, just as he or she alternates between the love and hate for food.

Another interesting aspect in Teresa's experience, common among other anorexic girls, is the way she clearly blackmails her family. Specifically, the anorexic behaviour comprises all three aspects of a blackmail situation: the blackmailer is the girl ; the blackmailed are her parents; and finally the hostage is her body. As a result, the girl feels that her anorexic state is a necessary tool to keep together the unstable and conflicting family environment. Better yet, the disorder serves as the aggregating element of a fundamentally conflicting couple. Consistently, the Kleinian School of thought (Klein,1921, 1958) emphasizes that the father-child interpersonal relationship may also play a critical role in triggering an anorexic behaviour. Commonly, in fact, the father figure does not seem to be totally and emotionally involved in his daughter's life. As a result, underlying the condition of Teresa's unhealthy behaviour may be her desperate attempt to receive her father's attention, namely an attention-seeking behaviour, in the hope of having him reconcile with his mother.

Furthermore, Teresa, as most other patients with eating disorders, is in denial, and the unconscious mechanisms underlying her psychological state often reinforce the symptoms.

In conclusion, anorexic patients are reluctant to treatment because it is through their illness that they display their need to communicate, thus hoping to resolve their emotional problems. Hence, recovering from such illness would mean for them to lose the power over their family environment, acquired at such high emotional and physical price.

CASE 2 – CARLA

Carla, a 19-year-old high school student, lives in a middle class family of six people: her parents, a younger brother and her grandparents. Her father is a car dealer, and her mother, a very young and friendly woman, has already retired in order to assist her old and ill mother.

Carla was accompanied to our eating disorder unit by her mother who had been advised by a nutritionist to seek psychiatric help for her daughter.

The patient, a very fashionable dressed girl, appeared a bit nervous, withdrawn and depressed at first. However, as the interview went on, she gradually began to feel more comfortable, thus becoming more cooperative. She was very fluent and articulate. There were no distortions in her train of thought and in her perceptions. Her cognitive abilities and her insight were unimpaired.

She had been suffering from purging behaviour, an eating disorder entailing overeating episodes followed by self- induced vomiting, for four years and had also taken diuretics and laxatives. She was 1.63 tall, and, at the time of our interview, she weighed 63.5 kg. Although she used to weigh less when she was 18, she never reached her ideal weight of 53 kg. As Carla was a professional swimmer, she had been on a diet since she was a child. However in 2000, after more than 10 years of training, an accident forced her to stop swimming. Because of the accident and of demanding school commitments, she never tried to swim again. Actually, her swim coach and her doctors told her she could have swum, if she wanted to, but without competing as she had always fervently done. Consequently, since her eating behaviours were no longer checked by her trainer or by her dietician, Carla got into the habit of overeating and vomiting right after. A slight improvement in her eating habits, however, occurred during a short dating experience she had with a swimmer (2002-2003). The experience made Carla feel better about herself; however, as soon as the relationship ended, things returned as before. Since then, the bulimic symptoms have become more frequent and serious. At present, she often eats huge amounts of food and vomits every day of the week and sometimes more than once a day. Specifically, she can not stop eating until she starts feeling sick. When that happens, she vomits fearing of becoming fat. After vomiting, she always feels weak, depressed and "dirty". These symptoms usually decrease during the summer and increase after the beginning of the school year.

Although Carla thoroughly described these incidences, more information was necessary to find a correlation between her past, her present life and feelings, and her behavioural disorder. Past history revealed that Carla was born at full term and had had a regular growth rate. In the course of her developmental years, she had become a very strong and sensitive person. Although she had always been a brilliant student, now she was no longer interested in school as she used to be. She considered it tiring and boring. Her relationship with her school mates was also disappointing. She reported going out only with a few of them and was now dating a school friend. When I tried to probe into her feelings about this relationship, she became shy, especially on her sexual habits. The only thing she admitted was that sometimes it was very difficult for her to enjoy her sexuality because of weight and body image problems. She also admitted that her boyfriend was often a bit selfish and did not really want to take care of her problems, including her eating disorder.

Carla reported that she wanted to go to college after graduating from high school and become a doctor. However, worrying about failing the entrance exam, she preferred not taking it at all, rather than failing it. Moreover, it emerged quite soon that she did not like speaking about her family. We did learn, however, that Carla and her mother were very close. On the other hand, her father was described as distant and inattentive whenever she tried to reach out to him. He commonly shunned away from her problems and avoided facing them. Similarly, neither her brother nor her grandparents seemed to be much interested in her life.

The first interview was completed by filling out a case file (CIDA, Di Pietro et al., 2000) and by administering the diagnostic tests.

The most interesting results were that Carla scored higher in the EDI and SCL 90-total scales. The EDI-2 scale analyses revealed higher scores in perfectionism, introspective awareness and maturity fears, whereas SCL–90-scale analyses showed a trend towards higher somatization scores.

Some interesting aspects emerged during our interview. For instance, Carla's strict conscience and her severe personality were in contrast with the lack of discipline and heavy impulsiveness of bulimic people. In effect, the former features seem to be directly related to Carla's desire for power and to her contempt for failure and weakness. Specifically, on the one hand, she thought that the state of being perfect and unyielding would have granted her people's admiration and acceptance. Most important, she believed that through perfectionism, she would have regained her self-esteem. On the other hand, she found it very difficult to establish any type of close interpersonal relationship fearing of being hurt and rejected after having lost her emotional control. Therefore, her stern rationality served as an effective means to avoid any emotional involvement.

After examining Carla's personality traits, a diagnosis of a probable case of obsessive-compulsive personality was made on the basis of the following observations: slight aggressiveness and anger, rejection of any kind of dependence, a peculiar tendency and strive for rationality and self control, and, finally, the use of defensive mechanisms, such as the "body-mind splitting "

Although the criteria for obsessive-compulsive disorder (OCD) have not been fully specified, it is important to underline that Carla displayed some forms of anxiety and rituals typical of patients with OCD. Carla's preoccupations and rituals, however, were largely egosyntonic and not egodystonic as in OCD patients (Halmi, 1999)(Holden, 1990). Specifically, the phobic thought of food and weight repeatedly entered Carla's mind but not necessarily against her will. Thus, the absence of OCD comorbidity in cases like Carla's is to be considered positively, for obsessive-compulsive behaviours may complicate the treatment of patients with eating disorders (Holden, 1990).

In conclusion, because Carla is a very resolute and resourceful girl, she could surely benefit from entering a psychotherapy program, although it may be long and hard to follow.

Case 3 - Antonella

Antonella, a 22-year-old young woman, was sent to our Eating Disorders Unit by a nutritionist. She was motherless, for when she was still a child her mother died of Familial Colon Polypsis (FCP). The patient was affected by the same disease, which as we will see later in the report, played a major role in determining her psychopathological profile. She lived alone with her father, for her two older siblings had moved to Northern Italy, where they ran a restaurant. We learned that she had been engaged for several years now and had never graduated from high school owing to the worsening of her disease. She tried to work as a restorer of antique furniture, but she soon had to quit because she had to attend to her father's needs and to take care of the house. Her father himself had been an expert in antique furniture; in fact, he used to work in the restoration of antiques and in the handmade furniture business sectors. Over all, thanks to her middle class sociocultural background, she was able to give us an objective and detailed description of her psychological distress. Before starting to probe into her disorder, however, we collected information regarding her present as well past medical history, which, in fact, started very early in her lifetime. Because of her mother's pathology, she was screened for FCP as soon as she was born. A very long history of her gastrointestinal pathology followed, for she was actually born with the stigmata of the disease. Specifically, at the age of 18, several centimetres of her colon were cut off and a transitory colostomy was built, but later closed. Ever since, to keep her dysplastic pathology under control, she had undergone follow-up medical examinations as well as follow-up nutritional check-ups at the Clinical Nutritional Division. From her psychological anamnesis, it emerged that she had a significant dysfunctional attitude towards food, reinforced by depressive moods and deep emotional weakness.

The day of our session, the patient appeared well-groomed for the occasion. She was cooperative and well-disposed even to talk about several emotionally painful episodes, thus establishing a solid interpersonal relationship with the specialist. She also seemed to recognize many contradicting and thorny traits of her personality, for she was quite capable of introspection or self-analysis.

From the psychological point of view, her decision to work as a restorer of antiques, along with the pleasure she found in doing the job, was quite intriguing. She said that it gave her pleasure and self-gratification. We may assume, in fact, that the job had acquired for her an important symbolic meaning: it stood for the reconstruction, or better yet, for the restoration and remaking of a diseased and frail body, made weaker and more rotten by the passing of time. However, what received more attention in determining the patient's psychological profile was the fact that the choice of her job recalled, at least indirectly, her father's former occupation. It outlined, therefore, a mixture of feelings that had developed inside the family and that yielded a complex mechanism of intrapsychic reflective mirrors in which the patient was the centre. Her siblings were equally accountable for such emotional miasma, since their transfer to Northern Italy was perceived by Antonella as an abandonment which further mined the weak foundations of the family cell. As previously stated, the symptoms of her pathology worsened when she was around 18, and the different surgeries that followed markedly ingrained in her mind feelings of body dissatisfaction, unworthiness and low self-esteem. Such psychological and physical discontent led to the development of a number of depressive symptoms, which, as the patient revealed, were worsened by her dietetic dysfunction. The disorder, in fact, had driven her to lose weight considerably, and to regain it way above her usual weight. Although the patient had subsequently managed to return to her regular weight, her wish for better results was not truly unrealistic. For this reason, Antonella persisted in her highly dysfunctional eating behaviours comprising frequent bouts of binge eating, even three times a day, and self-induced vomit.

Overall, this clinical case reflects the basic theme of a body perceived as a protective covering and highlights how nutritional behaviours may be negatively affected by the way a person perceives his or her body. Consistently, because of her illness, our patient had always perceived her body as maimed, dysfunctional, and deficient in some parts. Moreover, her emotional turmoil was further deepened by the fact that her physical deficiency was a constant reminder of her mother's illness, as she died of the same disease. Only later had this intricate interplay of emotions yielded the first clear signs of her mental disorder. During her childhood years, in fact, the patient had displayed only vague signs of a conflicting relationship with food, as she ate very little and irregularly; altogether, the food did not give her any pleasure. Then as her body grew uglier because of her illness, her feelings of being worthless and her low self-esteem increased. For instance, the patient found it very difficult and onerous to do certain simple tasks as driving in traffic. Such depressive symptoms were tightly bound to absurd eating behaviours, ranging from anorectic conducts to compulsive binges, followed by self-induced vomit. Therefore, it was plain to see that food became for Antonella an indispensable tool through which she managed to reach the physical side of herself that she totally rebuked, along with her entire medical history. A wide array of deep and unsolved conflicts seem to be crystallized around the basic theme of nutrition. Therefore, a deeper analytical approach of these conflicts would surely shed more light on the interplay between family dynamics and mental disorders that gradually develop over the years. Consistently, in the present clinical case, a better understanding of the interpersonal relationships characterizing the patient's family life has constituted a key element to uncovering the genesis of the her psychological breakdown.

CASE 4 – DANIELA

Daniela, a 24-year-old young woman with an imposing and robust appearance, came to our psychiatric unit in April 2004. It soon became clear, however, that beneath such striking appearance, a very fragile nature was hidden and was about to break any time. When she entered the room, she was on the brink of tears. Her eyes were not yet bright with tears, but they would have been no matter what one could have told her. Before entering the room, she glanced at her sister who had accompanied her. Daniela looked younger than twenty-four and her imposing appearance clashed with the way she spoke, with her gestures, and even with the way she sat. That evident fragility stirred an irrepressible but limited speech. One could envision that this first session would have translated into a sheer gush of emotions rather than into a true interview.

Actually, a nutritionist had advised her to seek psychiatric counselling after having failed to put order in her absurd eating habits which entailed days of bulimic crisis and repentances. She unemotionally described a chaotic world comprising laxatives, a seesaw of sizes, and twisted images which, when reflecting into a mirror, were hardly recognizable as one. One had the impression that she had told herself that same story over and over again. A casual listener, as I was at the time, may have perceived her story as distant and incomprehensible, but ,in fact, it comprised coherence, dignity and inner suffering. The inner suffering was the only perceivable trait, for nothing else could have possibly emerged from such hopeless and murky war report. As she continued her story, I kept reminding myself that, for her, I was just a mere object. To learn about her family members and the interpersonal relationships she had with them, as well as to bring her back to a more concrete reality in which I could have been a participant more than a mere observer, I asked her whether she had received any psychiatric counselling in the past. Interestingly, the talk about her family began with a person that was no longer there for her: her mother who had died two years earlier: "My mother died two years ago, after a long agonizing disease". While she reported that her mother had been the only person in the family to really understand her and help her, tears poured down her cheeks. Then, she continued to heighten her mother's benevolent nature and the last days and moments she spent with her. Particularly, her continual succession of thoughts encompassed a wide range of disconnected memories about her mother's long sufferings, unfaltering altruism, and insurmountable faith. She also allowed her mind to wander back to the runs to the hospital, to the doctors' vain attempts to raise her hopes about her mother's recovery and her struggle to believe in them. The terrible anxiety that overwhelms her today began while she assisted her sick mother. Next, she reported how she had replaced her mother in attending to her father' needs. She was expected to attend to her brother as well, although he was married and lived on his own with his wife. Finally, her sister, who had already reconciled herself to the tragic loss, was described as affectionate and nurturing as her mother used to be. Actually, she was painting a picture of a motherless and childish young woman left adrift in a world filled by false family images and immense solitude.

Her flow of words was incessant. One could have left the room and returned finding her still there unperturbed in her talk. Following her mother's death, she decided to lose weight. Actually, before then, she had never really felt the need to be on a diet, although her obesity was obvious. As she stated, everybody had always loved her for the way she was, without ever pressuring her about her weight, and paid her innumerable compliments. Therefore, owing to the fact that she had a supportive family environment and had not been pressured in any way to lose weight, it was difficult to unravel the mechanisms underlying her decision to do so. She herself confusedly defined it a mere challenge.

Therefore, she began a very poor, absurd, extremely restrictive and punitive diet: she took laxatives, hid food, threw it way, and vomited. No one in her family seemed to notice nor wonder about her weight loss (she dropped from a plus size to a regular one).

As for her friends, they kept loving her for the way she was and not for the way she looked. Moreover, now they were praising her willpower. She became relentlessly eager to fit into smaller and smaller sizes. In her distorted reality, she perceived the larger sizes as lurking vultures ready to attack her as soon as she dropped her guard. Then she mentioned the anxiety she felt whenever she looked into the mirror. A quick glance at the mirror was enough for to realize the changes in her body: smaller hips, a flatter belly, smaller bosom and slimmer thighs. The expression in her eyes had changed as well. Just as the mirror reflected her body, her eyes reflected her soul. A soul, however, that was too large to be contained in a body that had become so minute. Feeling so different from before, she gradually lost her identity: the line between what she actually was and what she yearned to be became finer and more fragile.

To maintain a steady weight was surely difficult when she had to cook everyday and attend to her father and brother. Actually, she really never complained about her everyday chores, but it was easy to empathize with her unconscious frustrations. Throughout the entire session, the flatness in her voice was temporarily broken only once by the following statement: "But my brother has a wife!". In her distorted world, rebellion was unconceivable by choice and not because of her family or social obligations. She perceived the events of her life as if preordained in a fixed set of rules devoid of logic and alternatives. Failures or mistakes were irreclaimable. However strange it may sound, she felt completely comfortable in her inertness, which demanded neither the capability of feeling well nor the right to feel sick. She willingly plunged in her self-pity, accepting all the gigantic and unrewarding efforts it entailed.

As a result, her dependence on past events, on other people, particularly the dead ones, and on the present circumstances, including the habit of taking laxatives, was total. This dependence allowed her no pleasure and, perhaps, not even pain. The sensation of feeling needed became the only tangible dimension in her life. Nothing could have changed the way she was. Nothing could have been otherwise. For instance, how could she have changed her huge hips, two sizes larger than the rest of her body? There was no other choice but surgery. However, surgery was not possible at the time.

In conclusion, based on the way Daniela expounded her story and on the way she displayed her emotions, we surmised that her eating disorder was a symptomatic expression of a more complex and deeply rooted psychological distress. In effect, we were dealing with a childish young woman who had been suddenly forced to face a tragic reality, probably too soon in her lifetime. A childish young woman still needing parental guidance and support and, thus, incapable of making good sensible decisions. The latter hypothesis was based on her wrong and impulsive decision to start a wrong diet and on the ensuing eating disorders. In the midst of the sudden changes following her mother's death, she found a sort of haven in the burden of her family commitments. Furthermore, although she realized that she was entrapped into a reality that she did not necessarily like and, most important, could not change, she willingly and passively accepted it. In the end, she found it reassuring, for as opposed to her baffled sense of reality, it was preordained. Accordingly, even the reason she gave for her dieting, "A posthumous gift for my mother," as she suddenly stated, gracefully fitted in the impressionistic but orderly picture she had painted.

I envisioned that she was probably willing to accept a second talk, maybe a third one, and, maybe, even a pharmacological therapy (sertraline); however, she was probably not going to accept a fourth one. Probably, I was never going to see her again.

She interpreted my role as a mere guidance, just like a neglected little girl longs for a nurturing mother figure. Thus, it was not so much a case of regression but rather of immaturity and childishness: a dependent personality, according to DSM . In effect, in making my diagnosis, I could have followed more closely the criteria available for such disorders. However, I believe that a psychiatric diagnosis demands the direct observation of the patient through his or her eyes in an attempt to unveil the hidden causes of the his or her inner distress. I have one last objection to make: Why did not she develop psychological dependence on her therapist? Maybe I did not give her the chance nor the time to do so.

CASE 5 – ELENA

Elena, a pretty 27-year-old teenager, first came to our Eating Disorder unit on September 2004, reporting no concomitant organic pathologies. She lived in Naples with her father, an urban policeman, and her mother, a housewife.

She wore hardly any make-up except for a dark red lipstick and kept her black jacket on the whole time even though the room was quite warm. Almost immediately, she told us that she had been working as a shop assistant but without getting paid. The grimace expression on her face clearly conveyed a great dissatisfaction with such situation. She was, in fact, considering quitting the job.

Although she seemed quite nervous, she displayed a very casual attitude which set a familiar tone throughout the entire interview. The first part of our conversation entailed her anamnesis, which was later added to the computerized case file (CIDA, Di Pietro et al., 2000).

As soon as we sat opposite each other, she began speaking about herself and the reason why she had sought psychiatric counselling. We learnt that, over the past year or so, she had been suffering from a Binge Eating Disorder, particularly the Night Eater Syndrome . Although she had not acquired an emetic behaviour, she was, nonetheless, worried about the negative effects that the intake of huge amounts of food (3 kg of bread, 2 kg of pasta, and whole bags of cookies) could have had on her health.

Surprisingly, she smiled as she spoke. Yet, those smiles surely seemed contrived. They seemed to hide a completely different reality: an unbearable anguish stemming from her incapability of resisting or sublimating her eating and violent impulses.

My "countertransferal emotions" was ambivalent: a mix between attraction and defensiveness.

Such ambivalence was significant for my diagnosis, for soon she began to show signs of a personality disorder.

As envisioned, those contrived smiles, which had brightened her face just a few minutes earlier, were soon stilted by an outburst of sadness that brought tears to her eyes . She confessed that she had not cried for years.

This chameleonic transformation was probably the result of her manipulativity: the expectation of being treated as a privileged person. Specifically, when she realized that her efforts of omnipotence had failed her, she was overcome with failure and disappointment. Consequently, she began to depreciate my presence. Could this have been a case of object devaluation?

At this point of the interview, I no longer doubted about the severity of her illness, revealed and confirmed also by the diagnostic tests she underwent.

As she continued telling her story, it was quite clear that we were dealing with a young woman that, throughout her childhood and her developmental years, had been neglected by her father and had been raised in a threatening family context. The story of her family encompasses, in fact, bleak episodes of physical and psychological violence, betrayals, adultery, and frustration. A whole series of micro traumas, which having resurfaced, seemed to destabilize her mental perception of herself and of her social environment.

She told us about her parents' quarrelsome relationship and how her father was hated by everyone in her family. As she stated, "No one ever came over to our house because no one could stand him. I hated the way he shouted at my mother and how he often hit her and threatened her. Being stronger than she, I would defend her by hitting him".

She talked more about the conflicting and rather pathological relationship she had with her father, who, as she reported, "seduced and deserted her." He was portrayed as cold and unresponsive to her solicitous efforts to receive his love and attention. As she stated, "When I would sit on his lap to receive some attention, he would grow ice-cold, giving me no caresses, no smiles." A more striking feature of their relationship was, however, the ambiguous quality of mixed emotions she felt for him after incidents of violence and non-violence: when he hit her, she would give him presents. However, when he smiled at her, she became suspicious. Not much was said about her mother except that she was loving and fragile.

As I listened to her narration, it became quite evident that her conception of reality, including her interpersonal relationships with her parents, was based on a dichotomy between good and evil. Similarly, she manifested a confused and contradicting self-image ("I am rubbish , so I deserve a lot more".)

She also talked about her unpredictable impulsive behaviour: " Once at the supermarket, a girl accidentally touched me with her bag and I split her lips with my head. The police arrived"

When these episodes occurred, she was often in a state of unconsciousness. More specifically, they happened in a twilight condition, or a state of reduced consciousness. She also reported of being affected by hallucinations and agoraphobia. The latter triggered in her panic attacks mixed with depressing states or latent anxiety caused by her fears of being helpless.

It came to no surprise to learn about these symptoms, for her eating disorder was the clinical demonstration of an affective disorder or latent anxiety.

Such consideration is consistent with recent studies showing the high interplay between Anxiety Disorders and Binging, and Purging Behaviours (Siracusano et al., 2003). Actually, such abnormal conditions seem to induce tranquillizing effects on social anxiety triggered by body dissatisfaction.

In conclusion, her tendency to act out archaic defence mechanisms (like the splitting), her lack of self-identity, and, finally, the occurrence of psychotic episodes, such as hallucinations and uncontrollable aggressiveness, led us to diagnose her condition as Marginal Syndrome (Kernberg, 1975), which characterizes the Borderline Personality Disorder.

Case 6 – Anna

Anna G. was now a thirty-year-old married woman and the mother of two children: an elementary school boy and a toddler girl. The day of our first session, she silently waited for us to invite her into the room. She appeared shy and quite placid in her manners; however, she gave the impression of being rather embarrassed and not totally convinced of why she was there. It was her mother who had persuaded her to come.

She must have been tempted to leave, for she rigidly and uncomfortably sat on the edge of the chair with her hands tightly holding her bag on her knees. Her features were rather indistinct and she hardly wore any make-up. Her voice was feeble too. Overall, she had a very childish appearance. While I collected information for the anamnesis , the supervisor, hardly listing to what we were saying, filled out the patient's case file. Not expecting the patient to talk and hoping to understand her expectations, I asked Anna why she had come. We learnt that she had been following a dietary and nutritional program at the Dietetic and Nutrition Section of the School of Medicine in Naples, but her compliance with the program had been very scarce.

"I'm not able to follow a diet!" was Anna's verbal expression of her distress. Managing to get thin and to lose weight (she weighs over 90 kg) had always been rather problematic for her, for she was unable to follow any diet plan. Her clinical case was compatible with an

Eating Disorder Not Otherwise Specified (EDNOS), in particular with a "Binge Eating Disorder" (BED). The patient had been suffering from bulimic crisis, characterized by strong compulsive components, for three years , specifically since the time she was expecting her second child. The "binge" episodes occurred daily and were essentially limited in the afternoon when Anna was at home and not working as a cashier in her husband's bakery shop. The dry tone with which she referred her lifestyle and occupation ("In the morning, I work at the bakery to give him a hand") revealed a certain sense of discontent in her life.

She did not seem too satisfied with playing the double role of wife/employee. Perhaps, her marriage was not giving her what she had expected. Whenever I asked her a straight question, she always replied evasively. Throughout the interview, in fact, reticence was a fundamental trait in her attitude. Because she was reluctant to talk about herself, she focused her attention on her symptoms. However, even then, her exposition was cold and detached. Her uncontrolled/compulsive food assumption represented the unconscious outlet of her dissatisfaction. It was her way either to retrieve something that had been lost or to compensate for something that had been missing. In fact, in the course of the interview, she started realizing that her eating disorders had probably stemmed from her efforts to fill the void in her life of which she had been hardly aware. Furthermore, she confessed that she had no idea of how to grapple with it. Her sense of alienation was becoming more and more concrete.

When I suggested that maybe the relation with her husband could have been the source of her dissatisfaction, she denied it. At this point, we wondered whether she was actually incapable of realizing the existence of a problem, or whether she was trying to hide it from herself and, even more, from us. Rather, she reported the conflicting relationship she had with her in-laws; however, because she was also aloof on this issue, the subject was completely dropped. The talk was then switched to her parents. Her father had had several affairs with different women, and, at the time, he was supposedly having one. Because of her father's unfaithfulness, she and her mother had suffered a lot. Interestingly, as opposed to her previous aloofness and discretion, Anna seemed now more impassioned in telling her story.

In fact, as she reported these incidences, we could tell (by the fervour in her eyes and by the excitement in her voice and, simply, by her uneasiness) that she was still deeply troubled by them, as if she had been, once again, the little girl of an unhappy marriage. In reporting her mother's present and past tribulations, she seemed to relive her troubled childhood in which her parents would continually argue. Because she had grown-up as an only child in a turbulent family environment, she had probably developed an extremely emotional bond with her mother. This emotional dependence persisted throughout her adolescence and adulthood, thus hampering her development into a fully grown-up, confident and self-sufficient woman. Accordingly, the hypothesis of a symbiotic relationship with her mother should not be ruled out as a possible phenomenon underlying Anna's inaptitude and insecurity to cope with her life.

Strongly empathizing with her mother's sufferings, she still deeply resented her father's inapt behaviour, blaming him not only for her parents' difficult marriage but also for her mother's unhappiness. Indirectly, she could not truly appreciate her husband, (seeing him almost as a father figure,) for she was afraid that he could become as unfaithful as her father

In this undifferentiated condition, Anna did not even seem to be in a position to be a good mother, since she had transferred her maternal duties onto her mother. Actually, she seemed to live her lifestyle in a very ambivalent way. On the one hand, she found it convenient to leave her children to her parents when she went to work; however, on the other , she demanded her role as a mother. In the end, she seemed totally baffled about her identity.

After approximately 40 minutes, the anamnesis clearly suggested a dependent personality resulting from a poor development of self-esteem. Therefore, her eating disorder became part of such "regressive" context.

At the end of the interview, no pharmacological therapy was prescribed, since sertraline and alprazolam had given her no relief. Rather, she was scheduled for a second interview for a diagnostic and therapeutic re-evaluation.

Follow-up: In the following interviews, the patient showed a reduction in her symptoms and an improvement in the quality of her lifestyle. Over all, the observed improvements result from the reinforcement of the Ego, and, hence, of her Self-esteem.

CASE 7 – ASSUNTA

Assunta , a 35-year-old woman suffering from bulimia nervosa came to our psychiatric unit following the advice of her nutritionist. Over the past few years, whenever she was left alone, she was taken by incontrollable and recurrent bouts of binge eating. As soon as our session started, a strong embarrassment seemed to characterize her attitude. However, as the interview went on, her embarrassment gradually vanished and was replaced by moments of cooperativeness and openness and by others of reluctance and impenetrability. It seemed as if a subconscious impetus for survival converged her attitude on the tracks of a true cooperative process; by contrast, her partial denial, mixed with reticence, seemed to drift her cooperativeness towards stubborn forms of obstructionism, as if she were trying to conceal her sufferings from us, but , above all, from herself, in an attempt to provide herself some type of psychological protection against her deeply rooted distress. Therefore, urged to provide some details about her life, particularly those that in some way triggered the onset of her disorder, she began describing the essentiality of her distress. Actually, the source of her disorder was rooted into a difficult family context. It was her father who played a major role in her entangled emotional life. He was a character that stood out against a conflicting family background which had been stirred by an excruciating aura of frustration deepened, in her point of view, by her mother's inapt behaviour to deal with the family problems. When we met Assunta , both her parents had already died. She was, supposedly, happily married to a man who was few years older than she and with whom she had had two children, now both adolescents. She confessed that she felt a certain sense of guilt towards her family, for she often yearned to be left alone in order to satisfy her bulimic cravings. After each bulimic episode, she always felt dirty, totally ashamed of herself and unworthy.

Her mood, clearly flattened by her depressive state, portrayed a rather bleak private and public life. She explained that she has two occupations. The first was to assist a physical and mentally disabled person in his own home, and, the second, probably stemming from her reparative needs, was to work as a volunteer for an organization of mentally retarded children. Her bulimic episodes occurred whenever she felt that her anguish was about to drift her towards an overwhelming state of depression. They represented a form of self-made medication needed to overcome such undesired state. She, therefore, had triggered a destructive mechanism in which what once may have served a potential therapeutic purpose, in reality, was now taking a "Janus-faced" psychopathological resemblance. Therefore, deprived of any therapeutic purpose, her bulimic cravings served no other purpose than that of arousing feelings of guilt not only towards Assunta herself, but also towards her own family. As she continued her story about her father, the resentment she felt against him changed into feelings of deep hostility towards her mother. She was portrayed as the culprit of her family's tribulations, lacking that centripetal force capable of restoring family harmony whenever it was broken by her husband's stormy and abusive behaviour. She was depicted as an emotionally fragile and weak woman who had reconciled herself to her husbands vexations, including his unfaithful behaviours. In the midst of such extremely tense family environment, our patient grew-up bringing her childhood and adolescent fears and apprehensions all the way up into her adulthood. Accordingly, she adopted stringent and aggressive behaviours as defensive mechanisms to conceal her deeply rooted fragility. So, she built a false psychological balance which, in fact, was broken when her father died of lung cancer. As she reported the incident of her father's death, it was clear that her mind was still unhinged by his death. During his short illness (her father passed away in a three months' time), she discovered a totally different person from the one she had known, and feared, in the previous years. Perhaps, the person she was now discovering was the father she had always wanted; unfortunately, it was now too late to make up for all the lost years What seemed to have stricken her the most, however, was the fact that her father, during the last days of his agony, had wanted her and not her mother to lie in bed next to him. It was plain to see that such unexpected circumstance was lived by Assunta as an almost acted out Oedipus complex, as she reported feelings of guilt and embarrassment. She began to doubt about her father's true identity: Was he that possessive, abusive and adulterous man she had known through her own experiences, but, above all, through her mother's eyes? Or, was he the loving father that had always loved being surrounded by his family and was now reaching out to his daughter to find love and comfort in the last days of his life? Such doubt was further elaborated in Oedipal terms. In fact, She retained her mother more responsible than her father for her family's conflicting and divided family. She was depicted as the offender who had failed to subdue her father's abusive behaviours because of her weakness. Therefore, she was considered responsible for having fuelled in her children deep feelings of fear and apprehension towards him. Interestingly, toward the end of this first session, the patient herself related her turbulent past experiences to her present depression and bulimic disorder. To begin treating her depression, an antidepressant drug therapy belonging to the class of serotonin re-uptake inhibitors was prescribed and supported by ten psychotherapeutic individual sessions.

DISCUSSION

The first session is generally oriented by the primary aim of creating a relationship and facilitating the patient's collaboration, not only in the diagnostic definition of the disturb, but also in the research for significant connections between these and other psychological trends, more or less conscious.

The patient should have new starting points for reflection, for example, on the historical causes that began the symptomatic behaviour, or even on the present background that sustains him.

The anamnestic collection represents a valid instrument through which such an objective can be reached. While the patient talks about himself the interviewer can steer the attention and the reflection – the pause – in areas which are judged significant; the waiting, then, will give the confirmation of how valid these new prospectives can be and considered as new on behalf of the patient.

We mustn't forget that, in the majority of cases, a patient begins a psychiatric interview in a mood of expectation, sometimes fear, that the interlocutor immediately gives definite answers to their ailment; very rarely, though, is he willing to accept that investigation should also be open to aspects different from the ailment and apparently far from the area of the ailment.

In other words, the time and space of the first interview must be used to evaluate the patient's motivation also, his insight capacity, the emotional possibility of creating a significant relationship with the doctor.

It is interesting to note that the observations reported in these notes have been drawn up in a formation and teaching university context, with two interviewers, but that this setting did not create specific interference, neither for the patient, nor for the interviewers. As was later verified, in all cases, it was possible to achieve the pre-fixed goals, even if in different measures from one case to another.

The first patient, in particular, who appeared to be the most difficult by definition of a treatment programme because he was supposed to show his functional opposition to the family context, re-took up contacts with our facilities to receive advice; of the other patients, some have undertaken a therapeutic journey with good results (Carla & Anna); others have a poor adherence to the treatment program but, however, maintain occasional contacts.

The identifiable dynamics in the course of the first interview are numerous: sometimes it was 'sui generis', as in the case of Teresa, in which an independence/dependence conflict was evident, which greatly embarrassed the interviewer, gripped in the paradoxical request of "Help me/Don't help me", expression symptomatic of the well known message just as paradoxical "You must be free and Independent", characteristic of certain anorexic families.

Other times you meet old and well-known relational problems, even if not resolved; the relationship with the absent father, which often maps the path to future emotional relationships, like the incapacity to create stable relationships (Elena) or the profound sense of guilt for not having known how to avoid the disappearance, or death (Assunta)

In all the cases observed, the defensive significance of ED seems to prevail, either to fill a " Void" or "to unload" a tension.

Just as frequently, the tendency with the relationship to the body appears a decisive psychological dimension for a physiological development of the personality.

The body is dominated and nullified, objectualized by a sadistic and oppressive Ego/Mind, but at the same time, in it's biological and physical aspects, it becomes cumbersome, demanding, unsatiable.

In this regard, the Palazzoni-Selvini's definition (Palazzoli S., 1963) of this aberrant mind/body relationship, seems particularly suitable, as in an "Intrapsychic Paranoia", we would just like to add that such a tendency seems to concern not only Anorexic patients, to whom Palazzoli S. was referring to, but also the bulimic patients, or BED observed by us.

The only difference seems to be that the torment, which in bulimics is expressed in all its phases and forms, in the anorexics, instead, is contained under spasmodic control.

From the cases observed, one particular case emerges, even though not infrequent: the relationship with the sick body (Antonella). In this case it seems really inevitable that all the anguish and the emotions takes the corporal and physical way: how can you have a quiet and non-conflicting relationship with a body that, irony of the process of fate, suffers from the same ailment by which the mother died? In this case, the pathology which pushes you to fill and empty out with good or bad things a malfunctioning wrapping seems physiological.

But only a long course of psychotherapy could maybe find complete and full answers to these and other questions.

BIBLIOGRAPHY

American Psychiatric Association (1994) Diagnostic and statistical manual of mental disorders, 4th ed. Washington DC

Bruch H. “Anorexia Nervosa: therapy and theory”. *Am J Psychiatry* 1982 Dec;139(12):1531-8.

Bruch H. Treatment in anorexia nervosa. Int J Psychoanal Psychother. 1982-83;9:303-12.

Karwautz A, Nobis G, Haidvogl M, Wagner G, Hafferl-Gattermayer A, Wober-Bingol C, Friedrich MH. “Perceptions of family relationships in adolescents with anorexia and their uaffected sisters”. *Eur Child Adolesc Psychiatry*. 2003 Jun;12(3):128-35.

Klein M: “Lo sviluppo di un bambino ”(1921) in: Klein M: “Scritti 1921 - 1958”. *Boringhieri,* Torino, 1978.

Klein M: “Il nostro mondo adulto e le sue radici nell’infanzia ” (1959) in : Klein M: “Il nostro mondo adulto e altri saggi”. *Martinelli, Firenze,* 1972.

Novelletto A. “L’anoressia mentale alla luce della patologia del Sé” , in Novelletto A. “Psichiatria psicoanalitica dell’adolescenza”. *Ed. Borla, Roma* 1993, pp 145 – 160.

Recalcati M. “Il corpo ostaggio. Teoria e clinica dell’anoressia-bulimia”. Ed. Borla 1998.

Winnicott D W : “Gioco e realtà ” (1971). *Armando editore,* Roma 1974.

Halmi K.A. (1999) Eating disorders: Anorexia nervosa, bulimia nervosa and obesity. *In K.E. Hales, S.C.*

Holden M. (1990) Is anorexia nervosa an obsessive compulsive disorder? *Br J Psychiatry,* 157, 1-5.

Lehnk C, Strnad A, Bailer U, Biener D, Fodor G, de Zwaan M (1998) Comorbidity of obsessive compulsive disorder in patients with eating disorders. *Eat Weight Disord.,* 3(1), 37-41.

Di Pietro G., Muscettola G., Bellini O., Sorge F.“Disturbi dell’Alimentazione: ipotesi per una nuova Cartella Clinica Informatizzata (CIDA-IIR) *Giornale Italiano di Psicopatologia* 2000; 6(2):223-239

Garner DM,Garfinkel PE,The Eating Attitude Test (EAT): an index of the symptoms of anorexia nervosa. *Psychol Med,* 9:273,1979.

Garner DM, Olmestead MP, Polivy J, Development and validation of a multidimensional eating disorder inventory for anorexia nervosa and bulimia (EDI), *Int J Eating Dis,* 2:15,1983.

Cuzzolaro M, Vetrone G, Marano G, Battacchi MW, Body Uneasiness Test, 1999. (BUT; manca la rivista su cui è stato pubblicato la prima volta!).

De Rogatis LR., Lipman RS., Covi L.: SCL-90: An outpatient psychiatric rating scale. Preliminary Report. In: Guy W (ED.) ECDEU Assessment Manual for Psychopharmacology. Revised 1976 *DHEW Pubblication N (ADM)* 76-338, 1976)

Beck AD, Ward CH,Mendelson M,Mock J, ErbaughJ: An Inventory for measuring depression. *Arch Gen Psychiatry.* 1961, 4: 561-571.

Apolone G., Mosconi P., Ware JE : Questionario sullo stato di salute SF-36. Manuale d'uso e guida all'interpretazione dei risultati. *A. Guerini e Associati Ed.* Milano, 1997.

Apolone G., Mosconi P.: The Italian SF-36 Health Survey: translation, validation and norming. J Clin Epidemiol, 51:1025, 1998.

Kernberg H Borderline conditions and pathological narcissism, 1975 – Ed. It. Sindrome borderline e narcisismo patologico – Bollati Boringhieri, MI, 1978 – 2000

SiracusanoA., Troisi A., Marino V., Tozzi F. Comorbidità nei Disturbi del Comportamento Alimentare: revisione critica della letteratura Noòs Ge-Mar 2003; Vol 9 N. 1: 7-26

Palazzoni Sellini M L'Anoressia Mentale Feltrinelli MI 1963

In: New Developments in Eating Disorders Research
Editor: Pamela I. Swain, pp. 169-182
ISBN 1-59454-542-1

Chapter 8

ARRHYTHMOGENICITY IN EATING DISORDERS

Yoshiyuki Takimoto* and Kazuhiro Yoshiuchi
Department of Psychosomatic Medicine, Faculty of Medicine,
The University of Tokyo, Tokyo, Japan

ABSTRACT

Eating disorders are complex conditions characterized by disturbances to eating behavior. Anorexia nervosa is a syndrome consisting of a combination of weight loss, amenorrhea and behavioral changes, whereas bulimia nervosa is characterized by recurrent episodes of binge eating. AN affects about 1% of all women between the ages of 15 and 25, and long-term follow-up studies have shown that AN has a mortality rate of about 1-6%, with ventricular arrhythmias being one of the probable major causes of sudden death. The risk of sudden death is thought to be higher in eating disorder patients, compared to coeval women, and therefore it is important to evaluate arrhythmogenicity in eating disorders.

The evaluation of arrhythmogenicity requires assessment of cardiac electrical instability, in which three factors need to be considered: 1) modulating factors, 2) triggers, and 3) substrates. Many previous studies have focused on the risk of fatal arrhythmia by evaluating substrates, and there have also been previous studies on substrates and modulating factors in anorexia nervosa. In this chapter, we review previous studies on cardiac arrhythmias and function in eating disorders, including our own studies on substrates in eating disorders. Hence, in one of our previous studies, substrates were evaluated for assessment of arrhythmogenicity in patients with bulimia nervosa, as well as in patients with anorexia nervosa. It was found that QT intervals were prolonged and QT dispersion increased in both anorexia nervosa and bulimia nervosa patients.

* Department of Psychosomatic Medicine, Faculty of Medicine, The University of Tokyo, Hongo 7-3-1, Bunkyo-ku, Tokyo 113-8655, Japan; Tel.: +81-5800-9737; Fax: +81-5800-9737; Email: taki-tky@umin.ac.jp

INTRODUCTION

Eating disorders are complex conditions characterized by disturbances in eating behavior. Patients with eating disorders show changes in their attitude towards weight and body shape, as well as in their perception of body shape. There are two major types of eating disorder: anorexia nervosa (AN) and bulimia nervosa (BN). AN is a syndrome that comprises a combination of weight loss, amenorrhea and behavioral changes. AN is subdivided into two subgroups: the restricting type (AN-R) and the binge eating/purging type (AN-BP), depending on the absence or presence of binge eating. On the other hand, BN is a syndrome characterized by recurrent episodes of binge eating and is subdivided into two subgroups: the purging type (BN-P) and the non-purging type (BN-NP), depending on the absence or presence of efforts to purge ingested calories through self-induced vomiting, laxative or diuretic abuse, fasting, or intensive exercise. AN affects about 1% of all women between the ages of 15 and 25 [1], and long-term follow-up studies have shown that AN has a mortality rate of about 1-6% [2,3].

SUDDEN DEATH IN AN

"Sudden death" is defined as the sudden and unexpected occurrence of death for which no satisfactory explanation of the cause of death can be ascertained. There are a number of case reports of sudden death in anorexia nervosa patients [4]. Isner et al. [5] have described 3 patients with anorexia nervosa who died suddenly, and suggested a connection between death and the degree of QT interval prolongation in an electrocardiogram (ECG) recorded 7 days before death occurred. In all 3 cases, microscopic investigation of the heart muscle revealed, among other things, an increase in lipofuscin. Based on the evaluation of five consecutive medicolegal investigations of young persons who suffered from eating disorders and who died suddenly, Rajs et al. [6] postulated that the cause of death was due to a circulatory catastrophe. In 4 of the 5 cases, intestinal hemorrhages of the myocardium, contraction bands, and uptake of basic fuscin were found at autopsy. Furthermore, the patients were found to have severe hypopotassemia and ECG abnormalities. Chikasue et al. [7] have reported that a histological investigation of an anorexia nervosa patient who died suddenly showed extreme atrophy of the cardiac muscles and moderate deposition of lipofuscin granules in myocardial cells. Therefore, it has been postulated that sudden death in AN patients may be due to cardiac arrhythmia [5,8].

QT INTERVAL AND QT DISPERSION IN AN

It has been proposed that deaths of AN patients are a result of cardiac arrhythmias. Determination of arrhythmogenicity in AN patients requires assessment of cardiac electrical instability, in which three factors are of importance: 1) the modulating factor, 2) the trigger, and 3) the substrate. Many previous studies of the risk of fatal arrhythmia have focused on an examination of the substrate. QT interval and QT dispersion are substrates which are associated with ventricular arrhythmias, and Isner et al. have reported long QT intervals in three young patients with anorexia who died suddenly, two of whom had ventricular tachycardia and syncope within the preceding 24 hours [5]. Cooke et al. have also described the cases of two patients who died suddenly, both of whom had relatively long QT intervals [8]. Hence, the question arises whether long QT intervals and large QT dispersions are typical features in AN. A number of studies have considered QT intervals and QT dispersion in AN patients, compared to controls. Hence, Cooke et al. [8] measured QT intervals and QT dispersion using 12-lead ECGs in 41 consecutive patients and in age and sex matched controls, and found that the QT interval was longer in patients with AN than in the controls, although the QT dispersion was not significantly different from the controls. Durakovic et al. [9] examined QT intervals and QT dispersion in 30 AN patients and 30 controls, and reported significantly prolonged QT intervals and increased QT dispersion in the AN patients, compared to the controls. Swenne and Larsson have found that QT intervals in AN patients were significantly prolonged, compared to controls, and that QT dispersion in AN patients was almost twice that of controls [10]. Galetta et al. compared QT intervals and QT dispersion in 16 AN patients with 16 women of normal weight and 16 constitutionally thin women [11], and found that QT intervals were significantly longer and QT dispersion was significantly greater than in the thin women and the controls. In contrast, Panagiotopoulos et al. examined QT intervals and QT dispersion in 62 adolescents patients with AN, and reported that the AN patients had significantly shorter QT intervals and reduced QT dispersion [12]. Vanderdonckt et al. have also suggested that QT interval prolongation is not a typical feature in AN patients, based on a retrospective analysis of 47 consecutive patients with AN, in which QT interval prolongation was present in 1 patient only [13].

As shown above, the results of previous studies of QT interval and QT dispersion in AN patients have not been consistent. The discrepancies between studies may have been due to the use of Bazett's formula to adjust for heart rate in measuring QT intervals, as it has been shown that this formula fails to adjust for extreme heart rates [14,15]. AN patients often have bradycardia [10], and therefore not only Bazett's formula but also another adjustment method is required to correct for the extremely low heart rate when QT intervals in AN patients are evaluated.

Another possible reason for the inconsistencies in the results of previous studies is that these studies did not take into account electrolyte abnormalities, which are sometimes found in AN patients and can result in alteration of QT interval. Indeed, Vanderdonckt et al. have shown that QT intervals are solely correlated with the serum potassium concentration [13].

Low body weight has been suggested to play an important role in prolongation of QT intervals in AN patients. Hence, Swenne [16] found that prolongation of QT intervals and an increase of QT dispersion in AN patients normalized within 3 days of refeeding that resulted in weight gain, although the serum concentrations of potassium and magnesium were, with few exceptions, normal before refeeding. Mont et al. [17] have also reported that after refeeding, a significant decrease in QT intervals and QT dispersion are observed independently of alterations of the serum potassium, calcium and magnesium concentrations. Unlike AN patients, those with BN do not have extremely low body weight, although BN is thought to have some psychopathological features in common with AN [18]. Therefore, examination of BN patients might help to clarify the role of low body weight in the prolongation of QT interval and increased QT dispersion in AN. However, no such studies have been reported to date.

We have hypothesized that QT interval and QT dispersion are not prolonged in BN patients. In a previous study [19], we examined QT interval and QT dispersion in both anorexia nervosa patients and bulimia nervosa patients, and excluded patients with abnormal electrolytes from the analysis. The QT interval was measured and adjusted for heart rate using both Bazett's formula [14] and the nomogram method [15], and in the following sections we describe our findings regarding QT variables in anorexia and bulimia nervosa.

Our Previous Study

Methods in our Previous Study

Subjects

Female patients aged over 18 years old who were referred to the Tokyo University Branch Hospital were enrolled in the study. The patients were diagnosed with eating disorders by well-trained clinicians according to DSM-IV criteria. Patients with abnormal plasma electrolytes or those taking medications, such as psychotropic or cardiovascular drugs, that might influence the electrocardiogram (ECG) were excluded from the study. Normal levels of potassium and calcium were considered to be between 3.5 and 5.0 mEq/l and between 8.5 and 10.5 mg/dl, respectively. The total number of patients examined was 179, and the control group consisted of 52 healthy female university students. All data were collected prospectively. After complete disclosure of the study methods, written informed consent was obtained from all of the subjects.

Measurement of ECG Parameters

Twelve-lead ECG recordings were obtained at a paper speed of 25 mm/s. All ECGs were magnified and measurements were performed manually to the nearest 0.25 mm in a blinded manner. QT interval was defined according to the criteria of Lepeschkin and Surawicz [20], and QT interval and RR interval were measured twice to confirm reproducibility. Reliability coefficients for the QT interval and RR interval were 0.90 (95% C. I., 0.88-0.93) and 0.97 (95% C. I., 0.96-0.98), respectively. PQ interval and QRS duration were also measured.

The corrected QT interval using Bazett's formula was calculated as follows:

$$\text{QTc} = \text{raw QT interval} / \sqrt{RRI}$$

where RRI refers to the RR interval just before the QT interval [21].

The corrected QT interval using the nomogram method was calculated with the formula:

$$\text{QTnc} = \text{raw QT interval} + \text{correction number [15]}.$$

QT dispersion was defined as the difference between the longest and shortest raw QT intervals [22].

Body Weight Variables

In addition to body mass index (BMI), the rate of body weight loss (BWr) was also calculated, using the following formula:

$$BWr = (BWh - BWt)/(\text{duration of illness})$$

where BWh refers to the pre-morbid average body weight and BWt refers to the current body weight. These variables were used because autonomic function is known to be affected by changes in body weight [23].

Statistical Analysis

All results are shown as means ± SD. One-way ANOVA and Dunnett's multiple comparison test were used to compare HR, QT interval and QT dispersion in each disease subtype group with those for controls. The relationships between the QT variables and the body weight variables were investigated using Pearson correlation coefficients. All analyses were performed with SPSS version 10.0.5J (SPSS Inc., Tokyo, Japan). A p value of < 0.05 was considered significant. Patients with ED-NOS were excluded from the analysis because of the small sample size.

Results of our Previous Study

Demographic Characteristics

A total of 179 female patients with eating disorders were examined, comprising 50 patients with AN-R, 37 with AN-BP, 65 with BN-P, 23 with BN-NP, and 4 with eating disorders not otherwise specified (ED-NOS) (Table 1, Table 2). The total number of patients eligible for the study, based on the above criteria, was 164: 43 AN-R, 35 AN-BP, 63 BN-P and 23 BN-NP patients had normal electrolyte levels, including serum potassium and calcium levels corrected for the serum albumin level. In the patient group, the mean plasma level of potassium was 4.0 ± 0.5 mEq/l, and the mean plasma level of calcium corrected for the albumin level was 8.9 ± 0.4 mg/dl. Three patients with AN-R, two with AN-BP, and one with BN-P were excluded due to low serum potassium levels; two AN-R patients were excluded due to low serum calcium levels; and two patients with AN-R and one with BN-P were excluded due to low serum levels of both potassium and calcium.

There were no significant differences in age between each eating disorder subgroup and the healthy controls.

Heart Rate

Dunnett's multiple comparison test indicated that HR was significantly lower in all ED subtypes, compared with the control group ($p < 0.001$) (Table 2). There was no significant correlation between HR and BMI, while HR and BWr were significantly correlated ($r = -0.29$, $p < 0.01$).

Table 1. Patient characteristics and electrocardiographic measurements in anorexia nervosa patients with normal electrolytes and in normal controls

	AN-R (n=50)	AN-BP (n=37)	Control (n=52)
Age(years)	19.1±4.0	23.8±8.9†	18.3±0.5
Height(cm)	157.1±4.0	158.5±4.3	158.4±7.4
BW(kg)	35.3±4.5†	39.4±4.1†	56.6±8.2
BMI(kg/cm^2)	14.5±2.0†	15.4±1.7†	20.3±2.0
Duration(months)	26.7±20.6	65.8±68.8	-
K (mEq/l)	3.9±0.4	4.0±0.5	-
Ca (mg/dl)	8.8±0.3	8.8±0.3	-
Alb (g/dl)	4.7±0.3	4.5±0.5	-
Hb (g/dl)	12.9±1.4	12.7±1.4	-
HR (beats/min)	50.5±10.3*	51.7±10.9*	68.0±9.7
QTc (ms)	437.7±38.7*	448.8±37.9*	407.3±20.5
QTnc (ms)	456.2±37.5*	463.5±35.3*	402.2±17.9
QTd (ms)	63.4±35.8*	61.6±20.4*	26.2±11.6

All values are expressed as means ± SD.

AN-R = anorexia nervosa restricting type; AN-BP = anorexia nervosa binge eating/purging type; BW = body weight; BMI = body mass index; K = plasma level of potassium; Ca = plasma level of calcium corrected by albumin level; Alb = concentration of albumin; Hb = concentration of hemoglobin; Duration = duration of illness; HR = heart rate; QTc = corrected QT interval; QTnc = QT interval corrected by nomogram method; QTd = QT dispersion.

*$p < 0.001$ *vs.* controls using Dunnett's multiple comparison test.

†$p < 0.05$ *vs.* controls using Dunnett's multiple comparison test.

QT Interval

Dunnett's multiple comparison test indicated that both QTc and QTnc were significantly longer in all ED subtypes than in the control group ($p < 0.001$) (Table 1, Table2).

There were no significant correlations between BMI and QTc or QTnc. BWr was positively correlated with QTc ($r = 0.38$, $p < 0.01$) and QTnc ($r = 0.45$, $p < 0.01$) in BN patients only (Table 3).

QT Dispersion

Dunnett's multiple comparison test indicated that QT dispersion was significantly greater in all ED subtypes than in the controls ($p < 0.001$) (Table 1, Table 2).

There was no significant correlation between QT dispersion and BMI. BWr was positively correlated with QT dispersion in BN patients only ($r = 0.47$, $p < 0.01$) (Table 3).

Table 2. Patient characteristics and electrocardiographic measurements in bulimia nervosa patients with normal electrolytes and in normal controls

	BN-P (n=65)	BN-NP (n=23)	Control (n=52)
Age(years)	23.2±4.9†	22.3±3.6	18.3±0.5
Height(cm)	155.4±6.2	157.6±6.1	158.4±7.4
BW(kg)	47.6±4.1	58.1±6.3	56.6±8.2
BMI(kg/cm^2)	19.6±2.2	20.8±5.1	20.3±2.0
Duration(months)	60.3±49.2	28.5±8.3	-
K (mEq/l)	4.1±0.4	3.9±0.3	-
Ca (mg/dl)	9.0±0.3	9.0±0.3	-
Alb (g/dl)	4.6±0.3	4.5±0.2	-
Hb (g/dl)	12.8±1.0	12.7±0.9	-
HR (beats/min)	58.2±10.6*	56.7±10.8†	68.0±9.7
QTc (ms)	460.9±32.8*	437.2±24.8*	407.3±20.5
QTnc (ms)	468.5±29.2*	440.3±21.2†	402.2±17.9
QTd (ms)	62.9±29.3*	47.1±19.2†	26.2±11.6

All values are expressed as means ± SD.

BN-P = bulimia nervosa purging type; BN-NP = bulimia nervosa non-purging type; BW = body weight; BMI = body mass index; K = plasma level of potassium; Ca = plasma level of calcium corrected by albumin level; Alb = concentration of albumin; Hb = concentration of hemoglobin; Duration = duration of illness; QTc = corrected QT interval; QTnc = QT interval corrected by nomogram method; QTd = QT dispersion.

*$p < 0.001$ *vs.* controls using Dunnett's multiple comparison test.

†$p < 0.05$ *vs.* controls using Dunnett's multiple comparison test.

Table 3. Pearson's correlation coefficients between body weight change and ECG parameters in bulimia nervosa patients

	HR	QTc	QTnc	QT dispersion
BWr	-0.29*	0.38*	0.45*	0.47*

*$p < 0.01$

BMI = body mass index;

BWr = rate of body weight loss; HR = heart rate; QTnc = QT interval corrected by the nomogram method.

Discussion from our Previous Study

The results of our study indicated that AN patients had longer QT intervals after correction for HR using both Bazett's formula and the nomogram method, compared with the control group. QT dispersion was also significantly greater in AN patients than in the control group.

Other previous studies have yielded inconsistent results concerning QT interval and QT dispersion in AN [8-10,12,13]. These discrepancies may have been due to the use of Bazett's formula only to adjust QT interval for heart rate, since this formula is unreliable at extreme heart rates [14,15]. In contrast, we used both Bazett's formula and the nomogram method, the latter of which is more reliable over the whole heart rate range.

The prolongation of QT interval and increased QT dispersion did not occur as a secondary response to abnormalities in serum electrolyte levels, because patients with abnormal electrolyte levels were excluded from the study. Franzoni et al. [24] have evaluated QT intervals and QT dispersion in 28 patients with AN, 20 thin female subjects and 20 female controls, and found that the AN patients had longer QT intervals and greater QT dispersion than constitutionally thin women and women of normal weight, despite normal serum potassium levels being present in all patients. Mont et al. [16] and Swenne [17] have also reported prolongation of QT intervals and an increase of QT dispersion in patients with AN, despite the presence of normal serum electrolytes levels, and Swenne and Larsson [10] reported that QT intervals and QT dispersion in patients with AN were not correlated with serum concentrations of potassium and magnesium. Hence, the results of our study were consistent with these previous studies.

The pathological bases of QT interval prolongation and increased QT dispersion in AN have not been clarified. However, these effects might be caused by low nutrition and/or myocardial hypotrophy [25,26], and we note that Galetta et al. [11] found a significant relationship between QT dispersion and left ventricular mass in patients with AN. Changes in ion channels that are active in cardiac repolarization may be involved in this mechanism, since abnormalities in potassium channels have been shown in hypotrophic myocytes and this may contribute to prolongation of the action potential [27]. Echocardiogram results may provide more information about cardiac function, and although we did not perform such tests, in the following section we provide a review of previous echocardiogram studies in eating disorder patients.

Use of Echocardiograms for Eating Disorders

Because mortality in AN patients is mainly due to suicide or cardiac failure, structural and functional cardiovascular alterations have been investigated by means of echocardiography. Anorexia nervosa is reported to be associated with a lower left ventricular mass (LVM) [11,26,28-30], but whether the reduced LVM in AN patients in previous studies reflects alterations to the myocardium is unclear. The integrated backscatter (IBS) signal of the myocardium could provide an objective approach for the detection of myocardial structural properties, and Franzoni et al. have shown that in AN patients there is a significant reduction in the cyclic variation in IBS, which is also related to left ventricular hypotrophy [31]. Left ventricular systolic dysfunction has also been pointed out in AN patients [26,30], although, in contrast, some studies have report that AN patients have normal systolic function [29,32]. Left ventricular diastolic dysfunction has also been found in AN patients [29,33], but such an assessment is not routinely performed. The myocardial performance index (MPI) is a quantitative measure of global myocardial function. Eidem et al. have used the MPI to evaluate left and right ventricular function in AN patients, and found that both functions were decreased [34]. Galetta et al. has found that SDNN in heart rate variability is positively correlated with the E/A ratio, and demonstrated a cardiovascular vagal hyperactivity in AN, which appears to influence the ventricular diastolic dynamics [29]. After recovery from low body weight, working capacity and diastolic function have been reported to improve, although echocardiographic evidence has been found that shows that impaired systolic function persists [33].

Whether these abnormalities in AN patients reflect chronic protein-energy malnutrition or are primarily related to lower cardiac workload is unclear. Anorexia nervosa is a condition of low hemodynamic load that leads to low LVM. Even with an adjustment for stroke work, however, LVM is lower than would be predicted based on height, because of the effect of body weight reduction [35].

Echocardiographic evidence of cardiac abnormalities other than LVM and cardiac function has also been obtained. Hence, Ramacciotti et al. have shown that silent pericardial effusion in AN patients is seven-fold more prevalent than in controls, and the separation of pericardial leaflets among AN patients is more frequent in those with a shorter duration of illness [36]. Frolich et al. have described ten case reports for inpatient anorexic female adolescents, who developed pericardial effusions in the course of their illness, and in whom pericardial effusion remitted completely or partially with a concurrent increase in weight [37]. Inagaki et al. encountered a case in which pericardial effusion remitted completely along with body weight increase and normalization of low T3 syndrome [38], and also found that plasma brain natriuretic peptide (BNP) levels increased with severity of illness, despite heart failure, and then decreased as pericardial effusion remitted. In all other previous studies, no signs of heart failure have been reported with pericardial effusion, and whether clinically-silent pericardial effusion in AN patients is an early sign of cardiovascular involvement remains unclear.

Mitral valve prolapse (MVP) has also been described in previous studies. Johnson et al. have confirmed the presence of mitral valve prolapse in 37% of AN patients, while similar echocardiographic findings were present in only 4% of controls [39]. Oka et al. have reported that MVP is present in 87% of AN patients and that heart rate is lower in AN patients with double MVP than in those with single or no MVP [40].

In our previous study, QT interval and QT dispersion were not significantly correlated with BMI in AN patients. Therefore, the prolonged QT interval and QT dispersion in AN might be caused not only by the subject's malnourished state but also by other factors, such as changes in autonomic nervous control [41]. In fact, autonomic alterations have been reported previously in AN patients [42].

Heart Rate Variability

AN patients present a number of changes in autonomic system functions, such as thermoregulation, vascular motility, heart rate and rhythm, and blood pressure. An analysis of R-R interval variability can be used to evaluate changes in the autonomic control of the heart rate. Several studies have reported that heart rate variability in AN patients is increased [11,17,43], whereas one study has reported a heart rate decrease [42]. Spectral analysis of R-R interval variability is useful for the evaluation of autonomic function. The high frequency (HF) components of the spectral analysis represents parasympathetic modulation, partly including sympathetic function, and this is reported to be greater in AN patients than in controls [43,44]. The low frequency (LF) components of the spectral analysis are reported to be lower in AN patients than in controls, suggesting a decrease in sympathetic modulation of heart rate [44,45]. However, Rechlin has shown that the values of the spectral power analyses are significantly lower in AN patients weighing less than 75% of ideal body weight, when compared to the results for controls, and has also shown that the heart rate variability parameters of AN patients with restored weight does not differ from those of controls [46]. The results of previous studies of heart rate variability are consistent. However, there is thought to be autonomic cardiac dysfunction in AN patients, and a few studies have also suggested autonomic nervous dysfunction in BN patients. BN patients are reported to have an elevated cardiac vagal tone [47].

Another possible mechanism might be the influence of intracellular abnormal electrolytes levels in cardiac muscle. Indeed, in our study QT intervals were prolonged and the QT dispersion increased, even though plasma and serum electrolytes were normal. However, findings of normal plasma electrolyte levels do not necessarily imply that intracellular potassium and calcium levels are normal. Hence, anorexia nervosa patients with normal serum potassium levels who were treated with an oral potassium aspartate supplement showed increased kalaemia and a significant reduction in QT intervals and QT dispersion, compared with untreated patients [24]. Furthermore, QT intervals and QT dispersion in AN patients have been shown to normalize after refeeding, as the serum potassium concentration in the normal range becomes elevated [17].

Contrary to our hypothesis, we found significantly longer QT intervals and greater QT dispersion in BN patients than in the control group. There have been no previous studies examining QT interval or QT dispersion in adult BN patients. The increases in QT interval and QT dispersion could not be explained by abnormal electrolyte levels, because BN patients with abnormal electrolytes were excluded from our analysis. Although malnutrition is considered to be an important factor influencing QT interval and QT dispersion, BN patients do not exhibit severe malnutrition. We suggest that one of the causes of the prolonged QT interval and increased QT dispersion in BN patients might be autonomic imbalance secondary to body weight changes [23,48], since the results of our previous study demonstrated significant correlations between both QT interval and QT dispersion and body weight changes in BN patients.

We acknowledge that our study has some limitations. First, although every effort was made to examine only those subjects taking no medication, it is possible that some subjects may have failed to declare their medication usage, and there are many drugs that could potentially influence QT interval. Second, we did not measure serum magnesium levels, which could also influence the ECG. However, the presence of low magnesium levels was thought to be comparatively unlikely, because BN patients do not suffer from malnutrition. Third, other factors that might influence QT interval, such as high free fatty acid (FFA) levels, hypoglycemia, and high estrogen levels, were not examined [49-52]. However, abnormalities in FFA, glucose and estrogen levels were also thought to be comparatively unlikely, again because BN patients do not have malnutrition or amenorrhea.

Conclusions

AN patients are at risk of sudden death. In terms of cardiacelectrophysiology, there may be a substrate associated with ventricular arrhythmias in AN patients, because QT interval prolongation and increased QT dispersion may be typical features in AN. Although BN is thought to have less associated risk of unexpected death, compared to AN, the prolongation of QT intervals and increase of QT dispersion in BN shown in our study indicated that BN patients have a risk of ventricular arrhythmias without the presence of abnormal electrolyte levels. In fact, Suri et al. [53] have reported serious cardiac dysrhythmias in two patients whose BN was not revealed during preoperative screening. Both patients with BN demonstrated QT interval prolongation and one patient exhibited torsades de pointes. It is noteworthy that one of the two patients had normal potassium concentrations. Our results suggest that general mood disturbance, including depression and anxiety mood states, cause prolongation of QT intervals in BN patients, which might lead to sudden death. Therefore, attention should be paid to cardiac function and ventricular arrhythmias, not only in AN patients with severe malnutrition, but also in BN patients with a history of AN. ECG examination in eating disorder patients without an extremely low body weight also appears to be clinically important.

REFERENCES

[1] Royal College of Psychiatrists: Eating Disorders. London: Royal College of Psychiatrists. *Council Report CR* 14,1992

[2] Sullivan PF: Mortality in anorexia nervosa. *Am J Psychiatr* 52:1073-1074,1995

[3] Bruch H: Death in anorexia nervosa. *Psychosom Med* 33:135-144,1971

[4] Neumarker KJ.: Mortality and sudden death in anorexia nervosa. *Int J Eat Disord* 21(3):205-12.,1997

[5] Isner JM, Roberts WC, Heymsfield SB, Yager J: Anorexia nervosa and sudden death. *Ann Intern Med* 102:49-52,1985

[6] Rajs J, Rajs E, Lundman T: Unexpected death in patients suffering from eating disorders. A medico-legal study. *Acta Psychiatr Scand* 74(6):587-96.,1986

[7] Chikasue F, Kojima T, Miyazaki T, Yashiki M.: A medicolegal case of anorexia nervosa. *Hiroshima J Med Sci* 37(4):157-60.,1988

[8] Cooke RA, Chambers JB, Singh R, Todd GJ, Smeeton NC, Treasure J: QT interval in anorexia nervosa. *Br Heart J* 72:69-73,1994

[9] Durakovic Z, Durakovic A, Korsiv M: Changes of corrected QT interval in the electrocardiogram of patients with anorexia nervosa. *Int J Cardiol* 45:115-121,1994

[10] Swenne I, Larsson PT: Heart risk associated with weight loss in anorexia nervosa and eating disorders: Risk factor for QTc interval prolongation and dispersion. *Acta Paediatr* 88:304-309,1999

[11] Galetta F, Franzoni F, Cupisti A, Belliti D, Prattichizzo F, Rolla M.: QT interval dispersion in young women with anorexia nervosa. *J Pediatr;*140(4):456-60.,2002

[12] Panagiotopoulos C, McCrindle BW, Hick K, Katzman DK: Electrocardiographic findings in adolescents with eating disorders. *Pediatrics* 105:1100-1105,2000

[13] Vanderdonckt O, Lambert M, Montero MC, Boland B, Brohet C.: The 12-lead electrocardiogram in anorexia nervosa: A report of 2 cases followed by a retrospective study. *J Electrocardiol.* 34(3):233-42.,2001

[14] Jackman WM, Friday KJ, Anderson JL, Aliot EM, Clark M, Lazzara R: The long QT syndromes: Critical review, new clinical observation and a unifying hypothesis. *Prog Cardiovasc Dis* 31:115-122,1988

[15] Karjalainen J, Vitasalo M, Manttari M, Maninïnen V: Relation between QT intervals and heart rate from 40 to 120 beats/min in rest electrocardiograms of men and a simple method to adjust QT interval values. *J Am Coll Cardiol* 23:1547-1553,1994

[16] Swenne I: Heart risk associated with weight loss in anorexia nervosa and eating disorders: electrocardiographic changes during the early phase of refeeding. *Acta Paediatr* 89(4):447-52.,2000

[17] Mont L, Castro J, Herreros B, Pare C, Azqueta M, Magrina J, Puig J, Toro J, Brugada J.: Reversibility of cardiac abnormalities in adolescents with anorexia nervosa after weight recovery. *J Am Acad Child Adolesc Psychiatry* 42(7):808-13.,2003

[18] Casper RC, Eckert ED, Halmi KA, Goldberg SC, Davis JM: Bulimia: its incidence and clinical importance in patients with anorexia nervosa. *Arch Gen Psychiatr* 37:1036-1040,1980

[19] Takimoto Y, Yoshiuchi K, Kumano H, Yamanaka G, Sasaki T, Suematsu H, Nagakawa Y, Kuboki T.: QT interval and QT dispersion in eating disorders. *Psychother Psychosom* 73(5):324-8.,2004

[20] Lepeschkin E, Surawicz B: The measurement of the QT interval of the electrocardiogram. *Circulation* 6:378-388,1952

[21] Bazett HC: An analysis of the time relationships of electrocardiograms. *Heart* 7:353,1920

[22] Campbell RW, Gardiner P, Amos PS, Chadwick D, Jordan RS: Measurement of the QT interval. *Eur Heart J* 6:81-83,1985

[23] Pellizzer AM, Straznicky NE, Lim S, Kamen PW, Krum H: Reduced dietary fat intake increases parasympathetic activity in healthy premenopausal women. *Clin Exp Pharmacol P* 26:656-660,1999

[24] Franzoni F, Mataloni E, Femia R, Galetta F.: Effect of oral potassium supplementation on QT dispersion in anorexia nervosa. *Acta Paediatr.* 91(6):653-6.,2002

[25] Thurston J, Marks P: Electrocardiographic abnormalities in patients with anorexia nervosa. *Br Heart J* 36:719-723,1974

[26] de Simone G, Scalfi L, Galderisi M, Celentano A, Di Biase G, Tammaro P, Garofalo M, Mureddu GF, de Divitiis O, Contaldo F: Cardiac abnormalities in young women with anorexia nervosa. *Br Heart J* 71:287-292,1994

[27] Abel RM, Grimes JB, Alonso D, Alonso M, Gay WA: Adverse hemodynamic and ultrastructual change in dog hearts subjected to protein-calorie malnutrition. *Am Heart J* 97:733-44,1979

[28] Galetta F, Franzoni F, Prattichizzo F, Rolla M, Santoro G, Pentimone F: Heart rate variability and left ventricular diastolic function in anorexia nervosa. *J Adolesc Health* 32:416-421,2003

[29] Galetta F, Franzoni F, Cupisti A, Belliti D, Prattichizzo F, Rolla M: QT interval dispersion in young women with anorexia nervosa. *J Pediatr* 140:456-460,2002

[30] Gottdiener JS, Gross HA, Henry WL, Borer JS, Ebert MH: Effects of self-induced starvation on cardiac size and function in anorexia nervosa. *Circulation* 58:425-433,1978

[31] Franzoni F, Galetta F, Cupisti A, Rolla M, Santoro G, Pentimone F: Ultrasonic tissue characterization of the myocardium in anorexia nervosa. *Acta Paediatr* 92:297-300,2003

[32] Moodie DS, Salcedo E: Cardiac function in adolescents and young adults with anorexia nervosa. *J Adolesc Health Care* 4:9-14,1983

[33] Murphy DJ Jr, Dickson TM, Brunner RL, Maloney MJ, Farrell MK, Meyer RA, James FW: Concomitant psychological and cardiac improvement during successful treatment of anorexia nervosa. *J Adolesc Health Care* 6:392-396,1985

[34] Eidem BW, Cetta F, Webb JL, Graham LC, Jay MS: Early detection of cardiac dysfunction: use of the myocardial performance index in patients with anorexia nervosa. *J Adolesc Health* 29:267-270,2001

[35] Romano C, Chinali M, Pasanisi F, Greco R, Celentano A, Rocco A, Palmieri V, Signorini A, Contaldo F, de Simone G: Reduced hemodynamic load and cardiac hypotrophy in patients with anorexia nervosa. *Am J Clin Nutr* 77:308-312,2003

[36] Ramacciotti CE, Coli E, Biadi O, Dell'Osso L: Silent pericardial effusion in a sample of anorexic patients. *Eat Weight Disord* 8:68-71,2003

[37] Frolich J, von Gontard A, Lehmkuhl G, Pfeiffer E, Lehmkuhl U: Pericardial effusions in anorexia nervosa. *Eur Child Adolesc Psychiatry* 10:54-57,2001

[38] Inagaki T, Yamamoto M, Tsubouchi K, Miyaoka T, Uegaki J, Maeda T, Horiguchi J, Yamane Y, Kato Y: Echocardiographic investigation of pericardial effusion in a case of anorexia nervosa. *Int J Eat Disord* 33:364-366,2003

[39] Johnson GL, Humphries LL, Shirley PB, Mazzoleni A, Noonan JA: Mitral valve prolapse in patients with anorexia nervosa and bulimia. *Arch Intern Med* 146:1525-1529,1986

[40] Oka Y, Ito T, Matsumoto S, Suematsu H, Ogata E: Mitral valve prolapse in patients with anorexia nervosa. Two-dimensional echocardiographic study. *Jpn Heart J* 28:873-882,1987

[41] Gold PW, Gwirtsman H, Avgerinos PC, Nieman LK, Gallucci WT, Kaye W, Jimerson D, Ebert M, Rittmaster R, Loriaux DL: Abnormal hypothalamic-pituitary-adrenal function in anorexia nervosa. Pathophysiologic mechanisms in underweight and weight-corrected patients. New Engl *J Med* 314:1335-1342,1986

[42] Rechlin T, Weis M, Ott C, Bleichner F, Joraschky P: Alterations of autonomic cardiac control in anorexia nervosa. *Biol Psychiat* 43:358-363,1998

[43] Petretta M, Bonaduce D, Scalfi L, de Filippo E, Marciano F, Migaux ML, Themistoclakis S, Ianniciello A, Contaldo F: Heart rate variability as a measure of autonomic nervous system function in anorexia nervosa. *Clin Cardiol* 20:219-224,1997

[44] Casu M, Patrone V, Gianelli MV, Marchegiani A, Ragni G, Murialdo G, Polleri A: Spectral analysis of R-R interval variability by short-term recording in anorexia nervosa. *Eat Weight Disord* 7:239-243,2002

[45] Kreipe RE, Goldstein B, DeKing DE, Tipton R, Kempski MH: Heart rate power spectrum analysis of autonomic dysfunction in adolescents with anorexia nervosa. *Int J Eat Disord* 16:159-165,1994

[46] Rechlin T, Weis M, Spitzer A, Karscka WP: Are affective disorders associated with alternations of heart rate variability?. *J Affect Disord* 14:392-395,1994

[47] Rissanen A, Naukkarinen H, Virkkunen M, Rawlings RR, Linnoila M: Fluoxetine normalizes increased cardiac vagal tone in bulimia nervosa. J Clin Psychopharmacol 18:26-32,1998

[48] Kennedy SH, Heslegrave RH: Cardiac regulation in bulimia nervosa. *J Psychiat Res* 23:267-273,1989

[49] Nakagawa M, Takahashi N, Iwao T, Yonemochi H, Ooie T, Hara M, Saikawa T, Ito M: Evaluation of autonomic influences on QT dispersion using the head-up tilt test in healthy subjects. *Pacing Clin Electrophysiol* 22(8):1158-63,1999

[50] Corbi GM, Carbone S, Ziccardi P, Giugliano G, Marfella R, Nappo F, Paolisso G, Esposito K, Giugliano D: FFAs and QT intervals in obese women with visceral adiposity: effects of sustained weight loss over 1 year. *J Clin Endocrinol Metab* 87:2080-3,2002

[51] Eckert B, Agardh CD: Hypoglycaemia leads to an increased QT interval in normal men. *Clin Physiol* 18:570-5,1998

[52] Larsen JA, Tung RH, Sadananda R, Goldberger JJ, Horvath G, Parker MA, Kadish AH: Effects of hormone replacement therapy on QT interval. *Am J Cardiol* 82:993-5,1998

[53] Suri R, Poist ES, Hager WD, Gross JB.: Unrecognized bulimia nervosa: a potential cause of perioperative cardiac dysrhythmias. *Can J Anaesth.* 46(11):1048-52,1999

INDEX

A

B

C

D

E

F

G

S

T

U

V